A SCOT AT WAR *WITH* WELLINGTON

A SCOT AT WAR *WITH* WELLINGTON

The Memoir of

CAPTAIN JAMES STIRLING OF THE BLACK WATCH

GARETH GLOVER

Pen & Sword
MILITARY
AN IMPRINT OF PEN & SWORD BOOKS LTD.
YORKSHIRE – PHILADELPHIA

First published in Great Britain in 2024 by
Pen & Sword Military
An imprint of
Pen & Sword Books Ltd
Yorkshire - Philadelphia

ISBN 978 1 39904 151 5

A CIP catalogue record for this book is available from the British Library.

Typeset by SJmagic DESIGN SERVICES, India.

Printed and bound in the UK by CPI Group (UK) Ltd.

Pen & Sword Books Limited incorporates the imprints of Archaeology, Atlas, Aviation, Battleground, Digital, Discovery, Family History, Fiction, History, Local, Local History, Maritime, Military, Military Classics, Politics, Select, Transport, True Crime, After the Battle, Air World, Claymore Press, Frontline Publishing, Leo Cooper, Remember When, Seaforth Publishing, The Praetorian Press, Wharncliffe Books, Wharncliffe Local History, Wharncliffe Transport, Wharncliffe True Crime and White Owl.

For a complete list of Pen & Sword titles please contact

PEN & SWORD BOOKS LIMITED
George House, Units 12 & 13, Beevor Street, Off Pontefract Road,
Barnsley, S71 1HN, UK
E-mail: enquiries@pen-and-sword.co.uk
Website: www.pen-and-sword.co.uk

or

PEN AND SWORD BOOKS
1950 Lawrence Rd, Havertown, PA 19083, USA
E-mail: uspen-and-sword@casematepublishers.com
Website: www.penandswordbooks.com

MIX
Paper | Supporting responsible forestry
FSC® C013604
FSC www.fsc.org

Contents

List of Plates

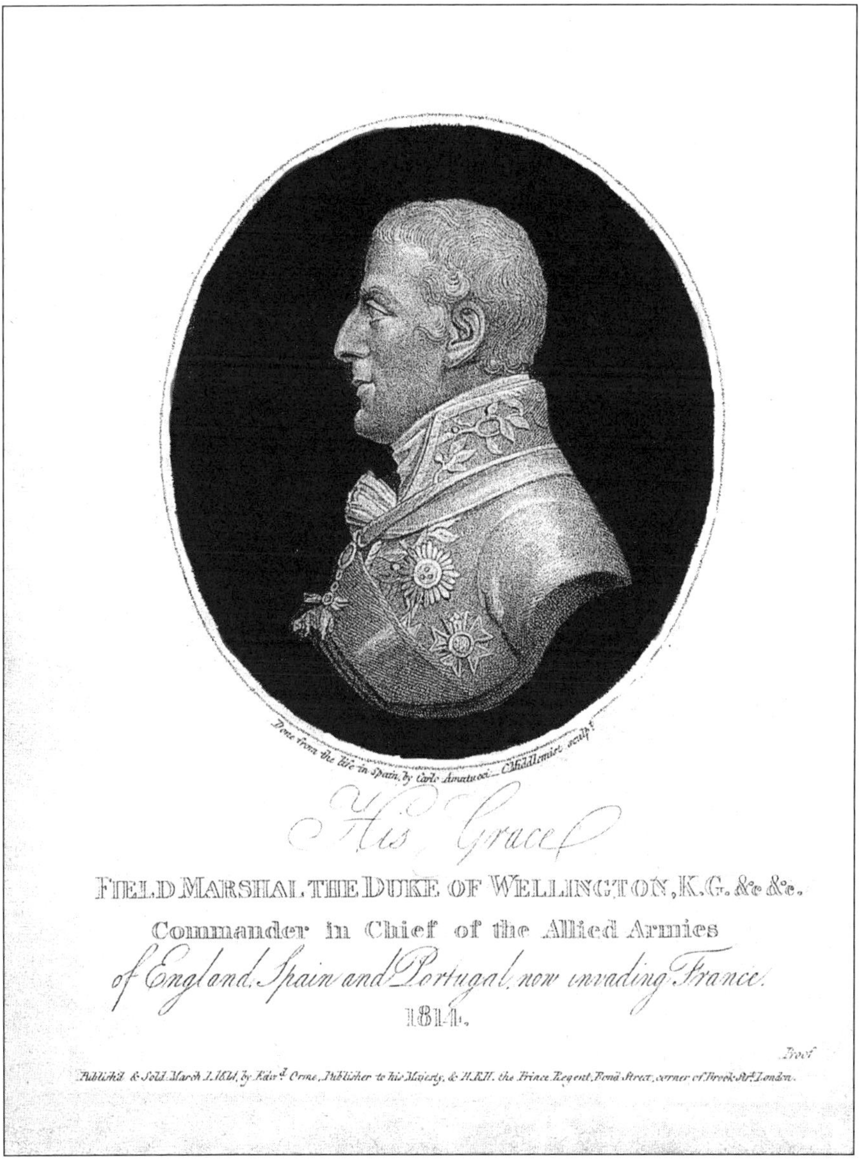

The Duke of Wellington.

James Stirling's Memoirs of the 42nd Foot

For such a famous regiment as the 42nd Regiment of Foot (The Black Watch), the number of published memoirs is surprisingly low. The discovery of the three handwritten journals in the collection of the National Library of Scotland[1] covering the period from August 1808, when the regiment left Gibraltar for Lisbon until the end of 1813, are therefore of significant importance in our understanding of the actions of this regiment during the Peninsular War.

Previous to this publication, the memoirs of the regiment have consisted purely of the following few. The anonymous *Narrative of a Private Soldier in the 42nd Highlanders*[2] published as early as 1821 is probably the best known, along with Sergeant James Anton's *Retrospect of a Military Life, During the Most Eventful Periods of the Last War*,[3] but the latter only served in the Peninsula from late 1813 until April 1814. Beyond these two, we only have Ensign John Malcolm's *Reminiscences of a Campaign in the Pyrenees and South of France in 1814*,[4] who again only joined the regiment in January 1814 and *Merely a Memorandum, From Spain to Waterloo in Wellington's Army*.[5] This last work provides the very brief recollections of Lieutenant Donald Mackenzie who served with the Black Watch from 1807 until 1821. However, whilst working on the voluminous memoirs of James Stirling for publication, I have often had recourse to compare his remarks on events with Mackenzie's version and it soon became patently

1 National Library of Scotland Archive and Manuscripts Collection, Reference MS 23629 to MS 23631.

2 *Personal Narrative of a Private Soldier Who Served in the 42nd Highlanders for Twelve Years*, published London 1821.

3 Published London 1841

4 Published in Constable's *Miscellany of Original and Selected Publications* in 1828.

5 Published by Guy Hutton-Wilson in 2005.

obvious, that although not identical, far too many phrases in both accounts are virtually identical, leaving no doubt that the author of one referred to the other and reproduced passages. Given that we know that James Stirling wrote his Journals between 1816 and his untimely death in 1818, and that Donald Mackenzie did not record his short memoir until at least 1821 (the last date mentioned in the memoir) but almost certainly written decades later than that, then it is certain that Mackenzie copied from Stirling. This unfortunately reduces the value of Mackenzie's memoir to historians; however, we do now have Stirling's entire memoir for the first time.

These journals cover his entire period of active service with the 42nd Foot, but unfortunately it then only covers the time he served with the Portuguese forces until the end of 1813. Given the fact that the journals end so cleanly with the end of that year, it seems likely that James did intend to record his service with the Portuguese Army in 1814; however his sudden death so soon after the war probably meant that he died before he could do so, but we will never know for certain.[6]

During the period 1815–18, James Stirling wrote up tidily the journals of his period of service, undoubtedly utilising a combination of small pocketbooks he had used to record his day-to-day thoughts and events, but at times also relying on his memory, which occasionally erred in the identification of specific regiments. The first of these volumes is annotated with the attached provenance as to their validity.

> The property of Major John Charles Bell RHP [Royal Hospital Pensioner], 53rd & 47th Regiments, of 34 Bruntsfield Gardens, Edinburgh; grandnephew of the writer of this memoir, viz Captain James Stirling 42nd Royal Highlanders who died in 1818 aged 25, past 3 months. This book has been handed over by the above Major Bell to Garthshore Tyndal Porter, 2nd Lieutenant Royal Artillery, great-great-grand-nephew of the author 1907.

6 The editor has trawled the internet and archival collections intensely, but has failed to find any evidence of an 1814 Journal ever having existed.

Our Captain James Stirling was the offspring of an illegitimate branch of the Stirlings of Craigbarnet. Mungo Stirling of Craigbarnet (James' great-grandfather) died in January 1733 and his wife succumbed eleven days later. Their only legal son James ['Burrie'[7]] Stirling (James' grandfather) inherited the estate, but lost almost all, having backed Bonnie Prince Charlie in 1745, and was imprisoned for some time at Dumbarton Castle. Being eventually released he rebuilt his fortune. Acting as a tobacco importer, he regained the right to his estates and built a much improved dwelling at Craigbarnet in 1786. He married Catherine Monteith of Auldcathy and the couple had two children named John and Charlotte.

On the death of James in February 1774, John (James' uncle) inherited the estate as the only legitimate son (as twelfth of Craigbarnet and second of Kirklands). John Stirling married Anne Murray, daughter of Sir Patrick Murray of Balmanno, but they had no children. His sister Charlotte married James Gartshore of Alderstone and had five children, all of whom eventually died without issue.

John died in 1805 and was therefore succeeded by his nephew, Alexander Gartshore (thirteenth of Craigbarnet), the third and eldest surviving son of his sister, who promptly took the additional surname of Stirling. Alexander Gartshore-Stirling was an officer in the Royal Navy and he married Ann Millar, daughter of James Millar of Glasgow in 1806.

However, James (Burrie) had sired further illegitimate children. An old work on *The Kirklands of Strathblane and its inhabitants from Early times*[8] includes a description of Craigbarnet and continues with the recent family history, introducing our James' father.

> There is a beautiful spreading old plane tree just at the entrance of the new avenue to Craigbarnet from the Strathblane side, and under its shade stood a cottage where lived a worthy pair, one of whose daughters was a pretty girl who was dairymaid at

7 It is sometimes stated that 'Burrie' was a derogatory nickname, based on the fact that the old family seat was built on a low-lying marsh, effectively 'boggy'. However, the replacement house built in 1786 was on a much improved site and it is stated that 'The fine public rooms and beautiful ceilings and general arrangements show that he was a man of both good sense and taste'.

8 By John Guthrie Smith published in 1886.

> Craigend farm, just across the public road. 'Burrie' [our James Stirling's grandfather] used to visit this lass, and by and by in this humble home a son was born to them who was named James Stirling [his father]. The young James after a time lived in the 'big house' and was treated like a [legitimate] son of the family, but on some occasion he received, or supposed he had received, an insult about his birth. High-spirited and energetic, he at once left Craigbarnet, and it was not for some considerable time that it was found he had enlisted as a private in the 42nd Royal Highlanders. He rose rapidly to the highest grade of non-commissioned officers in this regiment, and then at the request of the colonel, his father purchased a commission for him.

As we can see, James (the father of our memorialist) had enlisted as a private in the 42nd Foot in 1776 after a dispute with his father, however he afterwards forgave him and purchased him a commission in the 42nd Foot, becoming an Ensign on 8 July 1777 and serving in the actions in North America at Brooklyn, Brandywine and Valley Forge. He gained the rank of Lieutenant on 3 November 1778 and served in Flanders from 1793 to 1795. He then became a Captain on 24 January 1795; Major 14 December 1796, serving at Minorca in 1798 and in Egypt in 1801 and was wounded at the Battle of Alexandria.

At the battle, the Regimental history,[9] records that Major James Stirling commanded the left wing of the 42nd, while the right wing under Lieutenant Colonel James Stewart were positioned 200m to the rear as a reserve. Taking advantage of the early morning gloom, a demi-brigade of French grenadiers known as the 'Invincibles' with a 6-pounder cannon penetrated unobserved between the two wings. Being perceived, they were attacked by the right wing, while Stirling ordered his rear rank to turn about and engage their rear. Caught between two fires, the French tried to escape but came under sustained attack from other regiments as well and eventually lost

9 *Illustrated Histories of the Scottish Regiments, Book No.1 1st Battalion the Black Watch Royal Highlanders 42nd Foot*, by Lieutenant Colonel Percy Groves, illustrated by Harry Payne, 1893.

over 700 of their men before the remnant surrendered. Their standard was surrendered to Major Stirling personally, who gave it to Sergeant Sinclair of the Grenadier company to guard. However during later confused fighting, Sinclair was ridden over by French cavalry and the standard lost; it was then recovered by Private Anthony Lutz of the Minorca Regiment.

He became a brevet Lieutenant Colonel on 11 May 1802; and a full Lieutenant Colonel on 7 September 1804. As such he commanded the 1st Battalion 42nd Foot in the Peninsula from August 1808 to January 1809 and subsequently at Walcheren. He became a Brevet Colonel on 4 June 1811 and commanded the battalion again in the Peninsula from April to November 1812, including a short period when James senior commanded the brigade on the death of General Wheatley between September and October 1812. The brigade being removed to the 6th Division in the November, he commanded the brigade again from November 1812 to June 1813; until Major General Pack was appointed to command the brigade. He went home in the following November. He saw action in the Peninsula at the battles of Corunna, Salamanca, Burgos and the Pyrenees; receiving a gold medal for commanding the battalion at Corunna, Salamanca and the Pyrenees. He was subsequently promoted to Major General on 4 June 1814. He later became Lieutenant Governor of Cork in 1820 and died at Musselburgh on 12 December 1834.

James had married Jean Fisher and they had two children, Jean was born on 17 May 1785 and our James was born 29 October 1792. Jean subsequently married Paymaster John Home and had five children, James Stirling-Home who went to Australia; Alexander Home who became a teller in the Royal Bank; Gartshore Stirling-Home who became a Captain in the 5th Fusiliers; Jane Home who married a Major Bell; and Christina who married Captain Elphinstone of the Honourable East India Company.

As to our James (junior); he became an Ensign by purchase in the 42nd Foot on 14 August 1805 at the age of thirteen, vice Ensign Thomas Munro.[10] James then rose to the rank of Lieutenant without purchase on 27 August 1807. James served in the Peninsula with the 42nd Foot from September 1808 to January 1809, then at Walcheren and again in the Peninsula from

10 Thomas Munro became a Lieutenant vice Lieutenant William McKenzie, who became a Captain, vice Captain Davitts who was deceased.

May 1812 to August 1813 (from October 1812 as Aide de Camp to his father Major General James Stirling). On his father's retirement from active service, he joined the Portuguese Army from 9 November 1813 as a Brevet Captain in the 11th Line Regiment, remaining with them until 13 October 1814. He then became a Captain in the 42nd by purchase[11] on 11 May 1815. He was present at Walcheren, Corunna, Salamanca, Burgos, the Pyrenees, Orthez and Toulouse. He retired from the army in 1817 and died on 20 January 1818 aged only 25 years old. The cause of his death is unknown.

Major General James Stirling and Captain James Stirling are both buried in St Michael's Churchyard, Inveresk, Midlothian, Scotland (see the photograph section).

The Epitaph on the monument to Major General James Stirling reads:

> Sacred to the memory of Major General James Stirling, Lieutenant Governor of Cork, and for forty-two years an officer in the 42nd Royal Highlanders. With a wing of that national corps he annihilated the French *Invincibles* in Egypt, and took their standard with his own hand. He commanded that regiment through the Peninsular War, and after twenty-seven years of foreign service he retired in 1813 into private life, where, cultivating the virtues which adorn the Christian character, he died, full of years and honours, at his villa of Eskbank, 12th December 1834. His remains, borne hither by his veteran companions in arms, are here interred.

On the reverse of the above monument is inscribed the following simple record:

> James Stirling, son, Captain 42nd R[oyal] H[ighlanders] / Died 20 January 1818 Aged 25.

11 Vice Captain Walker retired.

The Early History of the 'Black Watch'

The six former 'Independent Companies' of Highland infantry were formed into the 43rd Regiment of Foot under the command of John, Earl of Crawford in 1740. They served at Fontenoy in 1745 during the War of the Austrian Succession and four months later against Bonnie Prince Charlie at Prestonpans. In 1749 the regiment was renumbered the 42nd following the disbanding of Oglethorpe's Regiment.

The regiment then served in North America during the Seven Years War, fighting at Ticonderoga in 1759. A 2nd Battalion had been raised in 1758, originally serving in the West Indies, but the two battalions served together in Canada in 1760 and both partook that year in the capture of Montreal. In 1761 the two battalions proceeded to the West Indies and partook in the capture of Havannah in 1762, however at the end of that year the 2nd Battalion was disbanded, all fit men transferring into the 1st Battalion. The regiment spent the next five years in North America combatting the Native Americans before sailing for Ireland in 1767.

In 1768 the regiment was made a 'Royal' Regiment and a Royal cypher was added to the centre of the Colours. The regiment then proceeded to America again at the outbreak of the American War of Independence and fought in almost every significant engagement there. A 2nd Battalion was again added in 1779, serving in the West Indies, but in 1786 this battalion was used to form the 73rd (Perthshire) Regiment of Foot.

With the end of the war in America, the 1st Battalion moved to Nova Scotia, eventually returning to England in October 1789, after an absence of 14 years. They were garrisoned in Tynemouth and then Scotland, where they remained until the outbreak of the Revolutionary War against France.

Following earlier service in the Revolutionary Wars in Flanders from June 1794 until April 1795, they returned to England but were sent abroad again to the West Indies in that November. Severe storms caused part of the fleet to return to port, but half of the regiment (five companies) successfully sailed on and reached Barbados in April 1796. These companies served in St Lucia, St Vincent, St Christopher, Puerto Rico and Martinique, before returning to England in July 1797. The five companies were soon reshipped to Gibraltar, where they were reunited with the other five companies, who had been sent to Gibraltar in 1796 after failing to reach the West Indies. The entire regiment then remained at Gibraltar for the next three years, apart from a period garrisoning Minorca.

In 1801 the regiment sailed with the expedition to Egypt, landing with the army at Aboukir Bay and fighting bravely at the Battle of Alexandria, where soldiers of the regiment are credited with saving the life of General Abercromby[1] and then joined the march to Cairo. Following this successful campaign the regiment sailed to England, arriving at Portsmouth in December 1801 and taking up garrison duties at Winchester, where the regiment suffered a very high rate of fever.

In June 1802, during the Peace of Amiens, the regiment marched to Edinburgh where no less than 475 men were discharged as invalids. However, in early 1803 the regiment received new Colours and in April they moved to Weeley Barracks. On 9 July 1803 a Second Battalion was formed and proceeded to join the First Battalion at Weeley in November 1803.

In October 1804 the First Battalion was ordered to proceed to Gibraltar again, while the Second Battalion sailed for Ireland, initially remaining in garrison at Dublin, before moving to Sligo and Dundalk. They remained here until they moved to Scotland in late 1807 to garrison Fort George. The 1st Battalion remained at Gibraltar until August 1808, when James Stirling takes up his narrative, on the eve of joining the Duke of Wellington's army with his regiment in Portugal.

1 He eventually succumbed to his wounds.

The Corunna Campaign: August 1808–January 1809

The Journal begins with Lieutenant James Stirling at Gibraltar, where the First Battalion of the 42nd Foot was stationed from September 1805 until August 1808. Unfortunately, the short passage to Lisbon proved extremely tedious because of contrary winds, only landing on 2 September, a voyage of some 15 days. They therefore missed Arthur Wellesley's first campaign in the Peninsula which culminated with the victory of Vimiera and subsequent Convention of Cintra.

Gibraltar, 12 August 1808

Orders having arrived for our regiment to embark for the army in Portugal, everything was in preparation and on 18 August 1808, we sailed for Lisbon upwards of 1,000 men strong in high health and spirits.[1] We had great fear that all active operations with the army had ceased and that we should be too late to join in the expulsion of the French army from Portugal.

September 1808

The passage had been tedious and not until the 1 September had we any certainty of what part we were to fit in the campaign. On that day we however received the news of the Battle of Vimiera,[2] its consequences and the armistice entered on between the two armies. We also had an order to land the

1 The history of the regiment by Archibald Forbes states that they arrived in Portugal with a strength of 826 men, but Dr Andrew Bamford's records of the Muster List of the 1st Battalion 42nd Foot, show that in September 1808, the battalion consisted of 943 other ranks. Adding commissioned and non-commissioned officers would bring the total to about 1,000.

2 The Battle of Vimiera or Vimiero was fought on 21 August 1808.

day following and take possession of the town and fort of Cascaes [Cascais][3] and relieve the French garrisons along the coast.[4] The 3rd Regiment (or Buffs) who also came into the river along with us,[5] were to land at Fort St Julien.[6]

On 2 September we landed in Portugal and were received with every demonstration of joy by the people, who appeared most anxious to get rid of the yoke they had so lately been under.

On entering the town we were met by the officer commanding, General Bessieres chef d'etat major, the commandant of the surrounding coast. He conducted us to the fort which was given up after the compliment of presenting arms with all its guns, magazines &c.

On the detachment of the French marching out, the English Jack[7] was hoisted and soon after the Portuguese Colour was shown. We found Cascaes [Cascais] to be a small town situated in the bay of the same name at the entrance of the Tagus. The fort is by no means strong either by sea or land and we found the barracks in it in a dreadful state of distress and dilapidation. The officers were billeted on the houses

3 The Citadel of Cascais had been badly damaged in the earthquake of 1755 and was only partly repaired.

4 The Convention of Cintra saw the French forces in Portugal under the command of General Junot surrender. As part of this agreement the French garrisons of the fortresses along the Tagus were relieved by British troops.

5 According to most histories of the regiment, this would appear to be an error, as the 3rd Foot are stated as not having arrived in Lisbon until March 1809. However, Stirling is correct in his statement as Sir John Moore's diary entry for the 3 September confirms that the fortresses of Cascais, Bugio and St Julien had been garrisoned the previous day by the 42nd just arrived from Gibraltar and the Buffs from Madeira. The Fort Bugio mentioned was actually Forte de Sao Lourenco on Bugio Island in the mouth of the Tagus.

6 The fort of Sao Juliao da Barra was a major fortress on the northern bank of the Tagus. The French used it as a barracks for their troops under the command of General Jean Travot. It ceased to be a military fortification in 1951 and is now used for the reception of members of the Portuguese government and their illustrious international guests.

7 The Union Jack, or more correctly Union Flag, as the Union Jack can only be flown from the bow of a Royal Navy ship.

of the inhabitants who received them kindly, but poverty had rendered them incapable of giving us anything but the accommodation of their houses.

Fort St Julien stands on the [eastern] point of the Bay of Cascaes [Cascais] nearest to Lisbon, [it] is partly cut out of the solid rock and justly esteemed a most admirable defence for the harbour. The view of Lisbon from hence and the surrounding country is most magnificent and the river beautiful and most capacious.

Nearly opposite to Fort St Julien is St Sebastian,[8] a small, isolated fort, forming a defence for the harbour on the south-west entrance.

On the 5 [September] instant the 18th Light Dragoons landed and were quartered in the fort until further orders.[9]

Sir Huw Dalrymple[10] had assumed the command of the army which was encamped about eight or ten miles from Lisbon. Our anxiety to know the terms of the Convention was allayed on the 9th when we heard with infinite astonishment and concern that the enemy, a beaten enemy, were allowed to embark their arms, baggage, Colours and even the pilferings [plunder] they had exacted. Nothing could exceed the just indignation of the Portuguese, who were exasperated to behold our simple generals afford such unparalleled terms (to a set of banditti), who without any cause or formality had entered Portugal with professions of friendship and ever since had plundered, oppressed and murdered whenever they had an opportunity. This detestable, this shameful pusillanimity of our chiefs, drew reproaches on the whole army and any individual of it felt the consequences of it, from the unprecedented impudence of the whole French army. Junot positively went so far as to

8 Fort Sao Sebastiao de Caparica is situated near Almada on the southern bank of the Tagus opposite the Torre de Belem.

9 Eight troops of the 18th Light Dragoons arrived in Lisbon in September 1808.

10 Lieutenant General Sir Hew Dalrymple took command of the Army in Portugal just after the Battle of Vimiera.

demand five vessels to carry home his share of the plunder, the frigate in which he was to proceed not being sufficient to transport his baggage.[11] These 24,000 marauders embarked with menaces of a return to destroy what they had left and it was with difficulty the Portuguese were restrained from open outrage. Jewels, money in bars of gold, and silver plate of every description and valuable paintings were in the baggage allowed to be carried off. At last however, a committee headed by Brigadier General Beresford[12] was appointed to examine into the complaints of the natives and it was the means of restoring a great deal of property. Not less than 53 boxes of indigo were found in Junot's baggage and a vast quantity of plate. But nothing could restrain the natives from showing their resentment and at one period General Kellerman[13] coming on shore to dine with some English general officer, was watched and assaulted, but by the bravery and generosity of the English seamen was rescued. At Oporto the disturbances were worse (greater) and notwithstanding the vigilance of the English commissioners, many fell victims (perished) to the rage of the Portuguese.

On the 12 [September] we heard that Sir Arthur Wellesley[14] who had gained the Battle of Vimiera was going to England and that the army was to be concentrated at Quelus [Queluz] near one of the royal palaces. Any change of quarters was much to be desired as from the liberality of the inhabitants and the abundance of new made wine, our soldiers were fast getting unwell.

11 Junot did request the use of five Danish merchant vessels to carry his 'personal effects', which was promptly declined on the directions of General Dalrymple.

12 Major General William Carr Beresford.

13 Cavalry General François Kellerman had led the French negotiations for the Convention of Cintra.

14 Lieutenant General Arthur Wellesley had been involved in the negotiations for the Convention of Cintra and was recalled to London alongside Sir Hew Dalrymple and Sir Harry Burrard to give evidence to the enquiry set up, following the public condemnation of the Convention of Cintra.

On the 12 about noon, we had a view of the Russian fleet escorted by six British sail of the line proceeding down the river for England[15] and the same evening brought us a Route to proceed to Quelus [Queluz] to join the division under Sir John Moore. We accordingly proceeded next morning and marched through a very fine country, richly adorned by many noble palaces, one belonging to the ci-devant Duke of Abrantes who had joined the field.[16]

About 10 o'clock we reached Quelus [Queluz] and were encamped and brigaded with the 4th and 28th Regiments. We found at Quelus [Queluz] a large part of the army and the General officers and Staff are quartered in the royal palace.[17]

The French troops had not put to sea, owing to some of the transports not being in a state to receive them. The weather up to the 24th instant, had been very warm and clouds of dust enveloped our camp, which increased the already prevailing disorder of sore eyes among the soldiers. On the 26th, the brigade was inspected by Sir John Moore and gave every satisfaction, but as yet all was uncertainty as to what our future movements were to be.

---

15 A Russian fleet commanded by Admiral Seniavin had been ordered to sail from Corfu to the Baltic via Cadiz. The fleet however did not stop at Cadiz but continued on until forced by severe weather to take shelter at Lisbon, where they were received warmly by the then neutral Portuguese, with promises of plentiful supplies. Soon after, the situation altered markedly. General Junot's troops arrived at Lisbon, only to find that the Portuguese Royal Family, nobility and a huge amount of treasure had sailed for Brazil on Portuguese and British ships. Soon after, Russia declared war on Britain in alliance with France, trapping Seniavin's fleet in the Tagus, with a British fleet ready to pounce if they dared to sail. Seniavin's allegiance was not particularly favourable to the French, many British officers serving in his fleet and readily providing a safe haven for British families seeking to escape the French invasion. At the demand of Admiral Cotton commanding the British fleet off Lisbon, the Russian fleet was not included in the Convention of Cintra. It was agreed that the Russian fleet would be held in security in Britain, the crews would be repatriated to Russia and the ships would be returned to Russia six months after peace was announced between the two countries. Seven Russian ships flying the Russian Ensign passed the bar on 12 September and sailed for Britain accompanied by ships of the Royal Navy.

16 General Jean-Andoche Junot was created Duke of Abrantes in 1808.

17 Now Queluz National Palace.

In October 1808, Sir John Moore took command of the army in Portugal and initially organised his army with the 1/42nd brigaded with 1/4th and 1/28th and five companies of 5/60th in Major General William Bentinck's Brigade of Lieutenant General Alexander Mackenzie Fraser's Division.

October 1808

Towards the 1 October an English frigate arrived with money for the army and also Captain Dalrymple[18] who had gone home with the dire Convention, returned with orders for the immediate recall of his father Sir Hew Dalrymple.

It was also stated about this period that the command of the army was to devolve on Sir John Moore[19] and that Sir David Baird[20] was to join him in Spain with 15,000 troops from England. On the 8th instant it was announced to the army in General Orders, that Sir John Moore would take on him the care and command of the army as affairs required Sir Hew Dalrymple and Sir Harry Burrard in England. A few more days informed us of our future movements which were to take place immediately in different columns into Spain. The force about to march might be estimated at 22,000 men with Sir John Moore as commander in chief, a circumstance which was hailed with joy by the whole army.

The march in all probability or rather campaign would be a long one, it was therefore necessary to provide an equipment to undertake it with any degree of comfort. In purchasing stores and mules, we found an insatiable desire to extort more money than the value, well aware that have them we must, at any price.

Major General Fraser was appointed to the command of the 1st Division of the army, which would move in the direction

18 Captain Leighton Cathcart Dalrymple, 15th Light Dragoons.

19 Lieutenant General Sir John Moore took command of the British Army in Portugal after the other senior officers went back to Britain.

20 Lieutenant General Sir David Baird.

of Ciudad Rodrigo, Sir John Hope and the cavalry proceeding by the Elvas road.

On the 14 October we received Routes to march to Abrantes by regiments, leaving our heavy baggage behind at Belem. Next morning we commenced our march at 6 o'clock and the road being very fine, we walked at a good rate. The environs of Lisbon are very beautiful and the surrounding country rich and tastefully laid out in gardens. About 10 o'clock we reached Sacavem, rather a pretty little village about nine miles from Lisbon. The greatest number of the officers were billeted on the house of a nobleman, which being unfurnished afforded but little comfort. The officer commanding [Lieutenant Colonel James Stirling, his father] was lodged in the house of a marquis, both of whose lovely daughters spoke English very fluently.

Next morning [15 October] at six o'clock, we crossed a tributary stream of the Tagus on a flying bridge[21] of boats and entered into a fine and richly cultivated country. It was for a considerable extent flat, but at the distance a lofty range of hills bounded the prospect, clothed by the green lime and dark olive tree. The country continues flat until we reach Villafranca [Vila Franca de Xira], is well peopled and plentiful, abounding especially in wine & salt. Villafranca [Vila Franca de Xira] is a small town on the Tagus, prettily situated and enjoying a considerable trade. Nothing could exceed the kindness we experienced in this little village, more particularly from our landlord Senor Juan Paulo, a wealthy merchant and chief magistrate of the place. Our worthy host had provided breakfast for us the following morning and we parted from him with every sentiment of gratitude and thanks for his warm hospitality.

21 A 'flying bridge' was formed of boats which were simply guided across by ropes.

Our march on the 17 [October] was through a hilly country, wooded with the olive, cork and chestnut trees. The soil was sandy, and the aloe grew along the road in wild luxuriance here and there formed into a sort of barrier or hedge to the garden of a cottage. We left for a time the Tagus and arrived at a small poor village called Azambuja where with great difficulty we could procure bread or vegetables. What was at last given we paid for dearly, having to lament in the morning the loss of a spy glass,[22] not only valuable in itself, but doubly so on entering on a campaign. No threats nor entreaties could recover it, yet in justice to our landlord every exertion was made on his part.

Next morning [18 October] the '*Generale*'[23] roused us from sleep at the early hour of four o'clock, having a march of five Portuguese leagues to perform, which have four English miles each.[24] Was it in our power to have our wishes granted none of us ever desired again to visit Azambuja, not only on account of its poverty, but from the propensity its inhabitants showed to covetousness, not to give it a worse title. However, it is not so much to be wondered at, as the law of Portugal allows theft to be committed four times ere it is punishable by death.

The road to Santarem is through a country very sandy, but variegated by the sombre tint of the olive tree and autumnal shades of the chestnut and elm. On approaching the town, the road ascends a very steep hill, winding round its side till it reaches the summit where the city stands close above the Tagus. The situation is most commanding, overlooking a great extent very picturesque and diversified country, through which the Tagus rolls its waters in silent majesty, the view being bounded by a lofty range of mountains. Santarem is a place of considerable extent is naturally very strong and encircled by fortifications in bad repair. It has many religious

22 Telescope.

23 Otherwise known as *Reveille*.

24 Every country's league differed and the league can be anything from 3 to 5 miles long.

edifices, some of these very large and the various monasteries possessing great riches.

On the 19 [October] we halted here and during the forenoon enjoyed the restricted society of the nuns, who wished us to be thoroughly convinced of their happiness and resignation to their confinement and duration.

Next morning [20 October] we again pursued our march through a flat country, well cultivated and after halting a few minutes on the road, reached a very small village called Galegam [Golega]. It was utterly impossible to have anticipated our good fortune here, for we were not only treated well and hospitably, but really elegantly and in a style we had never before experienced nor had we the most distant hope of doing so in such a poor collection of hovels. Our landlord was a rich proprietor and a wine merchant who with his family had retired from business and enjoyed himself in the country. His rotundity of body and rubicund cheeks promised good cheer nor were we desired, our honest hosts showing the example, we included the excellent wine most freely.

Not far from Galegam [Golega] we were charmed by a most picturesque and animated scene of nature. The village of Tancos, consisting principally of rustic and religious dwellings opens suddenly on the view, engulfed in high escarped rocks, whose bases are washed by the Tagus and their sides caressed with the olive, cork and chestnut trees. The opposite shore is equally precipitous and covered with underwood, in the middle of the river stands a dark piece of rock, commanded on all sides by the impending mountains, whose summit is crowned by the remains of a Moorish fort or watch tower.[25] The troops in the foreground and the small boats on the river with lattine [lateen][26] sails gave a peculiar animation to the scene, which

25 The Castle of Almourol.

26 A lateen sail is a triangular sail running fore to aft, mounted on a mast.

was highly deserving the attention of the draughtsman, had time and military rigour permitted.

On the Zezere rises the small village of Punhete[27] to which we crossed on a bridge of pontoons. This stream is very rapid and owing to its being more so than usual, Junot while proceeding to Lisbon was arrested in his progress some days, thereby giving the prince[28] and family sufficient time to embark. Our accommodation here was very indifferent and people were very reluctant to afford us anything, probably from the idea as it was a '*jour maigre*'[29] with them, it should also be the same with their visitors.

On the 22 [October] we marched for Abrantes where we had orders to halt for a day. There we were billeted in the palace of the Duke of Abrantes, the exterior of which displayed great magnificence, but the base walls alone remained inside. Abrantes is a town of Estramadura, is on the Tagus and gives the title of Duke to one of the most ancient and noble families of Portugal. Its streets are very narrow and consequently dirty, a public square occupies the centre of the town and the traces of a large castle yet exist.

Our good fortune enabled us to be present at the yearly entertainment of a bullfight. It was held in the public square, which was palisaded with wood on purpose and booths erected for the accommodation of the people. By noon the square was crowded, especially with the Portuguese ladies who strange to think held this brutal amusement in the highest estimation. There were on this day no horsemen and the contest was sustained by only three 'chulos'[30] or new dressed in light silk jackets with checks of various colours on their arms and armed with small darts to teize [*sic*] and irritate the bull. The animal

27 Now known as Constancia.

28 The Portuguese Prince Regent became King John VI in 1816, on the death of his deranged mother Maria I.

29 Day of Abstinence.

30 'Chulo' means cocky or arrogant, perhaps indicating their brash costumes.

came into the area and frantic, made directly at one of the pedestrians, who receiving him on the cloak, darted one of his javelins and escaped over the palisading. He was thus actively tormented for about a quarter of an hour, when accident prevented one of the men escaping and great fears were entertained for his safety. He however got himself between the bull's horns and as the attempts of the animal were fruitless to throw him off, until watching the opportunity and assisted by his companions, he flung himself off and most dexterously escaped without injury. Shortly after, the trumpet sounded and the matador appeared, who was greeted with loud applause. He boldly walked up to the bull and receiving him on his scarlet cloak, plunged the sword up to the hilt in the spine and caused instant death. All joined in acclamations of praise and the animal was dragged off by three finely caparisoned mules. This inhuman amusement was followed in the evening by a wretched comedy performed in the streets and the inhabitants treated many of the officers to sumptuous suppers afterwards.

[24 October] After a short but very profound sleep of two hours, we marched from Abrantes and crossed the Tagus in boats. On the opposite side we enjoyed a beautiful view of the town and castle of Abrantes which from its situation must have been formerly very strong. The country through which we passed was very sandy and the wild arbutus and olive tree grew in luxuriance, the distant hills were covered with chestnut trees.

At 12 o'clock we arrived and halted at a small miserable village called Gorio [Gavaio], where little or nothing could be procured. The accommodations was hereby far the worst we had met with, but the poor inhabitants were civil and kindly gave us every little thing they had. About half a mile from Gorio [Gavaio] is an old castle in a fine situation[31] and the hills close to it were covered with large herds of fine goats.

31 Almost certainly he refers to the Castle of Belver.

On the 25 October we left Gorio [Gavaio] for Nisa, marching through a rugged and very mountainous country with large masses of stores here and there along the road rolled down from the mountains by the torrents that fall in winter. Eris [Arez], a small village stands at the extremity of an extensive heath and has a most bleak wretched appearance. The sound of the highland bagpipe drew the attention of the people and its *melody* seemed to please them. The peasantry have no peculiar dress, but wore generally a short jacket of brown cloth, with short breeches, gaiters and a cloak of the same colour. About ten o'clock we saw Nisa surrounded by hills and abounding in wood. The town is partly enclosed by an old wall, strengthened by towers and now mouldering into decay. The *Capitao General* or chief man in the place, entertained the commanding officer and his friends with great civility and hospitable attention.

Next morning [26 October] we came to the famous pass of Villa Vella [Vila Velha de Rodao] about two leagues from Nisa and for the last time crossed the Tagus in boats. This is esteemed one of the best defences of Portugal, as a very few determined men, with its natural situation might defend the passage against an army. The scenery about it is noble and wild to a degree and the marching zigzag of the tracks down the steeps with the fineness of the weather, heightened the prospect greatly. Four companies being left at Villa Vella [Vila Velha de Rodao], the headquarters of the regiment proceeded to Salzadas [Sarnadas Rodao], a very wretched poor village. In such places the vicar's house is in general the best supplied and with little scruple the church often suffers.

Next day the 27 October brought us to Castello Branco [Castelo Branco], a very old town in the province of Beyra [Beira] and on the small River Lyra. It stands on the declivity of a rise, at the top of which is an ancient castle connected by a long extending wall. Our men were quartered in two large convents and the officers were dispersed among the inhabitants. My fortune brought me into the home of the wealthiest man in the town, who had lodged Junot on his way to Lisbon and by him was deprived of two carriages and four horses in lieu of contribution.

We remained here two days and left Castello Branco [Castelo Branco] on the 29 [October] in high spirits and excellent order. The face of the country still continued rugged and the soil scanty, yielding but little to the industrious rustic. Atalaya [Atalaia do Campo] where we halted for the night was poor indeed and our beds were our cloaks laid on heaps of rye and wheat in the corner of our parlour.

[30 October] With expectations of finding but little comfort on our next march, we proceeded to Compaheirha [Castanheira de Baixo] and with difficulty found quarters. In the evening we had a Route from the headquarters of the division for three companies to go on to[wards] Guarda, there to remain at Velha [Vela] a small village between Guarda and Belmonde [Belmonte] and the headquarters with the rest at the latter place.

Next day [31 October] we proceeded according to our new Route and passed the pretty little village of Coria [Caria] where finding excellent water we halted and partook of the supply in our haversacks. Pursuing our march, we ascended a very steep mountain on whose summit we had a most extensive and finely varied prospect. Below us as we advanced we beheld Belmonte, situated on a hill in the middle of a fine fertile plain, watered by many streamlets and bounded by a lofty range of mountain, whose sides new clothed by the chestnut tree. Far as the eye could carry, was a view of the '*closed kissing mountains*' near Alemeda and Guarda shrouded in snow.

Arriving at Belmonte the different companies journeyed on to their appointed stations and the officers and men at headquarters were billeted. We narrowly escaped a shower and from the advanced time of the year, we had reason to fear a continuance of bad weather. We found the inhabitants of this little village very civil, extending their hospitality as far as their scanty means would admit. We had expectations of a halt here for a few days and being very comfortable it was not at all disagreeable.

About three leagues across the valley lies the town of Gavillao [Covilha?], one of the first manufacturing places of Portugal and beautifully situated on the declivity of the mountain. The country abounded in game, especially hares, which afforded us both amusement and profit.

The scenery round Belmonte was most enchanting and highly diversified, commanding at one *coup d'oeil*,[32] hill, dale, wood, water and the distant mountains in their winter's clothing. The chestnut tree in great abundance round the little village and were at this season loaded with their prickly fruit, which serves as a great part of the subsistence of the peasantry, being wholesome and nutritious food.

November 1808

On the 3 November, we had orders to move to Guarda, on the following day, but the weather being very unfavourable, it was postponed to the 5th instant, when we proceeded to the small village of Vella [Vela] which lay embasoned in by high mountains in a thick wood, having a most romantic bold appearance. Here we met with civility from a nobleman possessing the principal part of the country and the only good home in the village. With very keen appetites we sat down to a sumptuous repast he had kindly prepared for us and very soon relieved the table of the load under which it groaned. With every wish of prosperity and gratitude for his noble hospitality we left the worthy senor for Guarda. The country was rugged and the roads very steep and out of all order. Many began to feel fatigued notwithstanding the

32 A glance that gives a comprehensive view.

inviting refreshment they had partaken of and it was only the sight of Guarda towering over its neighbouring hills that cheered their spirits. This was by far the most formidable march we had as yet undergone and tired and exhausted we reached Guarda and men and officers were billeted on the inhabitants.

Guarda is in the province of Beira, is situated on a hill, very high above the level of the sea and is by nature so strong that if fortified is capable of enduring a long siege. The town from its position is very irregular, streets narrow, with very few good houses, except those of the clergy and those in the public square. It was the see of a bishop suffrageous[33] to Braga and is very lucrative. The convents and nunneries are here very numerous both within and out of town, but the fair devotees by no means had the behaviour or appearance of women who had relinquished solemnly all worldly desires and pleasures. The weather had been very bad and gave us serious apprehensions of having often wet jackets on our ensuing march.

As we had anticipated we marched on the 7 November from Guarda under a copious shower of rain which continued until we arrived at a small village with scarce room to lay our heads on. A fire of wood in the old vicar's house served to dry our clothes for next day's ducking and to cook our humble fare, a wooden armoire[34] being our bed. Mulled wine from mother church made us forget all our miseries and cares and being Saturday now, we drank '*sweethearts and lovers*'.[35] Having amply remunerated the cure for all he had procured us, we set off in as heavy a shower of rain as ever poured from the heavens and in an instant our bodies were thoroughly moistened.

33 Having voting rights in the Archdiocese of Braga.

34 A cupboard or wardrobe.

35 The traditional Royal Navy toast for a Saturday.

Coming up with the other companies at Morisco [Monteiros?] we continued our Route towards the Spanish dominions, hoping for better country and accommodation. We soon gained the ancient town of Castell Mendo [Castelo Mendo], which is surrounded by old walls and ditches and where we left four companies to be quartered. We passed through a very wild, rocky and sterile country and crossing the Coa, came to Castell Bom [Castelo Bom], another old fortified place on a hill near the river.

After a very tedious march we at length arrived at Freineda, a very indifferent village, but the last we had in Portugal. Our landlord here, we found to be a most jealous devotee to the rosy God and we had great mirth with him until the copious libations he swallowed, took their full effect, when a strong able bodied Portuguese woman lifted him into bed. The Portuguese seldom exceed in wine and this was the only instance we had seen of complete inebriety.

Crossing the border into Spain James, like most of his contemporaries, found a marked difference in the country and people and evinced a great preference for Spain.

On the 9 November we commenced our march into Spain and crossing over a barren heath about two leagues from Freineda, we came to a cross, which the guide informed us was the boundary to the two countries. Very soon after a great difference was visible both in the appearance and language of the people. At a considerable distance we had a view of Ciudad Rodrigo and about a mile from it, forded a river[36] which took the soldiers up to the middle.

The situation of Ciudad Rodrigo on the Agueda is fine and over it is a neat well-constructed bridge, part of it modern and the other part ancient.[37] On our entrance we were greeted

36 The River Azaba.

37 The bridge at Ciudad Rodrigo is first-century Roman.

with cheers from all sides, firing of guns and waving of handkerchiefs from the windows. On coming to the square in the centre of the town we drew up and gave three successive huzza's which the people returned with great enthusiasm. The officers received billets in the best houses in town and the men were comfortably lodged in two large convents.

Ciudad Rodrigo is a town in the Kingdom of Leon, on the river Agueda in an extensive and fertile plain. It has often been taken and retaken by the Spaniards and Portuguese, but lately it has become a rendezvous for the former, previous to a war with Portugal. It is walled round and fortified, but very indifferently; a neighbouring hill appeared likewise to command it. The streets are narrow and the homes of the clergy the only tolerable ones. It contains a fine cathedral in the Gothic style built by Ferdinand 2nd of Leon[38] and is the see of a bishop suffrageous on [Santiago de] Compostella. It has seven gates and 12,000 inhabitants. In the Plaza Mayor are three Roman columns on a triangular base, with Roman inscriptions on the cornices. The plain which is bounded by a chain of mountains abounds in grain, olives, vines, almond trees and in some parts, sheep and goats have pasture.

The Spaniards have a decided superiority of appearance over their western neighbours, their features possessing more regularity and by so many of so dark a cast. Throughout our march in Portugal, we found the better sort of people very much attached to the English and everywhere showed a wish to accommodate and please us. They appeared to be but ill-informed and to be upwards of two hundred years behind England or France in every particular. The lower class possess no education, being only able to follow the priest in muttering an '*Ave Maria*' learnt by memory. They have meanness and poverty depicted in their visages, and the latter along with idleness, often induced them to lay their hands on anything belonging to us that came in their way. Higher and lower

38 King Fernando II (1157–88).

classes are dirty in their houses and persons. The Spaniards of Leon seemed to bear the national character of taciturnity and gravity in their aspect. Their dress which generally is a short brown jacket, vest, breeches and gaiters, is always covered by a large loose cloak, sensing to keep out the heat in summer and the cold in winter. A large round brimmed hat, or a pyramidical cap is the headdress. The women of the higher sort, dress in black, with a mantilla neatly placed on the head and falling down [onto] the shoulders. Their petticoats worn short, display a pretty leg and sandals lined their feet and ankles.

The peasant girls wear a sort of round white hat, large gold earrings, necklaces of the same, wound round their necks several times, ornamented with figures of saints and santas[39] and a chemise finely wrought, closed over the bosom. Their waists small and large sleeves open behind. The petticoat is generally of a dark colour, often yellow, very loose and short. Stockings of various dye's and finely ornamented. Strong leather shoes with large silver buckles complete the dress of the fair ones. They excel in dancing boleros, fandangos and Spanish contre dances[40] and often are accompanied with castanets, or an instrument called Pandero [Pandeiro], or a sort of tambourine. We found no regular troops in garrison, the inhabitants mounting guard over the gates and on the ramparts.

On the 11 [November] Sir John Moore came into town and was received by a salute of 21 guns and other demonstrations of joy. We received orders at evening parade to march next morning towards Salamanca, where it was presumed the army would concentrate. On the alameda or promenade, which no Spanish town is without we had an immense assemblage of

39 Holy figures.

40 Country dances.

people principally the ladies, who condescended to admire the music and the highland dress.

On the 12 [November], we left Ciudad Rodrigo towards Salamanca and our first journey brought us to a small village called St Martin del Rio [Martin de Yeltes], where meeting with an American in the service of Spain, we continued to fare better than we had any reason to expect.

Next day [13 November] we entered on the fine plains of Leon, covered with the olive and dwarf oak and interspersed with numerous villages. On the acorns of the latter, the Spaniards feed their pigs, which are reckoned very delicate eating. Our accommodations this night in the house of the padre cure, were far superior to what we had the preceding march and the country now fertile, needing but little attention from the husbandman. The roads from Rodrigo to Salamanca are reckoned bad, especially near the rock of Del Gitano[41] but as we approach the latter city we found them improve. Next journey brought us within three leagues of Salamanca after traversing one of the most extensive plains in Europe and passing through the villages of San Munoz, Calzada de Don Diego and Calzadilla [Calzadilla de la Valmuza] situated on the small river Balmuza [Valmuza], which we forded. These vast plains are cultivated with wheat, barley, rye and beans. They are well watered and in several parts are pastures for sheep and cattle.

From the small village of Barhadilla [Barbadillo] we proceeded on towards the long and justly celebrated city of Salamanca and where we promised ourselves a longer and more comfortable rest than what we had yet found on our march. At a distance we beheld the grandeur of its churches and convents

41 *A View of Spain* volume 2, by Alexander De Laborde states that the rock of Del Gitano was an encumbrance to the road between Ciudad Rodrigo and Sancti Spiritus, 1 league from the fortress.

and as we approached the town found an amphitheatre, on the river, over which is a beautiful and elegantly constructed bridge of 25 arches and nearly five hundred feet long.[42]

The people received us with the greatest cordiality and the men were well accommodated in one of the seminaries, whilst the officers obtained generally good billets on respectable families. We had scarcely been well settled in our respective quarters when an alarm was given that the enemy was advancing in strength from Valladolid and having here only three brigades of infantry, that we should be obliged to retreat. For a few hours all was bustle and concern depicted in our countenances, [at] the disappointment we were about to meet with, but it was discovered that it was the Spaniards had caused it, by a few hussars in new clothing entering Valladolid, their inexperienced comrades took the alarm and circulated the rumour which created such unpleasant ideas in our minds at Salamanca.

However, we had news at least bad enough to throw a damp on our hopes. We learnt the total defeat of Blake's army[43] and the Estramadura army of 14,000 were at Burgos. It was supposed before these disasters that the British and Spanish forces might have amounted to 113,000 men and the French army in Spain to 200,000 men.

Salamanca is the first university in Spain and is styled by the Spaniards '*the mother of arts and learning*'. The town is extensive, well peopled and is situated partly on small eminences and partly on a plain on the river Tormes. The university was founded in the year 1200, by Alphonso the 9th King of Leon[44] and afterwards better established by Alphonso the Wise.[45] The number of students had decreased

42 Salamanca bridge actually consists of two bridges; the fifteen arches nearest the city comprise the first-century Roman bridge, the outer ten arches are medieval in origin.

43 General Joachim Blake's army had been heavily defeated on 10 November 1808 at the Battle of Espinosa de los Monteros.

44 The University of Salamanca was established by King Alfonso IX of Leon 1n 1218.

45 Alfonso X of Castille (1221–84).

but at former periods they were estimated at 16,000 and were from England, Germany, France and Holland. There are nearly forty professors and upwards of twenty colleges, the students wearing black gowns, their heads shaved and a small cap covering it, the only headdress permitted except in bad rainy weather. The cathedral is Gothic and is one of the most magnificent in Spain. The chief entrance especially is grand and finely executed, having various bas reliefs, but those of our Saviour, our Lady and the Adoration of the Kings are particularly beautiful. The cloister is worthy of notice and the inside of this church is by far the neatest and the workmanship the finest in the country. The small chapels in the aisles are highly ornamented and contain several good paintings. One in particular of our Saviour and the Virgin by Leonardo de Vinci is executed in the best style. The floor is done in mosaic and there are two fine organs and a curious choir in wood.

The number of magnificent colleges, churches, convents and nunneries is immense and most of them are ornamented with great profusion. They had all libraries and manuscripts, more or less valuable, with relicts of saints and santas famous for their miraculous performances. The square may be reckoned one of the finest and most regular in Spain. There is a portico round it of homely arcades, the houses above rising to the height of three stories [*sic*] with each a handsome iron gilt balcony.

In the archiraltes[46] are medallions of the Kings of Castille and Leon down to Charles 3rd[47] and it has 4 grand entrances. The streets are narrow and unless in the grand square there are few good shops. The bridge before alluded to is attributed to the Normans.

The town is surrounded by old towers and walls, on which they had erected houses and a fine promenade goes round

46 This term is obscure, but it describes the wall between the arches, usually termed a spandrel.

47 Charles III reigned 1759–88.

under the walls, where our bands were sent every evening for the amusement of the Spanish senoras. There the people dressed more in the fashion of the French about twenty years back and both men and women displayed but little taste in their dresses. The hidalgo was generally shrouded in his large mantilla, with a large broad brimmed chapeau and altogether had a mean, indolent and dirty appearance. The females have long narrow waists, short petticoats and whether natural or artificial, show no deficiency in that part of their persons which was so much in activity in the boleros and fandango. We found every article of life in great abundance and certainly very cheap, when considering that by the 1st Division we had nearly 20,000 men in and about the town.

Our old host dreading the aspect of affairs left Salamanca soon after we arrived and retiring into Extremadura, gave his housekeeper orders to let us have everything we required in the house which we found during our residence most punctually obliged.

With the majority of the troops marching from Portugal finally arriving safely at Salamanca via their three separate routes, Sir John Moore now awaited the arrival of the additional 10,000 troops under Sir David Baird, which had landed at Corunna. However, Hope's column with all of Moore's artillery was yet to arrive and was in grave danger of being attacked by the advancing French forces as it took a circuitous route which passed close to Madrid.

December 1808

By the 1 of December we had heard of the arrival of Sir David Baird[48] at Corunna and that he had reached Astorga on the 19 November, uniting himself with the Spaniards under the Marquis de Romana.[49] Soon after this our news were bad

48 Lieutenant General Sir David Baird had gained great military experience in India and Egypt.

49 Pedro Caro y Sureda Marques de la Romana commanded the Army of Galicia.

and things assumed a very dismal fortune. Castanos[50] and Palafox[51] had both been overthrown, the French profiting by their victories were fast advancing towards Madrid, Sir David Baird could not effect a junction before the 7 of December and Sir John Hope[52] had not as yet approached Salamanca. Thus affairs stood in the beginning of the month and our fears were increased by daily observing stores, sick and Staff officers proceeding to Almeida and Portugal.[53] At Madrid the French had met with some resistance, but soon it was natural to suppose they would make themselves masters of an unfortified capital garrisoned only by its inhabitants. We had a current report that Sir David Baird had got orders to retreat on Corunna and that Sir John Moore was determined to retreat on Portugal, but Lord William Bentinck's[54] arrival from Madrid on the 2nd, seemed to alter our course, and we were to advance, edging towards Sir David Baird's corps. We had also the pleasing intelligence of the junction of the corps d'armee under General Hope, who had made a most narrow escape. The supineness, inactivity and evident treachery of the Spaniards had determined Sir John [Moore] to retire on Portugal and we now only advanced through the entreaties of Mr Frere our Ambassador,[55] who represented how disadvantageous a retreat would be to the Spanish cause at present and that an advance joined by Sir David Baird and the Spaniards, would have the effect of

50 General Francisco Javier Castanos, 1st Duke of Bailen. His army was heavily defeated on 23 November 1808 at the Battle of Tudela.

51 General Jose de Palafox y Melci, 1st Duke of Zaragoza.

52 Lieutenant General Sir John Hope commanded the third part of the advance from Portugal, consisting of Stewarts' Cavalry Brigade, Catlin Craufurd's Infantry Brigade and the entire six companies of artillery. This force took an incredibly circuitous route via Badajoz and the Escurial near Madrid to get to Salamanca, because Moore had been informed that the other routes were useless for artillery. It only luckily escaped the French advance, because Napoleon was unaware of its presence. The route marched by the 42nd from Lisbon to Salamanca was about 520km, whereas Hope's march was in excess of 900km to arrive at Salamanca.

53 This would likely indicate a retreat into Portugal.

54 Major General Lord William Bentinck.

55 John Hookham Frere, plenipotentiary to the Spanish Central Junta.

drawing the enemy's attention from Madrid and Zaragossa [Zaragoza], threatening their communications and favour the rallying of the Spaniards in the middle and southern provinces. It was however evident all along that our commander had no confidence in the Spaniards and had he acted as he wished we should have retreated on Portugal.

Lord William Bentinck took the command of our brigade,[56] inspected it and ordered everything to be in readiness to advance. Indeed, we had nearly been a month in Salamanca and its inhabitants here looking on us with eyes of discontent and anxiety for our departure. During our residence at Salamanca not one unpleasant event had occurred between the Spaniards and our troops and we only had to lament that our rest had been so prolonged. The town afforded the amusements of billiards and other games, whilst we found in the country, fine walks and excellent shooting. A great source of curiosity and amusement was visiting the various colleges, churches and convents. Into the latter we never gained admittance further than the iron grating in the receiving parlour, where we had to converse & pay our compliments to the devoted but fading victims to religion. Few of them were young, fewer still were pretty, but they sustained a frank and lively conversation and in their expressions were most complimentary to the English. The different orders have peculiar dresses, are more or less strict in their privations and religious exercises and their numbers seldom exceed forty sisters. Notwithstanding the severe discipline, they appeared delighted with their seclusion from the world and none of them ever expressed a solitary wish to be released.

By the 10 [December], all was on the alert and in readiness to proceed, our hopes being raised by information that Sir David

56 Bentinck had been appointed to command the brigade in October, but does not appear to have taken up his command until 1 December, being on detached service at Madrid. Lieutenant Colonel James Wynch, 4th Foot, temporarily commanded the brigade until his arrival. In December the Brigade consisted on 1/4th, 1/42nd & 1/50th, the five companies of the 5/60th attached to the brigade having been ordered back to Portugal.

Baird was at Astorga, his cavalry at Toro and [was] joined by [La] Romana.

On the 11 [December] General Paget's Division[57] marched

And we received orders to move likewise on the 12 [December].

After a long rest of a month at Salamanca we set off with every prayer for our success and desire soon to encounter our enemies. The weather was very fine, the men in high spirits, the artillery and cavalry well appointed, all bade us hope for a happy issue to our campaign. The country through which we marched was level and sandy, but the road was excellent, permitting us to march in subdivisions. The small village of Puente Saloco [Fuentesauco] contained us and for one night the accommodations were tolerable.

Next day [13 December] we joined the Commander in Chief at Alejos [Alaejos], after a march of six leagues through a country equally flat as our first day's march. Alejos [Alaejos] is one of the best of nearly thirty villages or pueblas, we saw at one *coup d'oeil* and possesses a square, two churches, a castle which appears from its regularity to be rather a modern structure, having a wall with bastions and a very deep ditch. We halted here one day, posting strong, out and inlying picquets, as by various accounts we are not far distant from the enemy. General Stewart[58] with a part of the 18th Hussars had surprised and taken a French post at Rueda & the prisoners consisting of two officers and about thirty-three men arrived at headquarters at Alejos [Alaejos] this morning. Several of them were badly wounded, but the Spaniards wished us to have no compassion on them, but to draw them out and shoot them.

57 Major General Sir Edward Paget commanded the Reserve Division.

58 Brigadier General Charles Stewart.

It was supposed the Commander in Chief had received here an intercepted correspondence, of some consequence, but its imports never transpired.

On the 15 [December] we marched for Toro, a city but little inferior in magnitude to Salamanca. By this movement we were performing a forward and flank manoeuvre, so as to unite the sooner with the forces under Sir David Baird. The weather fortunately was very fine, the roads good, the country and views rich and romantic, but the march most tedious being upwards of eight Spanish leagues, a distance which is equal to thirty-two English miles, not considering the fatigue necessarily attendant on a march with a large body of troops. Nearly exhausted by the heat of the day and length of march, we descried Toro on the ridge of a hill overlooking the Duero[59] and plain beneath. We approached the town by a bridge, half of stone, the rest of wood[60] and ascending the brow of a steep mountain reached the summit on which Toro is most commandingly situated. It is called an ancient town, was formerly much more extensive than at present and is surrounded by hard walls and towers, monuments of Moorish architecture. There was fought here a famous battle in the year 1476, between Alfonso of Portugal and Ferdinand of Castile.[61] It is on the right bank of the river, in the part of the country called Tras a Duoro, is famous for municipal laws, or Leyes de Toro[62] and excellent wine and fruits. It contains eight thousand inhabitants, about twelve or fourteen churches and convents, none of them much worthy of notice except the principal church, which seems to be of Saxon architecture and has curious work at the entrances.

We now are joined by Sir David Baird.

59 The river is known as the Duero in Spain and the Douro in Portugal.

60 The Puente Mayor.

61 The Battle of Toro on 1 March 1476 was part of the War of the Castilian Succession, between Ferdinand II of Aragon and Afonso V of Portugal.

62 The 83 Laws of Toro were established in 1505.

And on the 16 [December] were all on the move to the front in search of the enemy who it was supposed was not very distant under the command of Marshal Soult.[63] The country through which we marched this day was very different to that we had just passed, although there were many villages and well peopled, yet the country was dreary and uncultivated. It is very rare in any part of Spain to find a detached farmhouse, or to see a well-stocked barnyard, all the inhabitants concentrating in small miserable villages, the houses often built of mud. Villadiego [Villardondiego] was the name of our village and we were very badly accommodated. The weather had begun to get very cold and a large fall of snow in the evening by no means added to our comforts. The men here wore a dress completely made of sheepskin, a larger one hanging over their shoulders and both sexes wore large wooden clogs on their feet.

On the 17 [December], we again advanced through a naked, desolate tract of country, the snow which had fallen rendering the roads very unpleasant. We were quartered in a village called Villa Nova del Campo [Villanueva del Campo], the men were put into a country church,[64] where they kindled large fires and made themselves as comfortable as a damp Catholic church would admit of.

Next morning [18 December] we again pursued our way, which was impeded by another severe fall of snow and hard frost, which making the roads like glass, our artillery horses and baggage mules, were tumbling every step and became a most serious hardship. Owing to these embarrassments it was the close of evening before we reached our destination when tired and comfortless, we retired to ease our wearied limbs, chusing [*sic*] the softest plank in our woe-begone dwelling.[65]

---

63 Marshal Jean-de-Dieu Soult commanded II Corps in Spain.

64 Almost certainly the *Iglesia de Santo Tomas*.

65 It is likely that they were quartered near Villagomez la Nueva that night.

Next morning [19 December] the snow had gone off the ground and the weather was not so piercingly cold, but the bleak mountains on every side of us, presented no object of interest. Towards the afternoon we came to Grahal [Grajal de Campos], a village containing but little accommodation for the great numbers poured into it. About 3 o'clock after being settled in our quarters, a general alarm was given that the enemy was advancing on Sahagun, a place about a mile distant. In a few minutes the division was under arms and it caused a good deal of mirth to see old, lame and blind Spaniards crawling out of hovels in all kinds of habiliments and with the greatest celerity taking their wooden clogs off their feet and running in all directions except in that threatened, crying '*Viva!! Los Valerosos Ingleses*' [Viva, the Brave English]. Finding however that the alarm was occasioned by a commissariat, who hearing from the Spaniards that the enemy were entering Sahagun, instantly took it for granted and rode back to impart the intelligence. We re-entered our billets.

[20–21 December] Indeed, the accounts were so different that it was our victorious cavalry that were in Sahagun; Lord Paget being ordered in front to occupy the village mentioned, fell in with a detachment of the enemy's cavalry, who had occupied the town on the 20th instant and although inferior in point of numbers, our gallant hussars attacked and defeated them, taking upwards of 200 prisoners, among them several officers.[66]

Colonel Grant[67] and Major Jones[68] of the 15th were the only officers wounded and few of our men had suffered. It was however remarked that our hussars were principally wounded

66 The Action of Sahagun occurred on the morning of 21 December 1808. The 15th Hussars encountered two regiments of French cavalry in the early morning light, charged immediately and the French cavalry were broken and fled. There were a number of killed and wounded and 12 officers and 145 men were captured.

67 Lieutenant Colonel Colquhoun Grant commanding the 15th Hussars.

68 Lieutenant Charles Jones, 15th Hussars, was Brigade Major.

in the head, a circumstance too plainly demonstrating the little use of their helmets which were more for ornament than protection. Thus, in two encounters of our cavalry with that of the enemy they had been successful, and redoubled our wishes to share with them the dangers of the fight. We had every reason to presume the day was not far off, as Soult with two divisions [II Corps] was at Saldana and next morning would push us very near him.

On the 22 [December] we were under arms at break of day and at 10 o'clock received orders to march and be brigaded in General Sir David Baird's Division at Sahagun.[69] There the men were put into a large noble monastery[70] and the officers were put into billets, several of them however were obliged to take up their quarters with the friars.

In the General Orders of this day the Commander in Chief bestowed great and very deserved praise on the 15th and 18th Regiments of Hussars, for their gallant conduct since the beginning of the campaign and felt confident the infantry would emulate them when brought into the field. An incident of an extraordinary kind was related of the affair of yesterday, of an officer of our [light] dragoons, who had taken the horse and baggage of a wounded French officer and on examining the valise, found therein a 'silver ewer' and 'bason' beat together, along with the handles of 'silver knives and forks' and above all a finely embroidered *jacket*, which bore the '*Croix d'Honneur*'.

We had intelligence of Marshal Soult being at Saldana, and there with 18,000 men had taken up a strong position on the Carrion River. Our force at Sahagun might be estimated at 23,000 infantry and about 2,000 cavalry, with some odd detachments.

69 Bentinck's 2nd Brigade now in Baird's 1st Division (Baird preferring a command to simply being second-in-command).

70 Almost certainly the Monasterio de Santa Cruz.

Sir John Moore, receiving news that Marshal Soult had been reinforced and that Napoleon had launched all of his troops in his direction, called off the attack. James' account of the reaction by the troops to this bad news is very interesting.

> **On the 23 [December]**, we were out at daybreak, when various conjectures were hazarded as to the future operations of the army. Our breasts beat with anxiety and we were confident, let our enemies be whatever strength, that success would crown our efforts. At last, our doubts were cleared to the satisfaction of every single individual of the army and everything bade us trust that another day of glory would shine on the Colours of Britain. In the afternoon orders were issued for the troops to hold themselves in readiness to march at 7 o'clock in the evening; the artillery to be drawn up in front on the road leading to Saldana. The men's arms and ammunition to be inspected and all baggage and women to be brought together at a certain rendezvous.
>
> Everything showed that Sir John had adopted the glorious determination to attack the enemy and no decision could have been more eagerly embraced by his whole army. Everyone seemed animated with the same spirit and the enthusiasm that glowed in this handful of Britons is perfectly indescribable. We were to move in two columns at 8 o'clock at night and by break of day we should be close to our foes, who no doubt from their strong position, would give us a warm reception.
>
> At the appointed hour our men were under arms and in the most cheering spirits. The artillery were on the road, the baggage collected, the necessary arrangements made for the wounded in the convents, all with impatience awaited the moment of attack. The spirit that ran throughout our ranks, was the most impetuous we witnessed. Every heart beat high, every breast was buoyant for victory and every countenance demonstrated the eagerness with which they awaited the order to advance. Our grenadiers had reached the foot of the

convent stairs, when astonished and struck with dismay we heard Sir David Baird give these heartrending orders '*Go back to your quarters and be ready to march in the morning.*' For several moments the men stood transfixed and at length their disappointment broke out into a mummer and every countenance lost its high brought anxiety.

Indeed, the effect of this counter order on our soldiers, was the most extraordinary and from the greatest pitch of exultation and courage, at once a solemn gloom prevailed throughout our ranks. Nothing was heard on every side, but the clang of firelocks thrown down in despair which before they guarded as their dearest treasure and from the high order they were in, had placed in them implicit confidence.

The reasons for abandoning so grand a design where glory seemed calling for our commander to obey and secure a victory so decidedly within his reach, did not transpire until next morning. At 8 o'clock the very hour destined for us to march, Sir John received a courier from the Marquis de Romana, with intelligence of the advance of Soult who had received reinforcements from Palencia. These circumstances caused our general to relinquish an attack, which although successful could not have been of any ultimate advantage to the cause we were engaged in.

On the 24 [December] we received orders to march at 5 o'clock in the morning next day, an order but too sadly confirming the instability of all human affairs, for it was to retreat with all our gay hopes and desires withered and fled.

[25 December] Alas! Christmas day, when every peasant at home now enjoying the cheerful festivities of this sacred season, our spirits broken and our bodies exhausted, with no hopes of better nourishment we pursued our dreary march, knee deep in mud and dirt, drenched to the skin with rain and but few of us brought either shoe or stocking to our journey's end. Our situation now reminded me of Southey's poem on

Christmas day when travelling over the same unfavoured country.

'How many hearts are happy at this hour
In England! Brightly o'er the cheerful hall
Flares the heaped hearth, and friends and kindred meet,
And the glad mother round her festive board
Beholds her children, separated long
Amid the wide world's ways, assembled now
A sight at which affection lightens up
With smiles the eye that age has long bedimm'd
I do remember, when I was a child,
How my young heart, a stranger then to care;
With transport leap'd upon this holyday,
As o'er the house, all gay with evergreens,
From friend to friend with joyful speed I ran,
Bidding a merry Christmas to them all.
Those years are past; their pleasures and their pains
Are now like yonder convent-crested hill
That bounds the distant prospect, indistinct,
Yet pictured upon memory's mystic glass
In faint, fair hues. A weary traveller now
I journey o'er the desert mountain tracks
Of Leon, wilds all drear and comfortless,
Where the grey lizards in the noontide sun
Sport on the rocks, and where the goatherd starts
Roused from his sleep at midnight when he hears
The prowling wolf, and falters as he calls
On Saints to save. Here of the friends I think
Who now, I ween, remember me, and fill
The glass of votive friendship.'[71]

About 3 o'clock the Brigade of Guards halted at a small village and at 4, we were crammed into a parcel of old huts, drenched

71 From Southey's '*Written on Christmas Day, 1795*'.

to the skin, but glad to get any place to rest our wearied limbs. No roast beef or plum pudding graced our board this gay day and our havresacks [*sic*] were only replenished with a hard biscuit and a piece of cold beef. The march of this day was attended with every sort of sense and inconvenience of a retrograde movement. We now began to feel the horrors of war and taste the fatigues of a retreat in winter through a wretched country.

And what distresses had we awaiting us, when so much appeared the first day, especially what could become of our wretched females, who in multitudes were following the army, with poor helpless infants on their backs? The sensation of what should befall us, had our retreat continued, only served to make our feelings the most poignant, although we had every reason to presume that Astorga would be our rallying point.

We pursued our retreat on the 26 [December], our mules and baggage being sent off at 2 o'clock in the morning in order to cross the Esla at Valentia de Don Juan [Valencia de Don Juan]. At this place we halted for some time and received provisions. It stands on a very noble and picturesque situation overlooking the Esla, a river of some consideration, which runs into the Duero. Its principal ornament is a strong Moorish fort, the view from it is lively and commands a large extent of country, which if we might judge from the number of villages must be very populous.

After remaining one hour we descended a steep hill down to the river which the men forded, it taking them up to the armpits. Many of our poor women suffered here, for their obstinate perseverance in following a campaign, many of their famished asses, loaded with their panniers and children found the current so strong that there was no resisting it; and so perished. Unfortunately, these were not the days of chivalry, for our commanders constrained us to pass on, without any attempt to assist them.

After crossing the river we marched on to a small village called Villa Mairana [Villamanan] and from the distribution made of the troops, a momentary halt was to be expected. The rain had fallen incessantly since the direful morning of our retreat, the rivers in consequence were much swollen and the roads hardly passable.

We remained in our little village on the 27 [December] and comforted ourselves with mulled wine of the country which was in plenty and excellent. In the evening we received forage and provisions for some days and also orders to march next morning.

[28 December] Soon after daybreak we were on the march and joined the other corps of the division and were again in full retreat. The weather still was most unfavourable, the roads knee deep and the soldiers at every step losing their shoes and dropping behind. What a difference exists between that of an advancing and retreating army, especially when composed of English.[72] All their spirit and emulation to keep up, was now changed to dejection and disappointment.

We lingered on until quarters were allotted for us in a small village called Don Pedro [San Pedro Bercianos], where neither by love or money could we procure anything comfortable. We halted here on the 29 [December].

And on the 30 [December] again proceeded through a country which promised a better reception than we had experienced. The scenery was pretty, the vallies [*sic*] fertile and little rivulets ran through the vineyards which appeared abundant, whilst the mountains of Galicia and Asturia far behind were rearing their stupendous heads in the clouds.

On the 30 we began our march for Astorga, where it was natural to suppose the whole of the army would join. For the

72 A seemingly strange comment for a Scotsman, but at this time *English* was often synonymous with *British*.

first time since leaving Portugal we met some native soldiers belonging to the army of the Marquis of Romana, miserable and wretched they were and came on in straggling parties of threes and fours. About a league from town, we had a salute from a Spanish squadron of cavalry, tolerably well equipped, but their appointments were all English. They were accompanied by a few pieces of artillery.

On arriving at Astorga we were greeted with the pleasing intelligence of another advantage gained over our adversaries by our brave hussars; at Benevente [Benavente] on the 29th instant, the French cavalry a second time made their appearance on the heights over the Esla. The bridge had been blown up, part of the army was out of the town on the march towards Astorga, Sir John Moore, Lord Paget, General Stewart and the cavalry alone remained. The enemy crossing below the bridge, was at first charged by the Third Regiment of German Hussars assisted by the picquets, but by the steadiness of the French hussars, the victory remained doubtful. Immediately two pieces of horse artillery was brought up and by a well-directed fire obliged the enemy to retire and gain their ford. Our brave troops followed and dreadful carnage took place on the shore. One hundred prisoners were taken and General LeFevre[73] their commandant with several officers also were among the number.

Upwards of a hundred more of the enemy were slain[74] and our loss was one officer of Germans[75] and from 50 to 60 men. The force of the enemy was five squadrons of the Imperial Hussars [Chasseurs à Cheval] and the valour and firmness reported to have been displayed was honourable to

73 General Lefebvre-Desnouettes was captured and sent to England but broke his parole and escaped.

74 The French left fifty-five dead and wounded on the field while Larrey states that he tended to seventy wounded who got away. In addition, three officers and seventy unwounded men were captured.

75 Major Burgwedel (Beamish No.866) 3rd KGL Hussars was severely wounded and retired on half-pay in April 1811.

both parties. It was believed Bonaparte in person was on the opposite side of the river and if so, it was most grateful to our feelings, to think he himself was the spectator of the defeat of his fine household troops by a handful of British hussars.[76]

Astorga is a very ancient city of the kingdom of Leon, stands in an agreeable plain on the small River Tuerto [Jerga] and is strongly fortified by art and nature. It is surrounded by a stone wall, which is in certain parts strengthened by towers, and the gates with parts of the old castle of Astorga still exist. It has four churches, one of which is a cathedral of Gothic architecture[77] and has also two convents[78] and [a] good square or marketplace. The town is not large, streets narrow and dirty and the population is small in proportion. Near Astorga is the famous Lake of Sanabria,[79] which frequently by the report of the people is agitated as greatly as the sea and has an old castle in its centre, which must add grandeur to this curious scene of nature.

[31 December] In the morning we pursued our march at 8 o'clock with the expectation of having the heavens for our canopy and of ushering in a new year without hardly a hope of having bare subsistence for another day. We were now entering into a country totally different to what we had traversed, mountains gradually rose before us; and the valleys on each side were more wild and romantic than the highly cultivated fields of fertile Leon. About 5 o'clock we reached a few miserable dwellings inhabited by horror struck and famished peasantry. Close to them we halted and piled our arms in the snow. There appeared neither wood nor water near us to cook our scanty morsel. Impatient to satisfy the urgent demands of nature, the men pulled down doors, carried away chairs, carts

76 This is something of an overstatement, the numbers of cavalry on both sides engaged being roughly equal.

77 The Cathedral de Santa Maria de Astorga.

78 The Convento de Santi Spiritus and Madras Redentoristas.

79 Sanabria Lake is some 40km to the south-west of Astorga.

&c from the isolated houses of the helpless natives. No attempt had been made by the Staff to supply the troops with wood and it was impossible to restrain the urgent and absolute wants of a fatigued and half-starved army. Indeed, destruction and terror are the concomitants of a retreating and disappointed army and the miseries and dire distress at this period of ours, is beyond the power of description. The ground around us was covered with snow, the wind was piercingly cold and shivering with hunger, we crowded round a fire and eat [*sic*] our miserable fare of roasted potatoes. Our misfortune, our misery might have been very faithfully drawn in the little poem of the Winter's day.

'*When raging storms deface the air*
And clouds of snow descend
And the wide landscape bright and fair
No deepened colours blend
When biting frost rides on the wind
Bleak from the north and east
And wealth is at its ease reclined
Prepared to laugh and feast
When the poor traveller treads the plain
All dubious of his way;
And crawls with still increasing pain
And dreads the parting day.
When poverty in rich attire
Shrinks from the biting blast,
or hovers o'er the pigmy fire
And fears it will not last.
When the fond mother hugs her child
Still closer to her breast
And the poor infant frost beguiled
Scarce feels that it is prest.
Then let the bounteous hand extend
Its blessings to the poor
Nor spurn the wretched, while they bend

All suppliant at your door'.[80]

But alas! No bounteous hand was near to supply our ranks, on the contrary the terror and alarm of a retreat, had caused the peasantry to desert their villages on our approach and left nothing but empty dwellings.

No rest was now allowed us, for we hardly had been two hours on the ground, when an order arrived from headquarters to be again on the road at 8 o'clock. The moon shone in very silvery splendour and seemed anxious for the safety of the sons of Britain, guiding us by her light through the stupendous mountains and rugged sinuosities of the road. We continued our march through a most extraordinary and highly romantic country intersected with deep ravines and rushing falls of water, until 4 o'clock in the morning when we halted, at a few deserted houses, with little or nothing to sustain nature and no wood to warm us, we laid ourselves down and endeavoured to find rest in that which when it visits misery '*It is a comforter*'.[81]

January 1809

On the 1 January 1809 we were within two days march of Villafranca [Villafranca del Bierzo], a pass where everyone indulged the hope of a temporary rest in security. On that day we marched at 12 o'clock and the weather began to moderate, when we enjoyed a journey through a pretty, undulating and well cultivated country. It was everywhere interspersed with fine and very old vineyards, olive and chestnut trees. But notwithstanding the army was destitute of provisions, many of the men wanting shoes and already horses, mules and asses lay in heaps on each side of the road, some dying for want of food and through fatigue, others from want of shoeing. In fact,

80 This anonymous poem appeared in *The New Lady's Magazine, or Polite and Entertaining Companion*, Volume 3 (1819) but as this was after James' death, it must have been written previously.

81 From Shakespeare's *The Tempest*.

new scenes of wretchedness & misery presented themselves at every step and our track was strewed with every excess, that can well be imagined.

The 2 January brought us to Cacabelos, round which the country is romantic, very productive especially in white wines. About one o'clock we also reached Villafranca [del Bierzo] situated on the River Valcarse [Valcarce][82] and is almost surrounded by mountains whose heads were covered in impenetrable snows. There we only halted for a few hours, indeed nothing indicated Sir John's intention of taking up a position, for all the stores and magazines here were ordered to be destroyed, which caused a considerable effect on the men. Rations of spirits and stores were ordered to be distributed to the soldiers, but aware that all was on the eve of being destroyed they rushed into the stores and many it is to be presumed died afterwards of intoxication.

Shoes, English saddles and bridles, in fact every necessary equipment for our army were seen rolling down the stream to prevent their being of use to the enemy, altogether the scenes that passed here during a few hours, were most racking[83] & melancholy.

In the afternoon we left Villafranca [del Bierzo] and gradually ascended the mountains we had seen and dreaded so much before us. The scenery was sublimely romantic as we passed through the *puerta* or pass, which had it been judged expedient, might have been defended by a few battalions against an army. We journeyed on until we reached a few miserable huts, indeed the air was so frigid, we were perishing with cold. On our arrival however we were comforted by intelligence from the rear, of our dragoons and riflemen again giving the enemy a lesson, making them smart for their

82 The town lies at the junction of the River Valcarce and the River Burbia.

83 Painful.

temerity. General Merle[84] and Colbert[85] lead the enemy and the latter received a mortal wound in the forehead.

On the 3 [January] we again renewed our march through these stormy regions, moving through clouds until we nearly gained the summit of the sierra. The snow was knee deep on the ground and this march exceeded in horror, anything we ever could have anticipated. The road on each side lay strewed with the dead and dying, the piercing groans of women and helpless dying, famished children in their arms, awaiting with dismay the awful moment of dissolution. Sick and wounded with incalculable pain dragging their wasted bodies over these wintry regions, our poor maimed and faithful animals expiring under burthens, or shot to prevent them falling into the hands of the enemy, waggons overturned, all presented a scene of agony, destruction and distress, that no mind can fancy, no pen describe. Two miserable women on the very summit of this stupendous mountain, gave birth to beautiful children, whilst struggling on a bullock cart and providentially both the women and children survived their awful situation. These dismal scenes of heartrending distress were before our eyes, until the evening we arrived at Doncos, a small village where we remained until daybreak.

Next morning [4 January], when again we were to bear the terrible varied ruins of another march in the trackless snow. We this day began to descend the mountains and winding down their weary zigzag path, attempted to destroy several bridges in order to endeavour to retard the vigilant pursuit of our enemies, but from their near approach the next day we had failed in our efforts.[86]

---

84 General Pierre Merle.

85 General Auguste de Colbert-Chabanais. He was shot near Cacabelos on 3 January 1809 by Rifleman Tom Plunket.

86 It is likely this night that they halted in the vicinity of Raposeira.

On the 5 [January] we still lingered on the road every hour, every day presenting objects of misery and death too affecting to enumerate. The enemy were very close, all our sick were taken and the blowing up of the bridges had surely been badly executed, for it did not serve to impede the harassing progress of the French cavalry. Having no time to pay the troops or distribute the dollars conveyed with the army, they were to a considerable amount thrown down one of the mountains among the snow and it was to be hoped this treasure would fall into the hands of the patriots as soon as the snow went off the ground. The necessity of doing this also obliged us from want of animals, to leave behind and destroy several waggon loads of clothing and other stores brought from England for the use of the Spaniards, which would be a good prize to the enemy. In the evening the cavalry passed our division to Lugo and we were quartered in a small village called Matabaxo [Matafaxin de Abaixo].

On the 6 [January], we proceeded at 6 o'clock in the morning, the weather was better, but still every ten yards the road was strewed with the carcasses of our invaluable horses and mules and the tattered shoes of our soldiers barely covered their feet. Our provisions were never regularly distributed and often when it was attempted the violence of the soldiers destroyed a great part, often leaving but little to those who were to be supplied after them. About 3 o'clock in the afternoon we were put into a few houses, with orders to be ready to march at 11 o'clock at night.

Procuring some coarse bread, we laid ourselves on the ground and refreshed our weary members by a few hours of sleep. Fortunately we had the moon for our guide, but the want of food and rest, closed many an eye in everlasting sleep this night. Marching very slow, we often got fast asleep and continued so, until awoke by running against our neighbour, when having been in the same dilemma, was astonished to find himself roused and a mutual controversy took place. If for an instant the head of the column halted, our weak frames sunk to the ground and with the greatest difficulty could we bring ourselves again to march. Thus, until daybreak we jogged on dragging our exhausted bodies to Lugo, where we remained two hours without a morsel having passed our mouths for twenty-four hours and at last were ordered into a few houses on the left of the town, with orders to be in readiness to turn out on a moment's notice.

Lugo is an ancient town of Galicia, with a rich bishopric and is situated on an eminence on the River Minho, about 12 leagues from its source & over it there is a tolerable good bridge.[87] It was of late very much diminished in size and opulence, which is shown by its towers, gates and halls, which are going fast to decay. It has a cathedral, a Bishop's palace, several convents, hospitals and a plaza maior, with a fountain. About 2 o'clock our outposts were attacked by the chasseurs of the enemy, supported by two Spanish guns which had been taken from us, but as if by inspiration the drooping spirits of our men revived and the assailants were defeated. Our loss was on this occasion little or nothing, but we beheld the conduct of our brave men, who were labouring under starvation and fatigue with delight and admiration.

On the 7 [January] also, we were turned out by a second attack from our foe, who by the firing seemed to be advancing in increased numbers. We immediately marched towards the scene of conflict and took up an excellent position in a wood opposite the enemy. The soul inspiring effect this hope of attack had on us all, but principally on the soldiers, would have made anyone suppose all our misery and fatigue had never been felt, for the crest-fallen creature who but yesterday seemed to be on the brink of eternity, no sooner heard the shout of battle than he sprung up a hero and with ardour pressed on towards the contest. In this encounter the enemy was soon repulsed and

87 Ponte Vella de Lugo.

with the loss of several prisoners. The firing having ceased, we kindled large fires in the wood and began to cook our little morceau and be ready for action in the morning. The prisoners having informed us of three divisions having reinforced the enemy, Sir John expected confidently an attack in the morning and had given his orders accordingly.

General Frazer's Division[88] which had been sent off on the road to Vigo [from Ponferrada], to follow General Craufurd's[89] and Alten's Brigades,[90] was recalled and took up its position in the evening.[91] The night came on very bad and until daybreak it rained incessantly.

[8 January] Then the whole of our force was drawn out in order of battle; but to our great mortification, Soult did not quit his position nor showed any disposition to come to a decided contest, although at 8 o'clock Sir John quitted his strong position and marching to the hollow beneath, gave the enemy a great advantage if he had been inclined to come down. It was evident our commander would have wished to fight on the 8th, but Soult awaited the divisions of Laborde[92] and Loison,[93] who being on the march to join would have given him a great superiority and during that time our supplies should have been nearly exhausted.

Under these circumstances a retreat to Corunna was ordered at even[ing] and to endeavour to deceive the enemy our fires were to be kept blazing, whilst with silence we again prosecuted our dreadful march.

88 Lieutenant General Alexander Mackenzie Fraser commanded the 3rd Division

89 Brigadier General Robert Craufurd commanded 1st Flank Brigade.

90 Brigadier General Charles Alten commanded 2nd Flank Brigade.

91 From the comment appearing at this point, it would appear that the army split near Lugo, with part of the army marching to Vigo, whereas this had actually occurred at Ponferrada.

92 General Henri Delaborde.

93 General Louis Loison.

[9 January] After considerable difficulty and the loss of several men we reached Lugo and our division allowing the Reserve[94] to pass, became the rearguard.

The torrents fell on our emaciated bodies for three hours, whilst we remained in the town for the purpose of getting all on before us and shivering with cold and hunger, we proceeded at midnight, experiencing the same melancholy scenes we had before passed. We marched all night and still the day brought us the same tempestuous, stormy weather. Near Bamonte [Baamonde] our division was drawn up in a field, under a shower incessant of the most piercing hail and sleet and desired them to remain until the enemy [arrived]. However the Colours of the regiments alone remained on the ground, the soldiers betook themselves to the village, crawling into the houses they helped themselves to whatever they found. All discipline was fled, nor was it possible for officers to remedy it by any means in their power. Large fires were made of the wood of the houses and we there remained until 6 o'clock, when we again received orders to move. But our men were so scattered, so completely worn out by want and fatigue; that they would not or could not march and on the wet ground remained rather to be taken. Threats and entreaties were tried but to no effect and leaving a field officer[95] and other officers to bring them up in the morning, we pushed on towards Betanzos, with only about six hundred men of our brigade, out of a force of nearly 2,500.

[10 January] This was the third night our eyes had never been shut and enduring every privation we arrived barefooted at Betanzos next morning at 10 o'clock. To say that there was three dozen of pairs of whole shoes in the army, would be probably exceeding, indeed many officers came in here without shoes or stockings, their pantaloons torn up to

94 The Reserve was commanded by Major General Edward Paget.

95 A field officer was of the rank of Major or above.

their knees. We remained here the rest of the day and until 10 o'clock of the 11 [January] when most of our stragglers came up. Soult from the trial of our strength at Lugo, was sensible what an English army could do in fighting when pushed, therefore allowed us to march all the way to Corunna unmolested.

Betanzos stands on a hillside, with the River Mondeo [Mendo] running at the foot, which falls into the Bay of Ferrol. It is only three leagues from Corunna and the country is abundant in wine. It has a square and only one street.

Proceeding towards Corunna we blew up the bridge at Betanzos[96] and shortly after ascended a hill from whence we with unspeakable delight beheld the ocean and the end of our disastrous march. Blowing up another bridge over an arm of the sea,[97] we arrived at Corunna at 5 o'clock on the 11 January 1809, after having suffered every privation, disappointment and an accumulation of misery with the most dire calamities, that ever befell an army.

[11–12 January] There we found ourselves more comfortable than we had been since leaving Salamanca and had the transports from Vigo arrived, should have embarked immediately, but the wind was unfair and we saw ourselves obliged to wait with patience. Returns of all deficiencies were given in and the soldiers were supplied with stores. The sick at the same time put into hospitals and gradually recovering our lost discipline, we experienced every attention from the inhabitants who had formed themselves in[to] regiments in order to assist us and all seemed devoted to their country.

Corunna is a rich maritime city of Galicia, situated at the foot of a range of hills, built on a small *peninsula* and has an excellent harbour defended by the two forts of

96 The Ponte Vella.

97 The Ponte Romano de Burgo.

St Omaro[98] and St Antonio [Santo Antono]. The bay runs as far into the land nearly as Betanzos and the harbour is in the form of a crescent. It is divided into the old and new towns, which are both well built, the latter containing a citadel, covering the harbour and houses. The lower town is far superior and contains many good houses, churches and convents. The citadel has cost much labour and expense, in it are the houses of the Capitan General, Governor and Staff and also of other grandees, as also a theatre. The last side is entirely occupied by forts and batteries. There is a tower called the '*Tower of Hercules*',[99] it is strong and very solid and is supposed to be the work of the ancient Phoenicians. A very handsome lighthouse is erected near the town, to discover the face of the land at Cape Ortegal and is seen at a distance of 20 leagues. From Corunna a fine view of Ferrol is commanded, which is situated on the northeast side and used to be a famous port for the Navy of Spain but is now much reduced. The commerce of Corunna is not great and chiefly consists of hats, rope, lace, comb and linen manufactories.

The people of Galicia and more particularly the inhabitants of this town have showed no want of patriotism, had they been properly supported by their countrymen; but it was greatly to be feared it would soon be only repaid on themselves, as soon as we should leave them. The country people of this province are a quiet, simple, industrious race, enduring great fatigue and cold, with but little support. They are faithful, of honest principles, docile and submissive. From the latter quality and persevering industry, they are employed in the other parts of Spain and in Portugal, as servants and porters, are often ill-used and it is a common proverb in Spain, '*I was treated as if I had been a Galician*' '*Me ham tratado comma un Gallego*'.

98 The other fort at the entrance to Corunna was Fort San Diego,

99 The Tower of Hercules is the oldest lighthouse in existence, with Roman origins. It was previously known as Farum Brigantium.

The men are strong and very muscular, furnishing many young men for the army, which from their courage and pliancy, become good soldiers. The women are fair in general, but have by no means expressive features. All go barefooted or are sandalled and the language is a sort of patois mixed a good deal with Arabic.

On the 13 [January], we were ordered to be in readiness to march and occupy a position in front of the town, leaving the sick and baggage to be embarked as soon as the transports should come round [from Vigo]. On this day, we had two tremendous explosions, by the blowing up of two powder magazines some distance from town. The powder had been sent from England for the use of the Spaniards and it amounted to nearly 12,000 barrels, which as soon as it was discovered was all ordered to be destroyed. A whole village near the magazines was demolished, several inhabitants killed and among them also three or four of our artillerymen. Most of the windows of the town were broke and men, women and children kneeling and crossing themselves in the streets, terrified lest a following concussion should send them to destruction. There being no wind, we beheld an immense black cloud of smoke rising from the explosion, which rose to a great height and [it] was long ere it dispersed.

There being no accommodation for the cavalry or Staff horses to be embarked, there was orders to take them out of town and shoot them, a sacrifice most grating to their feelings! But to be done rather than allow our enemies to profit by leaving them in our stables. About 3 o'clock the regiments marched out of the town, towards the position taken up for the defence of our embarkation or resist any attempt which might be made by the enemy to '*Drive us into the sea*' as it had been ordered by Bonaparte at Astorga.

Sir David Baird's Division extended to the right of the village [Elvina] in a sort of semi-circle, General Sir John Hope's on a hill commanding the Betanzos road, on the right of our division, the Rifle corps [1/95th] communicating with that of Lieutenant General Fraser & the Reserve in a village on the road to Betanzos in rear of General Hope's Division. A howitzer, six or seven six-pounders were all the artillery and four Spanish guns in Reserve. The cavalry were sent onboard ship and most of their horses slaughtered.

On the 14 [January] the enemy commenced a cannonade, but soon desisted on its being smartly answered.

[15 January] On the following day all the sick and baggage were got onboard the transports and by orders we expected likewise that the whole army should embark without molestation on the 16 January.

Battle of Corunna

[16 January] But about midday the enemy showed every disposition to attack our position and try our courage under adversity. Sir John Moore had hardly mounted his horse to proceed towards the position, when he was met by a messenger and told that the enemy were under arms and on the advance.

About 1 o'clock the advanced posts were engaged and a regular attack was made on Lord William Bentinck's Brigade composed of the 4th, 42nd & 50th Regiments, who although possessing but a very bad position, maintained themselves against a very superior force. The Brigade of Guards were in their rear and General Paget was also ordered in support to them. The enemy opened eleven guns,[100] two large columns advanced from a road on our right, another on the centre and a fourth on the left wing, whilst a strong division remained as a Reserve half-way down the hill. Their various attacks were well directed and the artillery from the heights did our corps considerable damage.

100 Most accounts state ten cannon.

> At this period, General Sir David Baird had his arm severely shattered and [was] obliged to quit the field, relinquishing the command of the division to Lord William Bentinck. Our line advanced to meet that of the enemy and on finding theirs extend further than our right, the 4th Regiment formed an obtuse angle and gave the enemy a well-directed flanking fire. The 50th Regiment then charged and drove the enemy most gallantly out of the village of Elvira [Elvina], although not accomplished but with the loss of the two majors Napier and Stanhope[101] and also many officers and men.
>
> The Commander in Chief then advanced to the 42nd and said '*Highlanders remember Egypt*' and with them immediately charged the enemy, who instantly fled.

The 42nd and 50th advanced with the bayonet and drove the French from the village of Elvina, the 42nd halting outside the village as a reserve as Major Charles Napier's 50th Foot pushed through the village, suffering heavy casualties in the ensuing firefight.

> The enemy had directed his artillery towards the 42nd and when Sir John was in their rear, he received a wound by a cannon ball, which striking him on the left shoulder, carried in part of the collar bone, the arm hanging by the flesh. He fell from his horse, but showed no alteration of countenance, nor did he wish the surgeon of the 42nd to dress the wound.[102] He was taken off the field by the highlanders and expressed great satisfaction on hearing the enemy was repulsed. A blanket was procured and he was gently carried along by his faithful soldiers, now and then halting towards Corunna and apparently happy to hear the firing getting more feint [*sic*].
>
> The Reserve are ordered to advance to the support of the right wing, General Paget also beat back the enemy, who at

101 Major Charles Napier, 50th Foot, was severely wounded and became a prisoner of war, but was exchanged by March 1809. Major the Honourable Charles Stanhope, 50th Foot, was killed.

102 Surgeon John Erly, 42nd Foot.

> last finding himself repulsed, he made a grand effort on the centre commanded by Generals Manningham[103] and Leith,[104] and these also found the same steady and determined coolness of our troops. In every point the enemy were discomfited and night put an end to a very unequal contest, the enemy being flushed with victory; whilst our poor fellows had been deprived of everything but their innate courage and unconquerable spirit. In this action which crowned with glory the head of our gallant commander and added fresh laurels to those of our army, the enemy had against our small numbers upwards of 25,000 men and a well-served artillery.[105] In action we might have had 15,000 men, of which there were about 800 killed and wounded,[106] whilst the loss of the French exceeded 2,000 men.[107]
>
> About 10 o'clock picquets were planted along the line and our troops marched towards the point of embarkation. The transports were ordered to keep a lantern hoisted until they were filled with troops, but owing to the darkness and many pulling down their lights before they had their complement, all was in a short time confusion and every boat went to the first ship that would receive them.

The 42nd suffered a loss of 39 men killed and 117 wounded at Corunna. No officers were killed at the battle, but Major Archibald Campbell died of fever and Captain Duncan Campbell succumbed to his wounds within a few weeks. Captains John Fraser and Maxwell Grant along with Lieutenants Alexander Anderson, Duncan McInnes and William Middleton were wounded but survived.

Lieutenant Colonel James Stirling commanded the 42nd Foot in the action and received a gold medal in recognition. There were later rumours

103 Major General Coote Manningham commanded a brigade in 1st Division.

104 Major General Sir James Leith commanded a brigade in 2nd Division.

105 Oman puts their number at over 20,000 but Fortescue believes they only totalled 16,000.

106 This is pretty accurate.

107 French losses were similar to the British including 200–300 prisoners taken.

that the 42nd had been forced to retreat at Corunna, but the colonel wrote a letter to the Editor of *Blackwood's Edinburgh Magazine* from Musselburgh on 30 March 1830, which was published in Volume 27 in the May 1830 edition (Page 704).

In it he takes umbrage at the publication of *Annals of the Peninsular Campaigns*[108] that from some 'misapprehension' the 42nd had been stated as having retired at Corunna. He wrote:

'Having had the honour to command the 42nd Regiment in that action, I feel it incumbent on me to state to you, that what relates to the 42nd is very inaccurate; the 42nd *never retired*, as therein stated, or evinced occasion for a brief but animating address from the General.

'On the advance of the French to the village of Elvire [Elvina], Sir John Moore allowed the enemy to deploy and form their line at half musket-shot from us. He then gave me orders (about half past two o'clock) to advance and charge with the 42nd, accompanying that order, with the words "*Highlanders, Remember Egypt!*"; which is the only address they received from him, or anyone else. As soon as the regiment had given their fire and drove the enemy with the bayonet to the bottom of the ravine, Sir John directed me to halt the corps and defend that position; and turning myself round to him when he gave the order, I saw him at the moment struck to the ground off his horse, and I immediately sent a party to carry him from the field. The grenadiers and first company not hearing my word of command to halt, continued the charge a little in advance, as did the light company also, when I was ordered by Lord William Bentinck commanding the brigade, to recall them and form them in line with the regiment; and in that position, as directed by Sir John Moore, the corps continued in close action with the enemy, until night put an end to the contest; when the picquets were posted on the ground occupied by the regiment, who *then retired* as ordered, with the rest of the army to the bivouacs occupied by the troops at the commencement of the battle and which we quitted at ten o'clock the same night for embarkation. I have the honour to be Sir, your

108 *Annals of the Peninsular Campaigns from 1808 to 1814*, by Captain Thomas Hamilton, was published in 1829. Hamilton had served as an Ensign in the 29th Foot and was severely wounded at Albuera.

obedient humble servant, J Stirling Major General, Late Lieutenant Colonel 42nd Foot.'

Thus, by daybreak on the 17 [January] the greatest part of our worn-out army was onboard the ships destined to convey them home and about 9 o'clock the picquets and Reserve were also put onboard the ships of war. Ere this we had the melancholy news of the death of our gallant and much beloved commander in consequence of the very severe wound he received on the 16th. It was related that he died without a struggle, that his joy was great on being told the enemy had been repulsed and when expressing some wish to Colonel Graham[109] or Anderson[110] about his mother,[111] he expired. He was interred in the citadel on one of the ramparts in his uniform by his personal staff who had to regret in his premature departure from the world, a brother, an affectionate friend, liberal unaffected instructor in their future military career.

Sir John [Moore] throughout his long and meritorious service in the army, had ever sustained an unsullied and very high reputation as an officer, a gentleman and soldier's friend. He possessed eminent ability to conciliate even in the severity necessary to the support of discipline, with manners refined by a most excellent education, knowledge of the world, tempered by experience and thought, he drew the attachment and confidence of all under his command. When appointed to head the army in Spain, the regard he was held in by the troops was proclaimed as universal and in every period of the hard struggle he had to sustain that army placed in his known abilities, decision and interest for their welfare and his country's good, the most implicit confidence. Never had he given them orders to face their foe, even when bending under famine and

109 Major General Sir Thomas Graham, Lord Lynedoch, was aide de camp to Sir John Moore.

110 Lieutenant Colonel Paul Anderson Deputy Assistant Adjutant General.

111 His mother, Jean (née Simson) lived until 1820.

fatigue, than with alacrity, nay with soul inspired enthusiasm they obeyed with joy the summons and at last in their greatest extremity, when they beheld their beloved commander fall, in the midst of their undaunted ranks, they were going on to glory & to victory. In the heart of every British soldier that fought under the gallant Moore the same tribute of regard and sincere regret must be felt and every heart beat high in relating his virtues and talking of his short-lived glory.

Lieutenant General Sir John Hope had assumed the command of the army and gave orders for the embarkation and sailing on the 17th instant as soon as possible for England. Fortunately, the wind was on that day fair for our getting out of harbour, but it blowing fresh, some of the transports went on shore on a reef of rocks near the town, but no lives were lost, the boats of the men of war taking up the soldiers. To add to our confusion, the enemy determined to annoy us even to the uttermost and about 11 o'clock ere any of our ships had weighed, some guns were brought down to the beach and soon obliged our transports to cut cable and go off to sea. We sailed in company with a few other transports and although we were very much crowded and very ill off for every comfort or necessary, yet our hearts rejoiced that again we soon should touch our native soil and smile at the past, which however unfortunate had yet only withered our laurels, which were again in the mind of every Briton, revived by our best effort and we had the satisfaction to find it so in England, where they did us every justice, pitying our misfortunes but admiring our fortitude.

[23 January] After a tolerable voyage, endured in all sorts of distress and filth, we anchored on the 23 January at Spithead and the following day our wounded and sick were put into the naval hospital at Haslar.[112]

112 The Royal Naval Hospital Haslar at Gosport. Some of the regiment were also landed at Plymouth.

It is an aphorism[113] that disappointment is the road to wisdom and on landing again safe in England, we hoped our government would take its measures with more circumspection than the last disastrous campaign had been carried on with. To fully enjoy the luxuries and comforts of an English fireside, was to have suffered as we had, and no one that has not felt it, can imagine the degree of satisfaction on throwing off our ragged vestments, capable nearly of marching on a campaign themselves and exchanging them for new wholesome clothing.

On the 27 [January] arrangements were made for disembarking the army near their various allotted quarters, and on the same day we were gratified by receiving General Hope's dispatch and thanks from the House of Parliament.

By the 1 February the wounded and sick were all landed either at Plymouth or Portsmouth, many of them in a very dangerous state with a fever occasioned by bad living and fatigue. Of this we lost our major at Plymouth,[114] a character conspicuous for talent, genuine worth and fast rising to renown in his profession.

113 A pithy observation.

114 Major Archibald Campbell, 42nd Foot, died of fever at Plymouth on 27 January 1809.

Home Service: February–July 1809

The remnants of the battalion landed in England, some at Plymouth and others at Portsmouth. The wounded and sick were taken into the Naval Hospitals to recuperate, while the remainder were ordered to march by easy stages to Shorncliffe, where the 1st Battalion 42nd were brigaded with the two battalions of the 95th Rifles under the command of Major General Sir Thomas Graham.

January–February

The regiment was ordered to march by land to Shorncliffe in Kent and there to equip with all possible dispatch in order soon again to try our luck on other shores. Portsmouth is a town so well known that it hardly here requires to be mentioned, suffice it to say, that it has now become one of the most secure and capacious harbours of Europe, were fortified, containing immense magazines of naval stores and the finest dockyards in England or any other country.

Travelling the coast road we came to Chichester the capital town of the County of Sussex, with the see of a bishop. It is large, containing within its walls nearly 7,000 inhabitants and situated in a fine rich country. Near it we observed a handsome seat belonging to the Richmond family,[1] with many others diversifying the prospect, until 10 miles further we arrived at the pretty little town of Arundel. The town is on the small river Arun and is greatly beautified by the old castle in it belonging to the Dukes of Norfolk. It is a borough town of Sussex and sends two members to Parliament.

1 He refers to Goodwood House in Westhampnett, Chichester.

From Arundel to Brighton the country is flat and Worthing a small place on the seacoast, now much resorted to for sea bathing is the only place remarkable on the road. Brighton or Brighthelmstone[2] is now one of the genteelest sea bathing quarters, being principally the resort for the nobility whilst it is honoured by the presence of the Prince of Wales. The air is pure, the country open and the town has an air of gaiety and cleanliness. Passing on we progressively arrived at Lewes,[3] Horsebridge,[4] Battle and Hastings, where the Great William [The Conqueror] first landed in England in the year 1066.

The towns of Winchelsea and Rye next were passed, the former much decayed and the latter is only remarkable for its being one of the Cinque ports. [New] Romney is another & is situated in the extensive marsh of the same name in the County of Kent.

On the 9 of February we were snug in quarters at Shorncliffe, which although much exposed is reckoned, a healthy open quarter. It is in Kent and near it are the villages or towns of Hythe, Sandgate and Folkestone.

On the 18 [February] the body of the regiment arrived from Portsmouth and about a month after the remainder, in high health & spirits came in from Plymouth, the towns on the march affording every comfort and generous attention.

Shorncliffe, Kent, June 1809

A few months had only elapsed since Corunna saw us as an army of ragged, starved runaways, dismembered of all materiel but our innate invincible spirit, now we again appeared on the

2 The old traditional name for Brighton.

3 The villages are listed in an incorrect order in the original, with Lewes being listed after Battle. The editor has corrected the order.

4 Lower and Upper Horsebridge are one mile north of Hailsham.

> field, ready once more to defy danger and difficulty, in high health and spirits and with tolerable numbers. The volunteering from the militia had quickly filled up the large gaps,[5] that had been made in our ranks.[6] Reinforcements had also been sent to Sir Arthur Wellesley in Portugal to maintain the war there,[7] whilst it was supposed a large armament was fitting out to cooperate with the Austrians and although styled a '*Secret Expedition*', no doubt was entertained but that its destination was the Scheldt.
>
> By the exertions of Ministry, the Commander in Chief[8] and the Treasury, we were in complete order in June 1809 and marched to Canterbury so far on our road for embarkation. Here we were formed into a body and acquired discipline and correctness of movement under our Brigadier, General Montresor.[9]

The Narrative of a Private Soldier records that while at Canterbury, the regiment presented a sword to Colonel Stirling for 'his goodness and in token of our high opinion for his bravery'; every private having subscribed a day's pay and every non-commissioned officer two days.

> Our colonel, the most noble the Marquis of Huntly,[10] was to command the division of which the 42nd Regiment was to

5 The anonymous *Personal Narrative of a Private Soldier* states that the Scots and Highland Militia had been given leave to volunteer into the regulars and that Recruiting parties sent to Scotland successfully recruited 'a great number of excellent men' for the 42nd.

6 The battalion went to Walcheren with 758 men in its ranks. Reference the *History of 1st Battalion 42nd Foot* by Lieutenant Colonel Percy Groves.

7 The reinforcement to the Peninsula included the 2nd Battalion 42nd Foot, which mustered some 650 men, which meant that this battalion could not be depleted to make up the numbers of the 1st Battalion as would normally happen.

8 General Sir David Baird became Commander-in-Chief of the Army after the Duke of York was forced to step down in March 1809 following the scandal of Mary Clarke: the Duke returned to his post in 1811.

9 Lieutenant General Sir Henry Montresor. The 1/42nd served in Montresor's Brigade with the 1/9th and 1/38th.

10 General George Gordon, 5th Duke of Gordon, Marquis of Huntly.

form a part[11] and all in readiness, we marched for Ramsgate and embarked the same day, the 17 July 1809.

The scene on the magnificent pier was most lively and animated, everyone seemed inspired with the same enthusiastic spirit, the inhabitants partaking of the general joy and happiness, on seeing their heroes once more in the field & wished us every success, their hearts could suggest. The vessels being small we were sadly wounded [squeezed] having in our small collier brig,[12] fourteen officers.

As soon as the embarkation was fully completed, we sailed for the Downs,[13] receiving the cheers and good wishes of our fair country women on the pier. When we arrived in the Downs it seemed a forest of masts, although the part of our expedition from Portsmouth had not joined. The crowd that had collected in Deal to witness the departure of this mighty armament was immense and together with the Navy and Army on shore, rendered the streets of the little seaport almost impassable.

11 Marquis Huntly commanded the 2nd Division in the Right Wing.

12 Colliers were easily converted to also take horses, therefore were a popular choice for the Transport Board, particularly in summer when the need for coal was much reduced.

13 The Downs is a roadstead off Deal, it was used extensively during the age of sail.

Walcheren: July–November 1809

Only three months after the entire battalion had finally reformed at Shorncliffe, they received orders for Foreign Service again, this time to the Island of Walcheren. Despite continuing to reinforce the force in Portugal, the British government, in its wisdom, decided to make a major diversionary attack on Flushing (or Vlissingen) and Antwerp, where a large French fleet was based, in an effort to help the Austrians, who had recently declared war on France. The fleet of 230 warships and 350 transports, carried a huge force amounting to some 40,000 troops and 5,000 horses.

> The preparation of such vast means naturally created conjectures as to the effect they were meant to produce. The question therefore seemed to be, was it merely a '*coup de main*', or to carry on a regular campaign in the low countries of Holland. From the large naval force assembled, the first seemed most probable and Flushing [Vlissingen], the islands of Zealand and Antwerp, we supposed to be the points wished to be carried. The various arrangements that had already been made, were judicious and well formed, the force powerful and all appeared now to depend on a selection of commanders, capable of moving this tremendous instrument with skill and energy. The Lord Chatham, a brother of our great statesman was nominated to the army as commander in chief[1] and Sir Richard Strachan[2] was appointed over the naval part of the expedition, with other very able officers under him.

---

1 Lieutenant General John Pitt, 2nd Earl of Chatham, Master General of the Ordnance. He was the brother of William Pitt the younger.

2 Rear Admiral Sir Richard Strachan, 6th Baronet, commanded the naval fleet.

Although we had every reason to suppose our voyage would be of no long duration, yet it was better to be prepared for the worst, and the few days we had in the Downs, were busily employed in laying in stock and other necessaries requisite for a campaign, a lesson which we learnt from the last; and one that in future we constantly adhered to.

A report from France of the defeat of the Austrians in two successive battles, was the means of damping our hopes and might have frustrated all our expedition, but as it was Gallic fabrication, little credit was given to it.[3]

In the evening of the 24 [July] the sailing flag was hoisted,[4] but as there was no appearance of the Portsmouth division, it was merely to alarm the people on shore and to bring them to their stations onboard. It was two days after that we weighed anchor and steering completely outside the fleet, brought up again opposite Ramsgate. In the evening our attention was attracted by a sulphuric cloud, which slowly passing over the fleet, took the exact profile of the Right Honourable William Pitt, which we marked as ominous of our success and of his spiritual patronage.

On the 27 [July] towards the afternoon, we descried a brig of war from the westward and being the forerunner of the Portsmouth fleet, they soon after made their appearance. Everything being now ready, we weighed the following morning with a fine fresh breeze, producing a sight the like never seen in England before to such extent. Fortune & the winds seemed attached to our grand undertaking, for ere sunset we anchored off Ostend and there were hopes we might effect a landing the following day. No change had been made in our

3 Unfortunately, the news was but too true. Having initially been beaten as the Battle of Aspern-Essling on 21–22 May, Napoleon had won decisive victories at Wagram on 5–6 July and at Znaim on 10–11 July, forcing the Austrians to sign an Armistice on 12 July and a full peace treaty on 14 October.

4 The sailing flag was the Blue Peter.

ships, since leaving Ramsgate, so that hampered as we were, an expeditious landing was much to be desired.

On the 29 [July] we beheld the spires & the towers of Ostend and Brakenburg [Blankenberge] but weighing at nine o'clock disappointed us and our expectations of landing there. At first we bore down in the direction of Flushing [Vlissingen], but wearing again, we in the afternoon came nearly to our place [of] the former night.

30 July The following day however brought us nearer the point of action and our division came to anchor opposite the island of Cadsand [Cadzand][5] & near to the mouth of the Scheldt. This seemed to be the scene of action for our part of the grand operations and we were not long in doubt, for the signal being made to prepare for landing, the boats were hoisted out and with beating, buoyant hearts we were ready to step into them. But mortified and sulky, we saw soon after the '*Annulling signal*'[6] shown and we returned to our little pigsty or cabin. Cabin some of us had none, sleeping, eating and living on deck. We were preparing ourselves to endure a severe campaign, which seemed never to have existed but in our imaginations.

On the 31 [July] the same signal and preparations were made and to encourage our hopes still further we drew nearer the shore and beheld the walls which seemed destined never to be assailed. The men of war going in close, were fired on and soon after the countermand was thrown out. Suspense wastes the spirits and makes man tired of that he so anxiously desired to attain. It was so with our division, when . . .

5 Many of these islands in the Scheldt estuary now form part of the mainland, or have been joined together, by land reclamation.

6 According to Home Popham's signal book 62 was 'Annulling'.

On the 1 August the same part was played, by our commodore and with an additional order to hoist in all boats and be ready to sail.

It would have been difficult at the moment to determine whether we rejoiced or felt disappointed at the news given us in the afternoon by Captain Skeene [Skene][7] of the *Hussar* frigate,[8] that Sir John Hope[9] had proceeded up the river and that all was in our possession, except Flushing [Vlissingen], for it is in general galling to British soldiers to be left '*hors de combat*',[10] nor do they ever imagine they can be well employed, acting as a '*corps d'observation*' or as a deceit to draw off the enemy's attention. Thus, although we received with satisfaction the intelligence that Middleburgh [Middelburg] had surrendered and that Flushing [Vlissingen] was invested, yet we could not help murmuring against our bad fortune in being placed in a situation to deceive and to be deceived, which together deprived us of sharing the soldiers best creed '*Honour and Glory*'.

On the 3 [August] we got under weigh and following the *Redpole* Brig,[11] passed nearer to Flushing [Vlissingen], where the firing seemed to be kept up pretty sharply. Here we were surrounded by shoals and banks of sand and blowing very fresh, we anticipated a storm, which placed as we were, might have consequences the most disastrous.

The following day [4 August] continued boisterous but did not prevent us getting under weigh in order to shift our berth and endeavour to get nearer Flushing [Vlissingen]. However, the wind was so violent that we were soon obliged again to

7 Post Captain Alexander Skene RN.

8 HMS *Hussar* was a 38-gun frigate launched in 1807.

9 Lieutenant General the Honourable John Hope commanded the Reserve Army in the expedition.

10 Incapable of defending themselves.

11 HMS *Redpole* was a 10-gun brig.

anchor and a hurricane in the afternoon created most serious alarm. Many of the worst found ships began at close of night to drag their anchors and two large transports passed our little brig at the distance of a yard or two, with such violence that had they touched us, we must inevitably have perished. One of our regimental ships had drifted on a shoal, another broke her windlass, but from the activity of the soldiers in getting the cable round the foremast, she was saved.

Towards morning the wind abated a little and we had the pleasure to find that not so much damage had occurred as what we might have expected, from the tempestuous weather and vicinity of the sandbanks. The boats of the fleet were ordered to assist the shipping that had in the night gone on the shoals and fortunately no lives were lost.

On the 5 [August] we again attempted to extricate ourselves from the shoals and it seemed as if the attack of Cadsand [Cadzand] had been abandoned, for we steered well out and anchored on the tail of the bank. Our stock, provident as we had been, was now completely exhausted, having slaughtered all our live animals on the various orders given to land. We therefore delighted, found ourselves . . .

On the 6 [August] pass the blockading squadron and enter the river by the northeast mouth, proceeding as far up as the tide would permit.

Our attempt in the evening succeeded and we came to anchor close to the small town of Campvere [Vere], where our troops had made good their landing in the Island of Walcheren after a short resistance. Here three of our officers went on shore and brought us on board some excellent Hollands,[12] bread and tobacco. These we enjoyed from the exhausted state of our stock and we had reason to believe we should soon land on the opposite Island of [South] Beveland. The investment of

12 Hollands or Genever gin.

Flushing [Vlissingen] had been carried through and a regular siege was commenced. Next tide, we went further up the river and had gone nearly round the little, but fertile Island of Walcheren, which although but small is one of the richest spots imaginable.

On the 8 [August], as we had no orders to land, some of us went on shore and finding the people civil and obliging, walked into the country and purchased *de quoi* [enough] wine, very reasonable. Finding we were cut off by the tide from joining our ships, we were contented to take a homely Dutch dinner of eggs and ham and go on board in the evening.

Having received orders to land on the Island of South Beveland to cooperate with General Sir John Hope we landed . . .

On the 9 August, having nearly eight hundred men under arms. Immediately we proceeded on our march towards the villages allotted for our regiment, the road or dyke, running through the most highly cultivated country, abounding in barley, wheat, the most luxuriant pasture, orchards smiling with ripe fruit, indeed from our landing place to our small village of Ormskirken[13] it was selected for the headquarters, sending a few companies to the neighbouring farmhouses.

In the house of an old wealthy Boor [Boer], or farmer was received with civility and experienced every accommodation. As we had reason to prophesy a halt here for some time, to be situated thus and to be in good terms with the landlord, was no small good fortune. We found correct what from hearsay was acknowledged to be the peculiar property of the Dutch, neatness and regularity, in their domestic concerns. No sooner had we arrived at our wealthy Boor's [Boer's] extensive farm,

13 The identity of this village is difficult, the only other man of the 42nd to mention their quarters is Private Gunn who was in James Stirling's company, who clearly states that they were near the only town on South Beveland, which would be the town of Goes. Could it be Abtskerke?

Dutch peasantry going to church.

than our men were put into a large comfortable barn and we were proceeding to enter the best parlour when a pretty, towering Dutch girl, presented us with 'wooden shoes' in order not to soil the clean bright tiles with which the floor was laid.

The walls of this cleanly little apartment was ornamented with earthenware and a few plates of china, interspersed with others of copper and pewter and a few old family pictures. Wishing soon after to refresh ourselves, we took some of these sacred embellishments down and were on the point of using them, when the landlady with great agitation, begged us to desist and replacing the precious relicks [*sic*] gave us common white ones. Our bedchamber was detached and contained two recesses with very short beds, clean linen & feather beds being used both over and under the former as blankets.[14] There is no fireplace except in the kitchen, the rooms being heated by means of small stoves. The dairy of a Dutch Boer is the best part of his dwelling and it being close to our apartment, we anticipated the pleasure of regaling ourselves often in that of our worthy old host.

Meantime the siege of Flushing [Vlissingen] was carrying on with great activity and Sir John Hope was up as far as Batz [Bath] on the Island of [South] Beveland.

James had much time on his hands while on South Beveland and spent a great deal of time observing and recording remarks about the locals.

On the 15 August we learnt the news of the surrender of Flushing [Vlissingen] to our troops, after no great loss of men on our part and from our shipping passing up the river, we had hopes of quietly being employed on our alternate undertaking. Still however on the 20th no orders had arrived and our time passed pleasantly on, although in the way by no means desired, in riding our landlord's horses into the country or shooting or carousing on Schiedam.[15] We had no amusements that associated with the parties, being but a small village inhabited by plain industrious people. The Dutch may be divided into peasants, farmers, sea-faring men, merchants and tradesmen, those who reside on their estates and military men. The inhabitants of the islands of Zealand are generally speaking farmers, peasants and sea-faring men. The two former are industrious, stupid, good natured men, plain and simple in their manners and deficient in their education. The seamen are rough, honest & hardy people and has [*sic*] long been esteemed excellent sailors. The Boors [Boers] or proprietors

14 A form of duvet.

15 Schiedam near Rotterdam is synonymous with Geneva gin.

of patrimonial[16] bits of land, are little better than the peasant in point of education or manners & are very parsimonious in their way of living and throughout, the characteristic was frugality, regularity of expenses, void of all kinds of luxury. The diet of our Dutch Boor [Boer] was composed principally of tea, vegetables, milk, butter and very rarely butcher[ed] meat. At their meals they were regular; great attention paid to the religious part of them, the landlord before and after each [meal], doffing his bonnet and in a most reserved, respectful manner returning thanks for his family.

The men of Zealand are rather tall, ill made, awkward mien[17] with fair complexions. The women are in general fair, good eyes, bad teeth and a short thick squat make. Both sexes are simple and industrious, cleaner in their houses than persons, but although their vestments are coarse, yet they are always kept well brushed and decent.

The better sort of people imitate the French in their dress, but in general the genuine character is upheld in the country, by wearing an enormous quantity of clothes. The men from their infancy are accustomed to wear short breeches, very tight at the knees, which may so far account for their being so generally ill-shaped. The hat is broad rimmed, small crown, seldom a backcloth is worn, but the shirt which is plaited very nicely, is fastened at the collar by a gold or silver button according to the rank or antiquity of the wearer. The vest is very long, has a single row of silver buttons and the coat generally of a dark colour, being for the sake of frugality; has long skirts and partakes something of make, of those worn in England about three hundred years ago. The stocking is of coarse woven texture and the shoes also made very strong, are fastened by two large buckles. The various silver and other ornaments, descend from father to son and are religiously retained in the family. The women are occupied in regulating the interior

16 Hereditary.

17 Manner.

affairs of the farm & scrubbing the house &c in all of which they show a striking example of activity and cleanliness. They are mild and gentle in their manners, modest and obliging, not one in fifty good looking and not one in three fifties possessing a good set of teeth. Their figures are diminutive with a greater proportion of breadth than agrees with elegance and but little difference in the width downwards to the waist. Their countenances are small and round, wearing on their head a hat of nearly six feet in circumference, lined with damask or flowered linen. Under it is a stiff sash ornamented with a little paltry lace and a clasp of wire or gold or silver in holidays, bind their temples. Necklaces are worn round the neck, which although seldom uncovered, cannot boast of its fairness.

The petticoats are worn short, not descending further than a little below the knee and are thrown out to a distance from the legs, by means of cushions placed on the hips and by which when in the act of stooping, a person behind may behold the shapes far beyond the bounds of decency[!] They are well made in the legs and ankles, which it may be presumed induces them to wear their petticoats so short. The stocking is of a gaudy colour and they have shoes adapted for the field or church. On Sundays and holidays they are proportionately finer and the ornaments which have descended from their grandmothers are often of solid gold.

The language resembles the Scotch and is harsh and guttural, more adapted to speak to cattle or of profit and loss, than the effusions of friendship or love. Gallantry, conversation or politeness is but little known here and hours may pass without a syllable being spoken, nor a movement made except to light their pipes. Their favourite occupation is trade, or traffic of any description and as Goldsmith when speaking of the Dutch says:-

'*Industrious habits in each bosom reign;*
And industry begets a love of gain;
Hence all the good from opulence that springs,
With all those ills superfluous treasure brings,

Are here displayed'.[18]

The amusements of the Hollanders are but few, especially of the merchants and country people, who are more profitably employed in making bargains and sourcing their wheat than in playing at bowls, tennis or billiards, the common diversions of the other classes. But little attention appears to be paid to the education of the middling or lower classes and we met with very few in the country who could read or write their own language. Most of their books are printed in German character[19] and a Bible and Book of Psalms is generally all a farmer's library. The clergy are a respectable, modest, unassuming set of men and as their stipends are very moderate, they cannot afford to give themselves or children a liberal education. The people in their devotions are very strict and generally are Presbyterians. The police of a town and village are under the direction of a Burgomaster, secretary and under constables. The Burgomaster being the chief is chosen from the most esteemed and respectable. To him the people are very submissive and they hold the office in great respect.

No country is more favoured by the wanton gifts of nature, than the islands of Zealand. This happy soil teems with the most luxurious fruits, cultivation is displayed in every corner, no barren spot is seen to arrest the eye, indeed Ceres[20] seems to have chosen it for her residence for the eye delighted, wanders o'er her choicest gifts without one object to check its course, but in every step we tread on her select carpet, inhaling the soft and balmy fragrance of the various aromatics of the fields.[21] Cultivation seems well known in these islands for although the soil is excellent, yet it is much assisted by the industry of

18 From *The Traveller* by Oliver Goldsmith.

19 Dutch has many similar characteristics to German and he may easily have mistaken the one for the other.

20 Ceres was the Roman Goddess of Agriculture.

21 These words bear similarities with Byron's *Childe Harold*, but seem to be his own production.

the husbandman. The crops that are generally cultivated are wheat, oats, beans, peas, potatoes, kidney beans and clover, with the most luxuriant fields of pasture.

From the great lowness of the country beyond the beset of the sea, it is intersected with ditches, which renders the soil moist and must be a principal cause of the unhealthy state of the climate. The heat of the sun by day, causes strong vapours and dews to arise from the stagnated water in the ditches and consequently gives birth to ague and fever.[22] The inhabitants have therefore a sickly, discoloured appearance and as a proof that they also are subject to the baleful influence of the climate, the landlady of our house was fifty years old and had only passed the last ten years of her life without experiencing a shock of the ague. Had these islands been but a little raised over the level of the water, they would have been the Garden of Europe, but:

'*The pent ocean, rising o'er the pile,*
Sees an amphibious world beneath him smile;
The slow canal, the yellow blossomed vale;
The willow tufted bank, the gliding sail,
The crowded mart, the cultivated plain,
A new creation rescued from his reign.'[23]

When we heard of the fall of Flushing [Vlissingen], we were fully prepared for our grand '*coup de main*' or regular attack on Antwerp and its neighbouring forts, but although we had an order about the 18 [August] to be in readiness to march, it was again annulled and we were allowed to indulge in the lap of ease and plenty, whilst the fields ought to have been our couch and hunger or hard fare the sharpener to genius and intrepidity.

22 The fever soon to strike the troops was believed to derive from the miasmic vapours emanating from the waters rather than from mosquitoes.

23 From Oliver Goldsmith's *The Traveller.*

It would have seemed indeed that the heart when out of order, it affects the whole system, so it was with us, for the grand spring and head of the army, indulging in ease and luxury,[24] it by degrees infected the whole and we grumbled more at turning out at 6 o'clock in the morning, to a field-day than if we had been up to the middle all night in the trenches and no rations on return to camp. Shooting wild ducks, partridges & hares (in which the country abounded) drinking Schiedam at night, or forming parties of pleasure to visit the capitals of the two islands of Walcheren or [South] Beveland, were the severest part of our luxurious campaign.

Middleburgh [Middelburg] is situated nearly in the center [*sic*] of the island of Walcheren and contains about 26,000 inhabitants. It is divided by canals which come up to the doors of the houses and are well adapted for commerce, in which Middleburgh [Middelburg] partakes considerably. Its principal houses are the Stadt house, Market house and square, which is good enough for a small capital. It is about three miles from Flushing [Vlissingen], which is on the south-west point of the island and has always been considered a first-rate situation for commercial pursuits.

The smuggling carried on between the coasts of England and Flushing [Vlissingen] had been for a length of time very considerable, and by it many individuals had enriched themselves in a few years & by this precious and illicit life, now had sought a quiet retirement in the country.

The ground round Flushing [Vlissingen] is low, except towards the north-east, where there are some sand hills, which in a certain degree command the town and of which during the siege we took advantage. The country between Middleburgh [Middelburg] and Flushing [Vlissingen] is pretty and diversified.

Tergoes [Goes] the principal town of the island of [South] Beveland is large, ill built, is surrounded by a ditch, but in no

24 The Earl of Chatham was heavily criticised for the incredibly slow progress made.

other manner fortified. It has several good houses and shops, articles of life were moderate and in general good, the public inns often kept by Frenchmen.

By the 26 of August we had lost all hopes of finishing the grand work we had begun, but dreaded that the iron hand of death would lay many fine fellow low, that might have got it in a better cause. The fever had spread among our men to an alarming degree, often twenty men a day were sent to hospital, but as yet it had not proved very fatal, although from all appearances we would have very few men remaining fit for service. It came on quite imperceptibly and a strong soldier who went out to parade in the greatest health, often returned supported by his comrades.

In a few days we learnt that by a Council of War held by the Commander in Chief, the remaining part of our intended enterprise had been abandoned, that arrangements were to be made for the retention of the Island of Walcheren and that a portion of the troops would proceed to England.

On the 1 September we were inspected by our colonel the Marquis of Huntly and out of eight hundred effective men [which] we landed, we could now bring only the half into the field. We were informed however that the 42nd Regiment was to proceed to England and that orders for embarkation might be daily expected. Miserable termination to all our fond hopes and high-flown wishes, to that army which would have sought glory in every field it could be born, had it not been sacrificed by gross repose, indolence, luxury, error and ignorance and now left to feel the storms of disease and pestilence gathering round them, hurrying their brave hearts to an untimely grave.

On the 3 September we had a route to traverse again the few miles of our luxurious but fatal campaign and we proceeded

Publisher of death in Holland.

more like a procession, than the '*merry march of a corps of highlanders*'. Behind us came our victims to disease, huddled into cars[25] or carts and occupying a line of march of nearly one mile.[26] We succeeded in our march by coming on the beach [with] time enough to find that no arrangements had been made for our sick and that accordingly they must remain all night in the village of Bosland [Baarland]. The small remaining part of the regiment, with two companies of the 9th Regiment, embarked onboard the *Beleisle* [*Belleisle*] man of war[27] and together with her own crew we were pretty well cooped up. Captain Cockburn[28] her commander, had been on a separate service on the river and until his arrival we could not sail.

The poor people of [South] Beveland seemed to regret our departure, an idea of fire probably influencing them, of experiencing bad treatment again from their aggressors, owing to their having received our army so openly and behaving so temperately towards the enemy of their ally. On the 7th most of our men of war had withdrawn from their station above Bathz [Bath] and it was generally believed the enemy had taken possession of it.

Next day [8 September] we got under weigh with a fine breeze and as their pilots had imagined, were clear of all the dangerous shoals which are so numerous on the Dutch coast. The officers of the ship were very attentive and afforded every accommodation in our short but crowded passage, but an incident of a very serious nature had nearly made a tragical end to our ill-fated campaign.

25 Cars was an abbreviation of carriages.

26 Gunn of James' company states that on its first appearance in the regiment, the fever attacked twenty of his company alone. At first the water was blamed and they were ordered to boil it; then the fruit was blamed, which was stopped and finally the milk, which was also prohibited, without success.

27 HMS *Belleisle* was an ex-French 74-gun warship named *Formidable* captured in 1795.

28 Captain George Cockburn RN.

On the forenoon of the **[9 September]** after having been at anchor all night, we were steering on with a fine breeze, the men still heaving the lead, although both the pilot assured the captain we were out of all the shoals, and indeed he and the Master thought the same. However, all at once the lead came from twenty fathoms to ten and so on to five in less than a few minutes, when in the utmost rage, the captain ordered the ship to be put about and came to anchor, which luckily for us she obeyed. Had the lead been left off when the pilots directed, we should have all perished, for the state of the *Beleisle* [*Belleisle*] was so bad, that the iron pins [bolts] might have been taken out from her sides with the hand. Besides a ship crowded with nearly eight hundred souls, few of them could have reached the shore.

In the evening however, we got with the tide into the Downs, where but lately we had seen all that art and human foresight could bring together to accomplish an object and now we perceived with what ease all these mighty preparations could be frustrated.

On the 10 September we landed at Deal, about two hundred men strong, the remaining part of our poor fellows going to the hospital at Ramsgate, Margate and other military depots.[29] Marching to Sandwich from Deal, we went on to Canterbury where we were quartered, it was supposed for the winter.

The violence of the disorder had not abated by our leaving the detestable land, where it seemed we had imbibed so capaciously of the poison, that its sting was still to torment us and to add its strength to crumble us under our misfortunes. The officers and men now got worse, many of the latter dying daily and some of the former very little better. This disorder appeared to be what is generally termed in England, the ague, but of a nature far more virulent and fatal. Apparently, its symptoms were the same, which divided themselves into

29 On their return from Walcheren, the Return records only 204 men fit for duty.

fits of shivering and fever, and its various degrees again into '*Quotidian, Tertian and Quartian* [*Quartan*]'[30] once a day, once in the two or three days and often only once in four days. The fatality had become very great, both amongst the troops left in Walcheren and those who had returned to England, having as it were infused itself into the very veins and by degrees showing its increased and too fatal sting. Several officers and men did not feel its effects until a period of nearly six months had gone past in England, and only about six of the former escaped its contagious effects.

Towards the beginning of November by the great exertions of the medical people and from a greater knowledge of the disease, the fatality was diminishing, but still the disorder was creeping through individually in the regiment and in all probability would make them miserably weak and wretched for life.[31]

30 Quotidian fevers occurs for a few hours each day; Tertian fevers occur every 48 hours and Quartan occurs every 72 hours.

31 Private Gunn states that the men tried hartshorn (prepared from male red deer's horn), which they procured themselves and Peruvian bark was used, often seeing an initial improvement, but also often recurring weeks and months later.

Home Service Again: November 1809–April 1812

Nothing of importance occurred during the winter of 1809, but our army still maintaining their hold in Portugal and the Spaniards also endeavouring to shake off the yoke that Bonaparte wished to impose on them, imparted to us hopes still of sharing (as soon as health and numbers increased) in the satisfaction of emancipating the peninsula from the tyranny and oppression it was about to fall under.

At the beginning of spring 1810, our men were recovering and as a greater restorative (and often the best cure) the regiment was sent to Scotland their native country and quartered at Musselburgh near Edinburgh.[1] There we enjoyed the society and friendship of its kind and most hospitable inhabitants and of the gentlemen in the vicinity, together with the smiles of our fair countrywomen, those:

> '*Ancient bloom, the blush of chaste desire,*
> *The sprightly converse and the smile divine,*
> *Loves gentler claims, to milder climes retire*
> *And full in Albion's matchless daughters shine*'.[2]

By attention and care, regularity of food and exercise, combined with a pure and wholesome climate and situation, our men had almost all recovered

1 Gunn states that many of the men were given furloughs to recuperate with their family while in Scotland, which apparently worked.

2 This first appears in The Reverend J. Goldsmith's (a pseudonym for Sir Richard Phillips) *Geography for the use of schools* published in 1803. James has however misquoted it slightly, the original reading being
Youth's orient bloom, the blush of chaste desire,
The sprightly converse, and the smile divine,
Love's gentler train, to milder climes retire,
And full in Albion's matchless daughters shine.

sufficiently to be able to appear at parade and by degrees return to their duty. Relapses however often occurred and many of the soldiers although apparently well, still bore a sickly pallid countenance and emaciated bodies. Bathing in the summer, with now and then a moderate field day, however brought them fast round, and by the volunteering of the Militia we were again in considerable numbers, ere the winter of 1810.[3]

The winter passed away most pleasantly in festivities and social parties which are so numerous and splendid in that season, in and round the metropolis of Scotland. To them we also added our mite and by giving a ball in our mess room or town hall, we increased our popularity, and it was the only means we had of testifying our gratitude to our generous and kind neighbours.

The spring of 1811 effected a complete cure on our men and in August we again left our native soil for England and it was generally and naturally supposed ultimately for the peninsula. The regiment proceeded in smacks from Leith, when Sir Sidney Smith[4] and a numerous assemblage of the most respectable inhabitants of Edinburgh, were collected to offer their best wishes and a happy return. The crowd [was] very immense and it was gratifying that we embarked accompanied by the reiterated and sincere good wishes of every class of our countrymen.

The passage was moderate and disembarking at Chatham, we marched by Tunbridge Wells to Lewes in Sussex. At [Tunbridge] Wells we were received with kindness and a young lady treated our men to the number [42] of the regiment to a play, which was performing the evening they arrived. This is not mentioned as a single instance of gallantry shown to us by the fair sex, for on our arrival from Spain in 1809, the ladies on the road from Plymouth to Shorncliffe, gave our men flannel jackets and stockings, equalling almost yet in their patriotism, the Sabine women.

3 Other sources seem to indicate that the numbers volunteering from the Militia had declined significantly.

4 Vice Admiral Sir Sidney Smith. He had married Caroline Rumbold, widow of the diplomat Sir George Rumbold, in October 1810.

At Lewes the regiment passed the winter and in spring [1812][5] we received the joyful mandate to embark for Portugal, to join our army already glorious by its deeds and persevering exertions.[6]

Routes and Distances marched from 17 September 1808 to 1 April 1812

Names of Places	Leagues	Miles	Remarks
To Camp at Quelus [Queluz]	3	12	Army concentrated
Sacavem	3	12	Road
Villafranca [Vila Franca de Xira]	4	16	Road
Azambuja	3	12	Sandy deep road
Santarem	4	16	Hilly and strong
Golegao [Golega]	4	16	Deep sand
Total	**21**	**84**	
Nisa	11	16	Flat
Villa Velha [Vila Velha de Rodao]	2	8	Strong Pass
Sarnadas [de Rodao]	2	8	Strong Pass and Hilly
Castello [Castelo] Branco	3	12	Good Road
Atalaya [Atalaia do Campo]	4	16	Bad Road
Campaheinta	3	12	Bad Road
Belmonte	3	12	Country Hilly
Guarda	4	16	Mountainous
Castanheira	3	12	Mountainous
Castello Mundo [Mendo]	3	12	Mountainous
Freineda	1	4	Boundary Spain
Ciudad Rodrigo	5	15	3 English miles per league
St [San] Martin del Rio [Martin de Yeltes?]	5	15	

5 *The Personal Narrative of a Private Soldier* records that they remained at Lewes for eight months in total, where nothing happened beyond a planned review by the Prince Regent (travelling from Brighton) was cancelled due to very wet weather.

6 To Portsmouth via Eastbourne.

Names of Places	Leagues	Miles	Remarks
San Munoz	2	6	In Spain
Calzada de Don Diego	5	15	Good Roads
Total	**70**	**263**	
Salamanca	4	12	Flat Fertile Country
Fuentessauco	6	18	Flat Fertile Country
Alaejos	6	18	Flat Fertile Country
Toro	7	21	Fine Open Country
Villa Diego [Villardondiego]	8	24	Barren Country
Castello Verde	4	12	Barren Country
Castello Ponte	4	12	Barren Country
Gavahal	3	9	Plentiful in Rivers
Sahagun	1	3	Plentiful in Rivers
Barbarena	6	18	Retreat 25 December 1808
Valente de Don Juan	1	3	Over the Esla River
Villa Manana	3	9	Flat Country Abounding
San Pedro	2	6	In Wine and Wheat
Astorga	3	9	Romantic Country
Manzana [Manzanal del Puerto]	3	9	Romantic Country
Place Name Unknown	3	9	Bleak & Barren
Total	**134**	**455**	
Benhobie	4	12	Abounding in White
Cacabelos	8	24	Wine. Roads Better
Villafranca [del Bierzo]	3	9	Impenetrable Pass
Huerncias	2	6	Romantic Country
Ponteferrada [Ponferrada]	3	9	Romantic Country
Doncas	5	15	Very Mountainous
San Martin Lugares	4	12	Very Mountainous
Manillias	3	9	Flat but bounded
St Juan de Cabo	3	9	By the Galician
Lugo	5	15	Mountains. High
Betanzos	11	33	Military Road
Corunna	4	12	

Names of Places	**Leagues**	**Miles**	**Remarks**
From Portsmouth by			
the Coast to			
Shorncliffe	41	123	Good Roads
From Shorncliffe			
To Canterbury			Embarked for Service
And Ramsgate	12	36	In Walcheren & Beveland
Total	**242**	**779**	
Landed in Beveland			
To Armskirken	2½	8	Delightful Country
Return to England	2½	8	
To Canterbury	6	18	
To Ramsgate	6	18	Embarked for Scotland
To Musselburgh, Scotland	2¼	7	
Embarkation for			
England	2¼	7	
Gravesend to Lewes	20	60	
Lewes to Portsmouth	20	60	Embarked for Portugal
Total	**383½**	**965**	

Peninsula Campaign of 1812: April–22 July, Battle of Salamanca

While the 1st Battalion had been at Walcheren and subsequently forced into a long period of recuperation to rebuild its strength on Home Service, the 2nd Battalion had been in Portugal, where they were involved in the long painful retreat to the Lines of Torres Vedras, including the Battle of Busaco and the subsequent advance back to the Portuguese border in 1811, where they were engaged in the victory of Fuentes d'Onoro.

The campaign of 1812 in the Peninsula was to be a pivotal moment in Wellington's attempts to drive the French out of Spain. In January 1812 a surprise assault on the Fortress of Ciudad Rodrigo was successful but with heavy losses; the Fortress of Badajoz similarly fell on 6 April. Wellington had successfully wrested control of the two main invasion routes into Portugal, but at significant cost to his army. The 2nd Battalion 42nd Foot served at both sieges, but only suffered losses of fifteen men at Ciudad Rodrigo and was spared at Badajoz, being part of the covering force.

However, the rigours of campaigning in Portugal for close on three years had taken its toll from fevers and sickness, the number of effective men slowly dwindling from 586 in July 1809 down to 368 in April 1812. It was therefore decided, as part of the reinforcements for Wellington's army, to send out the 1st Battalion to replace them, the fit men transferring into the 1st Battalion and the officers, NCOs and unfit men of the 2nd Battalion returning home.

> From the situation in which Britain had placed herself, in her assistance to and cooperation with Spain and Portugal, in endeavouring for the common welfare of mankind and particularly of Europe, to rid the peninsula of the yoke of

the French, it was necessary for her to show that energy & attention on her part should not be wanting and by the means of her fleets, armies, arsenals and treasury, to aid and assist those who with her, fought in the grand & common cause.

With these ideas the greatest disposable force had been sent to the shores of Portugal, and these maintained themselves since the commencement of the Revolution.[1] The young and free born Britons, had no sooner learnt the use of arms, than they were sent out to fill the vacancies of this long campaign and with cheerfulness and alacrity, obeyed the summons in assisting their country's allies & in keeping the battle from their own dear soil. Carrying on the same determination with which she had begun, England continued to send regiments and detachments out, and these were daily embarking and sailing for the golden, now rendered the bloody Tagus, on whose banks many a parent has to regret a dutiful & beloved son, many a child, a fond father and many bewail the loss of their dearest and best of friends.

The 30 March 1812 brought us our long looked for orders and our destination was Portugal. The many glorious deeds done and victories gained by our brave companions in arms, had long inspired our ranks with envy to join them and the Route for embarkation, awakened in us the most lively sentiments of happiness & joy.

1 April

All regimental affairs being settled, we marched on the 1 April for Portsmouth in three divisions and arrived successively on the 3rd, 4th & 5th. Our noble colonel the Marquis of Huntly, ever anxious for the promotion & happiness of his regiment,

1 British troops had been at Lisbon from 1797 to 1802 to help deter a Spanish invasion and again since 1808, but James is wrong in appearing to state that the British had maintained forces in Portugal continuously since 1793.

had arrived at Portsmouth and saw the last division onboard; whose appearance drew forth his great approbation and praise.[2]

The frigates, the *Brune*, *Romulus* and *Freija*[3] were allotted to carry us to our destination, but it was supposed we should wait for a convoy with more troops. On the Saturday before sailing [4 April], the officers of the regiment were elegantly and sumptuously entertained by the noble Marquis, when he was conspicuous for that affability and liberality of sentiment which characterizes the whole of his proceedings.

Every article necessary for officers and men, was now to be procured and the little time we had to spare, was therefore fully employed. As the wind seemed to be coming round to a favourable point, on Sunday [5 April] they ordered all on board their respective ships in readiness to sail. However, we did not get under way until Tuesday morning [7 April], which allowed us sufficient time to lay in a good stock, besides other little comforts for the ensuing campaign.

Our frigates sailing without having charge of any convoy, gave us reason to expect a quick passage, and the wind being fair we passed through the Needles and stood down Channel in fine style. The captain and officers of the *Brune*, were very civil and polite, offering and rendering every assistance in their power, to make us comfortable. In crossing the Bay of Biscay we had many on the sick list, although the weather was fine and wind favourable; but nothing could enable them to resist or keep off this most disagreeable nausea.

2 *The Personal Narrative of a Private Soldier* states that the battalion boarded the three frigates 900 men strong. On arrival at Portsmouth they boarded immediately, apparently disappointed that their Colonel had not provided bread and beer on the beach for the men.

3 HMS *Brune* was the 38-gun ex-French frigate *Thetis*; HMS *Romulus* was a 36-gun frigate which had been converted to a troopship; HMS *Freija* was a 40-gun ex-Danish frigate. Private Gunn says that he was on the '*Seahorse*', however HMS *Seahorse* was in dock for all of 1812.

On the morning of the 10 [April] we descried Cape Ortegal[4] on our larboard[5] bow and came well up during the day; but alas, as fortune would have it, the wind became perfectly foul and afforded us the unpleasant prospect of not being able to weather Cape Finisterre[6] for a considerable time. At Corunna we spoke the *Myrtle* sloop of war,[7] who gave us no news, but was in the same situation as ourselves, with a small convoy endeavouring to weather the cape.

After beating and tacking for three or four days, we experienced a pretty severe gale of wind accompanied by thunder and lightning. In the morning we were far to leeward with our sails rent & some of our masts sprung, and our attendant friend, the foul wind still requiring from us to fresh exertions of patience. At last, after six days of delay & impatient anxiety, tired with viewing daily the rocky coasts of Galicia, we passed the cape and having a fair wind, had a view of the Burlings[8] on the evening of the 17 [April]. They consist of several detached rocks, separated from the mainland, a distance of about 3 leagues, the largest has on it a signal tower and was the prison of some French soldiers.[9] Going at the rate of nearly nine, or ten miles an hour, we reached the Tagus, in whose bosom we brought to anchor at nearly eight o'clock having gone since morning 140 miles.

17 April

Our entrance this evening into this noble river, was most majestic and sublime. The sun was just setting, tinging the

4 Cabo Ortegal is the northernmost cape in Spain, some 50km north-east of Corunna.

5 'Larboard' for left-hand was not replaced by 'Port' until the 1850s. The obvious similarity to Starboard was seen as a potential problem.

6 Cape Finisterre or Cabo Fisterra is the westernmost point in Spain, which lies 75km west of Corunna.

7 HMS *Myrtle* was an 18-gun sloop.

8 The Berlengas are an archipelago of small islands lying 10km off the coast of Peniche in Portugal.

9 The Fort of Sao Joao Baptista das Berlengas was used as a penal colony.

mountains with his golden streaks, when our three frigates opening their bosoms to the favouring breeze, rapidly glide[d] through the water. The delightful situation of the city of Lisbon, its majestic churches, convents and nunneries, the distant view of the country up the river, the lands on each side, tastefully interspersed with gardens & the dark olive & vine tree; together with the lofty mountains.[10] Fort Bugio[11] at their feet, presenting his formidable front to the sea, formed & completed one of the finest scenes ever witnessed.

We had heard from our pilot who came from Mafra, that Badajoz had been taken on the 10th instant,[12] but of course [we] gave no great confidence to this sort of foreign news-monger, however on coming to anchor we had the confirmation of this gratifying intelligence from a lieutenant of the *Latona* frigate,[13] who was going to England with part of the prisoners taken there. Our loss was reported to be considerable, consisting of upwards of three hundred officers & 4,000 men killed and wounded.

On the 21 [April] we took leave of the briny element and its inhabitants and disembarked surrounded by multitudes of English & Portuguese spectators, of all sorts & descriptions.[14] The barracks at Campo d'Ourique[15] were allotted for us and were the best in Lisbon.

Our arrival was immediately of course reported to the great commander of the forces, but we were led to understand we

10 Lisbon, with its tiers of whitewashed houses, made a lasting impression on those arriving by sea and new to the scene. However, on landing this favourable initial impression was sorely dented by the stench of the effluent running in the streets.

11 The Fort of Sao Lourenco do Bugio is located in the middle of the estuary of the River Tagus.

12 It had actually been taken on 6 April.

13 HMS *Latona*, a 36-gun frigate, had been converted to a troopship.

14 Private Gunn states that they landed at '*Black Horse Square*', the British soldier's name for the *Praca de Comercio*. The Praca de Comercio is a large square on the harbour front, built on the site of the Ribeira Palace which was destroyed in the 1755 earthquake. At its centre stands a large statue of King Jose I on horseback, leading to many British soldiers who landed here to refer to it as '*Black Horse Square*'.

15 Campo d'Ourique is a suburb of Lisbon lying to the west of the city.

should not be ordered to join the army until ready for the field & we exerted ourselves to procure mules and other animals for the transport of our baggage.

Every Tuesday a fair of cattle is held at the Praca de Rocia [Rossio] & where everyone endeavours to ask a higher price than anyone should think the animal worth. Our heavy baggage was put into store, and our campaigning equipment only consisted of two sorts of panniers, wrought of basket [wicker] and neatly covered with hides. These contained tea, sugar and in their other separate divisions, cold beef or other eatables and one was entirely for the carriage of linen and clothes. They were poised, on mule back, by strong broad leather straps and the bedding, cloak &c went in the centre. Those articles and two small casks of spirits generally completed an officer's travelling equipment.

Lisbon whose name is derived from Olisippo,[16] is an ancient and large city and the capital of Portugal. The situation is extremely fine and the air is esteemed salubrious and a good climate. Great commerce is carried on by all nations and its port is considered one of the best in Europe, although sometimes exposed to southerly and other winds. The earthquake in 1755[17] destroyed a great part of this city, but it now contains many fine edifices and especially churches and convents. It likewise has some fine pracas or squares and the Praca de Comercio is exceedingly handsome. Its curiosities are but few, however the aqueduct is a most noble structure of art and is of the most beneficial use to the inhabitants and supplies them with the most charming water. Its length is 1,500 paces [3,750ft or 1,143m], the width of the grand arch 287 feet [87.5m] and its altitude 208 feet [63.4m].[18]

16 The Ancient Celtic name for Lisbon.

17 On 1 November 1755 an earthquake and subsequent tsunami destroyed some 85 per cent of the city and killed up to 40,000 people.

18 The Aguas Livres [Free Waters] aqueduct provided fresh water, piped purely by gravity to the city from mountains 58km away. It was completed by 1748 and survived the earthquake unharmed. The measurements here describe the aqueduct where it passes across the Alcantara valley just outside Lisbon.

The churches of the Estrella[19] and St Roque[20] deserve attention and in the latter are some very old and fine mosaic. The dirtiness of Lisbon is almost proverbial and makes it very disagreeable to walk 'uncovered' either by day or night, unless at the imminent risk of getting a 'ducking'. In wet weather it is entirely impossible to walk in the street owing to the *water-spouts* by the sides of the houses, a '*river*' in the middle and a '*dunghill*' between.

The inhabitants of Lisbon are in four classes, the fidalgos or nobility, clergy, merchants and labourers. The first are quite distinct from the others and are extremely proud & tenacious of their rank. The greatest intrigue and duplicity prevails among them and many live a most vile, loose, debauched life, although they must be said to be attached to the sovereign and it is an honour to be styled son of the '*Casa Real*' [Royal House]. The clergy are in general, respectable & well informed and seem to mix but little with society. The merchants are attentive to business and just in their dealings, many also are very opulent. The lower class are laborious and hardy and are most civil, docile and obedient. All hard drudgery is done by the *Gallegos* and a Portuguese servant must hire one, to carry a portmanteau to the neighbouring door. Likewise, the water from the different fountains is carried by them.

The Portuguese are very attentive to politesse and the lowest or meanest individuals pull off their hats to each other at an immense distance, advance and (if friends) embrace each other. The same politeness is used on entering, or retiring from company, demonstrated by numerous bows, compliments or curtsies. Their salutations are very long and repeated, whilst making their *obeisance.* The women even to their uncle, cousin or other near relation seldom tender their hand and in company to their most intimate male

19 The Estrela Basilica or the Royal Basilica and Convent of the Most Sacred Heart of Jesus.

20 The Igreja de Sao Roque was the first Jesuit church in Portugal.

friend only salute him with the usual compliment. Women of equal rank embrace each other, although only half an hour in each other's society. Both sexes are fond of gaudy dress and the women wear an immense number of rings and other trinkets. No woman can go out of doors without their friend's permission and must always be attended by a *Duena*,[21] however notwithstanding these precautions, there are nearly as many '*filles de joie*'[22] as in London. They are in general well made, [with] regular features, black and expressive eyes, slender bodies and active, and have prepossessing and unaffected manners. Their dress is seldom varied and is the Spanish ladies costume, with the difference of being a little Englified [*sic*]. Although some of the officers got acquainted with the inhabitants, yet it was not general and our order to join the army was no matter of regret.

On the 8 May, we set off to come up with the 1st Division of the Army, who were in winter quarters near Nisa. Our first day's march was to Sacavem, a distance of nearly two leagues from Lisbon, the road being entirely paved all the way to Villa Franca [Vila Franca de Xira]. It must be understood that the leagues in Portugal are by no means limited to a certain number of miles, some being three, four and even five miles in length. Sacavem had formerly been a pretty village, but almost all the principal inhabitants deserting it, on Massena's advance, it was now neglected. We found however a tolerable good inn, where almost all the officers dined. When formerly here [in 1808] I had my billet on the house of a marquis, whose daughters, most amiable women, had both fled on the approach of the enemy and the house was now empty. Our orders were to march as early as possible, in order to avoid the heat of the day and this obliged us to go soon to rest.

21 Portuguese – Housekeeper.

22 French – Prostitutes.

We commenced our march on the 9 May at ½ past 4 o'clock and crossed a small tributary stream of the Tagus on a flying bridge of boats.[23]

[10 May] We found the road today the same as yesterday, only a little mixed with sand. The surrounding country was pretty and varied and rendered our march pleasant and interesting until we reached a small village called Alpidrinha [Alhandra], from whence the famous lines of Torres Vedras, extend their formidable barrier to [beyond] Mafra, a distance of 25 leagues. At 10 o'clock we entered Villa Franca [Vila Franca de Xira], which although still a good village, has been much destroyed. Indeed, the scenes described by the people of the rapacity and wantoness of the enemy were shocking and fully accounted for the great appearance of poverty here visible. The house where we were formerly billeted was still the best in the town, but its proprietor apologised that his present circumstances would not allow him pleasure of entertaining us as he had done before. The wanton barbarity of the enemy was here peculiarly displayed, by breaking all the fine mirrors in the house and cutting the paintings with sabres. We here found several good shops and sellers of spirits &c being so well situated on the high road, they had a great supply of everything for the army. Here we found *no* amusement or excitement whatever, either by day or night and less on our following day's march . . .

[11 May] . . . to Azambugio [Azambuja], which was in a complete state of ruin and dilapidation and it was with considerable difficulty that we found quarters and there were a few wine houses lately established. The country around here is delightful and if properly attended to would produce anything, but the wretched state of the people and their natural disinclination to innovations, prevent any regular cultivation.

23 A flying bridge of boats was formed by a cable being extended across the river and the boats crossing, by attaching themselves to the cable.

Next morning [12 May] we proceeded on our route to Santarem, a distance of 4 leagues over a fertile and most luxuriant country & where the riches of nature were sown in profusion, but were ill improved, with the exception of the vine and olive tree. About a league from town we crossed a stone bridge, over which Massena on his retreat took up a most strong position and we were obliged to renounce the contest of the bridge, finding him so strongly posted. Before arriving, we went up a most severe, long and tedious hill, at whose summit stands Santarem, commanding a most charming prospect of the surrounding country.

Santarem was formerly a fine and opulent city, but now stands amongst the number of those which French barbarity and the ravages of war have ruined & destroyed. It is situated on the Tagus, in a fertile and abundant country, especially in olives, wheat and wine. Here they have two harvests and everywhere the ground is most productive. A great number of its fine churches were entirely demolished and those that remain are stripped of their internal ornaments and plate. Likewise, all the nunneries and convents suffered the same fate and one in particular was made into a theatre and afterwards burnt. The nuns were very polite and unrestrained in comparison to other orders and on our former march, placed cockades in our hats and presented us with sweetmeats, so in return for which we sent them the band. Three of these poor women, had just now arrived and with horror were beholding the wreck of their convent and elegant little chapel. Santarem commands a most charming prospect from the northeast and would if well supplied with provisions be a very strong position.

On the 13 [May] our march to Golegam [Golega] was exceedingly cool and pleasant, the road now and then winding on the Tagus, the banks shaded by the elm and willow tree, the perfume of the wild lily and the breeze off the water served indeed to make the 4 leagues appear as nothing. Our old host was not at Golegam [Golega], we therefore went to another billet, which was very fair and the people civil. There was in one of the rooms an excellent painting of the Goddess Ceres,[24] but all her attendants could not prevent French barbarity from destroying the lovely face of their deity, with several sabre cuts. Golegam [Golega] is prettily situated at the extremity of an extensive and very fertile valley and a small river, which debouches itself into the Tagus, passes and winds through the country below.

[14 May] Our following day's march was even more agreeable and variegated by the beauties of nature than to Golegam [Golega]. Keeping still close to the Tagus, we passed through many villages charmingly situated and especially through Tancos, a little village in the vale of the same name. Four wretched huts were the only ones remaining and had it not been for the old Moorish castle that stands in the river[25] I could hardly have brought it to my recollection. These villages were all reduced either by the enemy, or our own soldiers, who often could not on a retreat be restrained from marauding, although the most exemplary punishments were inflicted. Their unfortunate inhabitants wore a pallid and dejected countenance & bespoke the utmost poverty and want, and their usual subsistence consisted of salad, bread & oil.

On the River Zezere stands the town of Punhete,[26] where we were quartered for the night and on it is a bridge of boats firmly secured and chained as the rapidity of the stream is very strong, so much so that in winter the boats are lifted and there is no communication with Lisbon. Punhete has been greatly destroyed and has every appearance of wretchedness. In their desire for plunder the enemy had burnt down a church and

24 The Roman Goddess of Agriculture.

25 The Castle of Almourol is built on a small island just off the northern bank of the Tagus near Tancos.

26 Now known as Constancia.

hearing that the treasures were buried under where the dead are buried, they turned up dead bodies & their bones and skulls were even laying in the streets. I was in the same house as formerly, but the proprietor was so miserably reduced, that he could afford us neither beds nor oil.

[15 May] Next morning on leaving Punhete, we had a fine view of Abrantes, at the distance of 3 leagues and ascending the hill also on which it stands, we commanded a prospect of the river and the country to an immense extent. Although we were to march to Abrantes by our Route, yet an officer of the Quarter Master General's Department ordered us to occupy some small villages about a league from it. The town is strongly fortified and professes an excellent situation for defence, standing on the Tagus, over which there was only a bridge of boats. The fortifications are still continuing & will render it one of the strongest holds in Portugal. As we did not enter the town we had no idea what state it was in, but as it had not been a possession of the French for some time, it may be supposed not to be so much destroyed as the others. Our villages were very bad and the by-roads to them were equally so, being dirty and narrow. For this day's march we found the country well cultivated, although the soil was sandy and by no means very arable. The method of ploughing here attracted our notice, about thirty oxen ploughs preceding each other, in a regular oblique line, each turning up a furrow and so until in a very short time the field is ploughed. In harrowing, the horses are in pairs to the number of 30 or more and form a circle in the field and at a full gallop go round the extent of it and gradually diminishing their circuit, complete their laborious task very soon indeed.

[16 May] Gaviao our next morning's march was a small miserable village and being on the high road was almost destitute of inhabitants until several sutlers opened shops and sold their articles well to troops passing.

[17 May] Here the country was very arid and our march to Gafete was over immense plains of sand, here and there interspersed with the wild scented underwood which abounds through Portugal and Spain. At Gafete we came up with the army and took the place of our 2nd Battalion viz 1st Brigade of the 1st Division,[27] right column of the army under General Sir Thomas Graham. This day the officers of the 2nd Battalion gave us an excellent dinner and exceeded far any expectations we could have formed of it, in considering there were nothing here to be got. No small degree of sociability prevailed between the officers of the two battalions, many of whom paying heavy contributions at the shrine of Bachus[28] and not till bright Aurora[29] appeared did they move from the table. Gafete was a small village and afforded no amusement, except coursing and shooting, at the distance of a league from town. The brigade consisted of the [1/]42nd, [2/]24th, [2/]58th and [1/]79th Regiments and was in general called the Highland Brigade, although the 24th & 58th were English regiments and but very weak.

The order for drafting the 2nd Battalion into the 1st appeared and in consequence the necessary arrangements were taking & everything was in hurry and bustle.[30] The [2/]24th and other regiments had been ordered to Abrantes to receive new clothing, therefore no fears of an immediate movement on our part was entertained. But the life of a soldier is so inconstant, that for an hour we cannot make sense where the next our quarters may be.

The commander of the forces was in the north, with some divisions of the army, while General Sir Rowland Hill was supposed to be actively employed in the south. We now had been four days at Gafete but the different arrangements were

27 The 1/42nd was appointed to 1st Division on 23 April but only joined on 17 May 1812.

28 Bacchus, Greco-Roman God of wine and festivity.

29 Aurora, Roman Goddess of the dawn.

30 On 19 May, the 2/42nd was ordered to draft all fit rank and file into the 1st Battalion and the remainder to return home to recruit.

not yet completed. When fostering the idea of remaining here for some time yet . . .

. . . An order arrived on the 20 [May] to march immediately to Castello de Vide [Castelo de Vide], a town 4 leagues off on the Spanish frontier. This sudden move threw the officers of the 2nd Battalion into great perplexity as they had in general disposed of their mules and other animals to the officers of the 1st.[31] Our only conjecture on this unexpected move was that General Hill was about to attack the enemy's position at the Bridge of Almaraz and that Sir Thomas Graham was ordered to support the left with his column.

On entering Castello de Vide [Castelo de Vide], we had a most severe shower of hail and sleet, which completely ducked us and forms one of the pleasures of a campaign; however it is in the fields after such a shower of rain that affords a person the greatest '*gout*' for the glory of a military life.

We found the whole of the division quartered in the town, consisting of a Brigade of Guards and another of Germans, along with the other corps composing the Highland Brigade. Castello de Vide [Castelo de Vide] is had now for some a pretty large town and is very strongly situated but has no fortifications except an old citadel and wall which is in several places destroyed. Opposite on a promontory of a ridge of rocks, stands a chapel of St Antonio,[32] where annually penitents go on their knees up to the summit to obtain absolution. Marvao, a place of considerable strength and regularly fortified, stands on the ridge of [a] hill with Castello de Vide [Castelo de Vide], at about the distance of a league. The country here is rich & well cultivated and the market was well supplied with everything.

31 Both battalions marched together until all arrangements for the transfer of men were completed on 4 June.

32 Santo Antonio das Areias.

Our route was fixed on the 21 [May] when we marched at 4 o'clock, the Brigade of Guards and Germans,[33] marching on St Vicente [San Vincente de Alcantara in Spain] & ours more to the right. At 8 o'clock we forded a small river and it was here that separated Spain and Portugal, although the language of the latter continued to be spoken. The country around here was rather rocky and barren, however in the intervening valleys and slopes of the hills, were some luxuriant '*quintas*' and vineyards.

Hardly had we crossed the streamlet when orders arrived by an orderly dragoon to return to our quarters at Castello de Vide [Castelo de Vide]. He likewise conveyed the agreeable intelligence of General Hill's success at the Bridge of Almaraz, taking several pieces of cannon and some prisoners. Our support was therefore useless and on arriving at Castello de Vide [Castelo de Vide], orders were received to transfer the officers & men of the 2nd Battalion immediately.

On the 25 [May] the 1st Battalion was completed to 1,200 rank and file and with officers and sergeants made a total of 1,350 souls, a number which very few regiments could boast of.[34] After remaining four days in this town, the division was ordered back to their several old cantonments, the Guards & Germans were quartered at Nisa and our brigade in Gafete and Alpahao [Alpalhao].

The 1/42nd had been assigned to the 2nd Brigade of General Thomas Graham's 1st Division in the General Orders dated 23 April, replacing the 2/42nd. The Brigade was commanded by Major General William Wheatley in the absence of General Edward Stopford. The 1/26th had also left the Brigade, transferring to Gibraltar to recuperate, being replaced by 2/58th. The Brigade in mid-June therefore consisted of 2/24th, 1/42nd, 2/58th,

33 The Brigade of Guards consisted of 1st Battalion Coldstream Guards and 1st/3rd Foot Guards. The German Brigade consisted of 1st, 2nd & 5th Line Battalions King's German Legion.

34 The regimental histories state that the 1st Battalion numbered 1,160 rank and file at this time, which would certainly make it one of the strongest battalions in the army.

1/79th and a company of 5/60th Riflemen. A General Order transferring 2/58th to the 5th Division was published on 1 June, but Oman states that the regiment remained with the brigade until after the siege of Burgos in the autumn, which would seem to agree with Stirling.

On the 4 [1] June[35] the affairs of the two battalions being arranged, the remains of the 2nd Battalion marched for Lisbon, the most welcome one they had performed for the space of nearly three years which they had served on the peninsula. Their toils and fatigues had now for some time ended, while ours were only commencing and the very morning they marched for Lisbon and towards the happy shores of Albion, we began our march for the north of Portugal, which happiness and joy had long forsaken. Our Route was for Nisa, which is on the high north road and this together with the march of the Guards,[36] indicated that our illustrious commander meant to beat up the enemy's headquarters at Salamanca. Nisa is a town of considerable size and had at one period been fortified, but in point of comfort, or beauty, the rapacity of war has completely ruined it. Sir Thomas Graham here inspected the 42nd Regiment and was pleased to express his most heartfelt satisfaction at again seeing it so very effective and in such fine order.

[2 June] Next morning we crossed the Tagus at the famous pass of Villa Velha [Vila Velha de Rodao] where there is now an excellent bridge of boats,[37] in lieu of flying boats which were formerly there. Just over this impenetrable pass stands, or stood, the village of Vila Velha [de Rodao] now laid in

35 Unfortunately, none of the various accounts by the 42nd detail their route to Salamanca; but it is certain that they arrived in view of Salamanca on 17 June as James states; however, this means that working backwards his dates on the march do not tally with his stated encampments. Given the number of halts he identifies, the regiment must have begun the march on 1 June not the 4th. Did he misread his old notes?

36 The 1st Brigade of the 1st Division consisted of 1st Battalion Coldstream Guards and 1st Battalion 3rd Foot Guards, with a company of 5/60th.

37 Pontoon bridge.

ruins and where we this day halted on the declivity of the hill, enjoying a cool breeze and a charming prospect. After a long and fatiguing march, the headquarters of the regiment halted at a village called Sobral [Cebolais] de Cima but small & miserable enough, beautifully situated in a most luxuriant valley, buried (as it were) between the immense hills.

[3 June] Castelo Branco was our next day's march and where we found the 6th and 7th Divisions billeted, consequently the town was so crowded that several officers resorted to a bivouac. Castelo Branco is a town in the province of Beyra [Beira] and is situated on the River Lyra. It is a place of great antiquity and once of great strength. It contains many large edifices and buildings, churches and convents, together with a palace of the Bishop of the See, and likewise an old castle, connected with a ruinous wall, which mostly surrounds the town and in many parts of it, is to be seen the neighbouring country for an immense distance.

The destruction here was the same as we perceived in every other town that had been so unfortunate as to receive the common marauders of the peninsula. Every house of any consequence was gutted of all their articles and very different was it, when we before passed, each day sumptuously entertained and served in plate, to now when nothing but bare walls and a few broken chairs and tables remained.

Having laid in here an addition to our stock from the various suttlers . . .

[4 June] . . . we set off next morning on the road to Ciudad Rodrigo and marched through a pretty country to a little village called Lardosa and which was not so much destroyed as the others in proportion. There we had the good fortune to be in a house where the people were very civil and especially the ladies, who although rather vying towards antiquity, were very good looking and were by far the most free and pretty women, we had yet met on our Route.

[5 June] Next morning's dawn, we reassumed our journey long before our charming hostesses could bid us adieu and at ½ past 11 o'clock we came to Campinha [Capinha] where for the first time our regiment bivouacked. The scenery round this little spot was delightful and the fruit trees, especially the cherry, grew in wild luxuriance. Although the face of the country now got mountainous, yet it was well cultivated and most of the little huts possessed the comfort of a small garden, very well stocked and by no means had the appearance of inactivity or laziness, so universal in other parts of Portugal.

[6 June] Our following day's march was most fatiguing, owing to the great steepness of the mountains we had to ascend, which were cut in many parts, by deep ravines and gullies formed by the immense torrents in winter. At the summit of the last that we ascended, a most extensive prospect presented itself and within its bounds, we had a *coup d'oeil* of nearly eighty miles round. In the valley into which we were descending, were our old quarters Belmonte and several other villages. In a fine situation on the acclivity of the opposite hill, stands Covillao [Covilha], one of the largest and most opulent cities of Portugal.

After a very severe march we reached Covillao [Castelheiro?], a small wretched village, only fit to contain 4 companies of the regiment and the remaining six proceeded onto another small village on our Route. Here we were three in one small apartment in the house of a carpenter, one of the richest inhabitants of this little abode. He and his family gazed with utter astonishment and surprise at all our little comforts and our dinner and breakfast canteens really attracted their greatest admiration and curiosity. I slept most profoundly on one of those large trunks or ark's, which are generally found in the houses of the lower class and a[t] 4 o'clock started for our daily performance.

[7 June] The country still continuing mountainous and rugged, our following day's march was as fatiguing and long as that of yesterday and to add to our misfortunes, the guide had most materially taken us out of our road, for at midday we only reached our destination Agoas Bellas [Aguas Belas], a place deserving the title of a village, but where we had fine water, which the name implies and an excellent bivouac.

It was rumoured that at Renda [Rendo] our next day's march, the army should concentrate and that also it would be necessary to wait a few days to allow the cavalry time to join the rest of the army.

[8 June] At Renda [Rendo] we were bivouacked in a most delightful spot, shaded with the broad spreading chestnut and the soft verdure of the ground, up to the knees, the River Coa on the left of our line and near the situation General Craufurd with the Light Division made a gallant stand against superior forces.[38] The Coa here was slow, tranquil and perfectly fordable and gently gliding in its course through a most charming, variegated country. Our soldiers with the idea of remaining in this romantic spot for a few days, had employed the day in making huts with the branches of the trees; but always liable to be deceived, an order at 4 o'clock gave us the Route to march next day, to our infinite regret.

[9 June] Leaving our delightful encampment, at 5 o'clock we marched to a small village called Bismula, where we were all put into quarters such as they were. Our Reverend Padre in whose house we were, complained loudly of the devastation committed in his little parish by the enemy.

38 The Action of Sabugal took place on 3 April 1811. Wellington's main force was ordered to make a frontal attack on General Reynier's Corps at Sabugal, while the Light Division with two cavalry brigades would make a march around the left wing of the French. Unfortunately, heavy fog delayed the main attack, but Major General William Erskine pressed his flanking movement (commanding in Craufurd's absence in England). The Light Division fought hard but were in great danger of being overwhelmed, when the fog lifted, revealing the frontal attack to Reynier and causing him to order his troops to retreat.

[10 June] At Bismula we halted one day, which was employed in arranging all our little affairs, for the prosecution of our journey. Everything of the people was preserved and taken care of, with the greatest secrecy and it was only by the patronage of the vicar, we [were] promised some bread and wine at a very dear rate.

[11 June] We had no anxiety to remain here, where everything was so scarce and so extravagant and our Route came in [during] the night to march towards Fuenteguinaldo [in Spain], the headquarters of the army . . .

[12 June] . . . and the following day to Pistores [Pastores], a small village about a league from Ciudad Rodrigo. Here the whole of the army were nearly connected, the 6th & 7th Divisions being on our left and the Light Division and some cavalry in front.

[13 June] We had one day's halt here and we took the opportunity of riding into the city [of Ciudad Rodrigo]. It was most materially changed since I last was there, and of our old billet not one stone was left on another, nor of its old possessor could we learn any particulars, except that he was dead. All the houses near the principal breach and the churches were in ruins, with these excepted, not many of the houses in town seemed much injured.

The two breaches were in a state of repair and three or four very formidable redoubts had been constructed on the less defencible [*sic*] fronts of the ground round the town.

Ciudad Rodrigo is in the Kingdom of Leon and had a bishoprick [*sic*] of great value. It is situated in an abundant and fertile country and on the Agueda, over which it has a very handsome stone bridge. It has been the point of dispute between the Spaniards and Portuguese many times, but it has been in the hands of the Spaniards since 1707,[39] except when the French left a garrison in it.

39 Ciudad Rodrigo fell on 4 October 1707 following a Spanish siege commanded by the Marquis de Bay.

The fine large Almeda,[40] under whose kind shade we were wont to pass our siestas was entirely cut down and nothing but its fountain could recall its site to memory. There are still some good linen and other shops, but they by no means possess the dashing appearance they formerly had.

In the afternoon we returned to camp, but little satisfied with the city . . .

[14 June] . . . and next morning we traversed the famous plains of Leon.

James made some immediate comparisons between the Spanish and Portuguese.

The difference that 4 leagues made between the Spaniards and their swarthy neighbours [Portuguese] was most obvious and in their mutual detestation of each other, they tried which should show it most and especially expressed their feelings to us. The language was completely changed, although there is a similarity to the Portuguese and the former is most majestic, although at first a little harsh to the ear.

The Spaniards are all in general of a black tawny colour, their features regular and they are well made. The women in point of beauty far exceed the men & are in general slender and possess a handsome figure and shape and are anxious above all things to have small feet. Their dress although but little varied, is excessively handsome and the genteel manoeuvres of the fare are kept in constant practise.

In their conversation and manners they are perfectly different to the men, who have a sullen and grave gloom on their countenances, whilst those of the women are animated and full of expression. The title of *Don* and *Donna*, is given indiscriminately to everyone and although '*Buestra merced*' [Your Grace] or you is used, yet to the nobility '*Nossa Senoria*'

40 Spanish for a plateau area. Here however it would appear to refer to a shaded walk.

or your 'Lord or Ladyship' must be paid great attention to. They are more cleanly in their houses than in their persons, although it is rare to find a bed void of troublesome gentry of different descriptions. They are very abstemious both in their eating and drinking and a drunken Spaniard or Portuguese is seldom seen. In their visits they are not so formal as their western neighbours, yet the noblesse pay their visits in great state. In their religious ceremonies they are very devout, but under this head, much might be said for even under the sanctified cloak of religion are too often practised the most vile intrigues and are perceivable when performing their devotions in church. Mass is held every feast, saints or holiday and on Sundays, but it is only during the time they are really at prayer that they restrain themselves from other employments and pleasure.

Their amusements are bullfights, shooting, boulyards ball [boules?] and the young men generally play on the guitar, with which they serenade their fair ones in the night, with love songs composed by themselves. Dancing and singing are also two of their great divertments [*sic*] at the former, the women are excellent performers and dance the bolero, fandango and other national dances, with peculiar grace and activity.

Our march on the 14 [15 June] was very short, agreeable and interesting, nor was the idea of soon coming close to the enemy the least of our enjoyments. We on the 14th [15th] encamped in a wood near the village of Tamames, where the Spaniards suffered a defeat shortly after the commencement of the Revolution[41] . . .

[16 June] . . . and [next day] we bivouacked near Matilla [Matilla de los Canos del Rio], another small village not far distant from Salamanca. We now are in great expectation of

41 An odd mistake by Stirling. The Action at Tamames occurred on 18 October 1809, when the French General Marchand, commanding the weak 6th Corps, was defeated by a force under the command of Spanish General Del Parque.

Man and women of Castile.

seeing the enemy and on the 15th [16th] our cavalry and light infantry were partially engaged when we lost three officers of the German Hussars and some men wounded.

Various were the conjectures as to the strength of the enemy and we supposed they had garrisons in the forts they had made in town and entrenching themselves in position.

On the 17 June we were gratified with a sight of this venerable city, from the heights over it and close to the River Tormes on which the town is situated. We rested here for upwards of 3 hours, during which time the cavalry, supported by the 6th and 7th Divisions crossed the ford at St Martin [Santa Marta de Tormes], above the town, which they effected without any opposition at 2 o'clock.

The French had retreated, setting fire to several houses near the redoubts, in which they had left strong garrisons. At 3 o'clock we crossed the river at the same place as the other part of the army, except the 3rd Division, who forded below the city. The river was pretty deep and rapid, causing very considerable alarm to the 'final part' of the army. We were bivouacked in a pretty situation, close to the banks of the river. It appeared by accounts given by the people that the enemy retired about midnight and were about 12,000 men and [left] 1,000 picked men in the redoubts.

Our light troops were close up with the enemy, who were only about 3 leagues off, in order to harass or retard the siege of the forts. The joy the inhabitants testified at our appearance, was manifest and grateful, and our old acquaintances received us in the most-friendly manner, but it was most deplorable to behold the altered and timid state, to which the finest city of Leon and mother of Spanish literature had been reduced in the short period of 3 years. The house of my old patron was deserted, as it was close to the principal fort and a church which stood before it had been demolished in order not to afford our men cover to fire into the redoubt. All the churches and convents were gutted and destroyed and few public buildings escaped the ravages of the enemy.

The two redoubts were modern and although small, of considerable strength and connected with a fortified convent [San Vincente], with loopholes and a deep fosse,[42] drawbridge and bastion.[43] There were about 8 pieces of cannon and two howitzers, which were before pointed towards the west, but now were turned towards the town.

[18 June] The investment took place immediately and our trenches were commenced by parties from the 6th Division[44] who were in town.

On the 19 [June], the trenches were opened and a battery of 4 eighteen pounders and 2 [3] howitzers was finished to bear on the front angle of the old convent [San Vincente], the first point required to be breached. At daybreak of the morning of the 20 [19 June],[45] this battery opened and in less than eight hours the angle of the convent was beat down and breached. All the day there had been a considerable deal of musketry from the redoubts and our men put into the opposite houses.

[20 June] The battery was now changed in order to bear on the right angle of the convent and one of 5 nine pounders [two 24-pounder howitzers – this was increased to five cannon that evening][46] was erected before the smallest redoubt. Several other guns were expected up and my hope was entertained of the loss of their forts.

42 Fosse – a deep ditch or moat.

43 There were three forts which mutually supported each other. The forts were converted monasteries which had been greatly strengthened, named San Cayetano, La Merced and the larger San Vincente and were defended by around 800 men under Colonel Duchemin with 36 cannon.

44 Major General Sir Henry Clinton's 6th Division was given the task of besieging the forts.

45 The siege battery opened on the morning of 19 June.

46 This information is taken from the Journals of Sir John Thomas Jones Royal Engineers, who was a witness. James seems to be ill-informed regarding the artillery used in the siege, which he was not an eyewitness to.

> Salamanca is an old, rich and well peopled city, in the Kingdom of Leon and first university of Spain. It is beautifully situated on the River Tormes, over which there is a most magnificent stone bridge of very fine architecture and strong. The churches, convents and seminaries of arts and sciences, were formerly very numerous and the buildings were very fine, but the rapacious hand of war has been stretched over them and almost all are in ruins. The cathedral above all is most admirable and strikes awe and respect into the mind of a beholder. It has not so many of those gaudy ornaments and bigoted toys, that in all other churches on the peninsula contain,[47] but the architecture both within and without is light and elegant and principally scriptural representations. It has two superb organs and the choir, altar and smaller chapels, display a great degree of taste and airy lightness not usually found in Catholic places of worship. The new college is a fine edifice, but is not finished nor would in all probability never shall be.[48] There is only one square of any consequence and it certainly is very regular and tastefully arranged.[49] The houses are of three floors & each window with venetian blinds, green iron curtains. The under floor are shops and above every arch is a bust of a king or prince of Spain. Formerly there was held an excellent market here, but it is much reduced, although before we left it everything was to be procured.

The short period of rest for the army while the forts were besieged were over, Wellington was forced to postpone the siege and ordered his forces forward to meet the advance of Marshal Marmont, who was trying the relieve the garrisons in the forts. Wellington stood in his path and offered battle, but after three days of probing, Marmont retired, leaving the forts to their own devices. James relates what happened to the regiment that same day.

47 There speaks a Scottish Protestant on Catholic tastes!

48 It has of course been completed and the University of Salamanca continues to flourish today.

49 The Plaza Mayor built between 1729 and 1755.

On the morning of the 20 [June], most unexpectedly were we disturbed taking our humble repast under the umbrage of our spreading elm, by an order to be in readiness to march immediately, communication being received of Marmont's advance having been considerably reinforced. At 10 o'clock we were under arms and marched towards the heights above and to the right of Salamanca and waited under a most severe storm of rain and sleet, for nearly two hours. At last, we advanced in regular order to the heights about a league from the town and the brigades to march by companies preserving proper distances and afterwards to form in line of battle. The advance of the army was rapid and our second line was forming, when a sharp fire of musquetry commenced in front and also several cannon shots. Everyone was buoyed up with the hopes of a general action, seeing every arrangement made and our capital position crowned with troops.

The 7th Division being on the right of the 1st line, had possession of a small village, of which the enemy appeared to wish to possess themselves, the 68th and 51st Regiments[50] of light infantry were ordered to occupy and retain it as long as possible, which was until recalled by Lord Wellington and their resistance had caused the firing we had heard in front. It was now too late in the day to suppose the enemy should make any attack and they had halted, taking possession of San Christoval and other villages round our position. The position was most commanding and the arrangements to resist any attack were likewise fine. Our first line was supported by the cavalry and artillery, judiciously placed and a 2nd line, or sort of reserve to every division was about 2 hundred yards behind the first and ready to afford assistance whenever they might be required.

[21 June] Sleeping beneath our arms piled, we were formed in line at daybreak and waited so for an hour, but no attack took place. However, our advance posts were engaged at 11 o'clock

50 Major General von Bernewitz's 2nd Brigade of Major General Hope's 7th Division.

and the enemy tried to push them, but in vain. At 2 o'clock the light companies of our brigade were sent to reinforce and relieve the Guards, when a regular chain of posts were formed all round our position and at the distance of [a] musket shot from the enemy. This day was fine and we had an opportunity of judging of the force of Marmont, which taking the columns in the village, those that were continually kept moving and the great display of waggons, mules, baggage &c, which were all taken care to be shown, could not have been estimated at more than 20,000 infantry and 2,000 cavalry and artillery.[51] By the movements of the enemy on the 21st, every precaution was taken against an attack . . .

[22 June] . . . on the following morning and the outposts were under arms at 2 and the whole line at 3 o'clock. However, to our very great disappointment, they declined paying us a morning visit. Marmont seemed anxious to possess a small commanding hill on the right of our position to reconnoitre it and on which we only had a small detachment of cavalry, which were obliged to retire on the advance of Marmont himself and a superior force of cavalry, supported by some infantry. Our force was however immediately supported by the two battalions of light Germans and the regiment of Brunswick Oels and the audacious enemy was immediately driven off in most gallant style, our Germans pursuing them almost to their villages. Our artillery in this little affair threw some shells into the columns of cavalry with great effect and this smart though comparatively small business, was nearly ending in a general action. Marmont had now surveyed the strength of our position and forces, quietly retiring to his former positions and no evident signs of attack were seen for the remainder of the day, whilst most audaciously he was threatening to attack us with far superior forces. Our ideas therefore of being attacked were but faint and as we had imagined . . .

51 Fortescue estimates that Marmont had about 25,000 troops with him.

. . . on the 23 [June] he commenced his retreat at 1 o'clock & most happy at having escaped our clutches, the bird next morning had fled. Their rear guard were followed up by a part of our cavalry, but they did them but little injury. The villages they had left, presented a shocking display of wanton barbarity and not three houses were found in one of them, that was not burnt or ransacked of every article. Marmont's plan of retreat must have at once been decided on, on gaining an insight into our strength and position and most opinions were, that he had not more than 25,000 men, infantry, cavalry & artillery, whilst our force far exceeded this and occupied an excellent position.

Although everything ought to be left to the superior judgement and knowledge of the commander in chief, yet everyone on seeing 25,000 men retire untouched, before an army of 35,000 or 40,000 British troops, in the highest order and spirits, could not help expressing their feelings of regret, that an attack was not made on our part, which nearly as sure as certainly, would have annihilated their whole army, together with baggage, artillery, stores &c and put them at all events in a state not to again confront us as they had done. Many arguments since have decided, that had we withdrawn all their cavalry to the hill on our right on the 22nd and bringing up the guns, marched down in solid columns and surprised them, while in confusion they must have been all taken or defeated.

At 5 o'clock in the evening, fearing that a body of the enemy might cross the river at Alba de Tormes, the 1st and 7th Divisions with their artillery, marched down to the ford, in order to be ready to act if wanted.

[24 June] The batteries and fire against the forts had still been kept up[52] and on the 24th instant, one of them[53] was stormed at 10 o'clock by the light companies of General Bowes' Brigade, but the attack had failed from some unavoidable cause and

52 The guns had actually been put back into the batteries on 23 June.

53 Fort Cayetano was attacked, but it failed.

the general wounded and taken, with Brigade Major Hobart[54] and several other officers, killed and wounded. Major General Bowes[55] after died of his wounds in the fort and there was interred.

A sharp firing on the other side of the river, caused us to cross and we advanced for about a league and there took up a position. At 2 o'clock we again marched to the ford and there remained three hours without crossing. As the movements of the army were so uncertain, we could not hazard to cook anything and it was fortunate as we again were ordered on the advanced and chosen position. We therefore at 4 o'clock were in a second position & disposed in columns of regiments out of sight, hoping there to remain during the night, but an order arrived to recross and to bivouac on our old ground. There we reached at 9 o'clock nearly famished, but fatigued, we stretched our heavy carcasses on the verdant carpet and beneath the shelter of our old branchy friend, not thinking of eating.

On the 24th and 25th a new battery was made of 4 x 24 pounders and red hot shot being prepared, they opened in the evening . . .

. . . and on the 26 [June] continued until a part of the convent took fire and during the smoke and confusion, dispositions were made for assault, which succeeded and the garrison surrendered prisoners of war to the number of 700 men strong and artillery. The strength of these two [three] small forts was more than we formed any idea of and cost nearly 250 men and some good artillery men amongst them.[56]

We remained in our bivouac until the 27 [June], when we marched by corps on Valladolid, General Sir Thomas Graham's

54 Major Paul Minchin Hobart died of his wounds on 1 September 1812.

55 Major General Barnard Foord Bowes died on 24 June 1812.

56 Fortescue estimates Allied losses of about 350 men during the siege of the forts.

consisting of the 1st, 6th and 7th Divisions. The country round Salamanca was pretty and irregular and very productive, but on this day's march, we travelled across immense plains, covered with the dwarf oak and olive trees. In a very thick wood of this description we were bivouacked the first night, in very close order, so much so it was with difficulty we got sufficient space for officer's tents. We now began to feel the want of the good water and plentiful wood of Portugal and our men had to go far before they found the former at all.

[28 June] Next morning we proceeded on our Route and traversed a plain, but most beautiful and abundant country and the fields were covered with the most luxuriant crops of wheat and barley. The enemy had carried on their usual enormities and destruction; we found all the inhabitants returning from their coverts, deploring the loss of many of their valuables, but particularly all their wine vaults had been broken open and plundered. We encamped this day in a bare plain, of ploughed ground, where little or no water could be procured. Marmont from his inferiority of forces, would not make a stand previous to reaching Valladolid near the Duero.

On the 29 [June] our advance was partially engaged with the rear of the enemy and on this day headquarters were at Alaejos. Our whole corps d'armee was bivouacked in a space of 300 yards, with not so much would suffice to cook the men's dinners, but a pretty purling stream which ran through the camp, made up so far for the other deficiency. The enemy had retreated very slowly and in high order and our cavalry were obliged to dislodge them only this morning from the ground we now occupied.

[30 June] Next morning owing to the proximity of the enemy our baggage was ordered to halt, until further orders and we bivouacked near the ancient little town of Medina del Campo. Part of the enemy had crossed the bridge at Tordesillas and

1. Cascais Citadel.

2. Praca de Comercio or 'Black Horse Square', Lisbon.

3. Original map of the Peninsula by James Stirling, showing his marches.

Map of The Peninsular,
The Original was annotated by James Stirling with the marches of the regiment in 1812
The Editor has added the marches for the Corunna Campaign and March into France

1808-9	GREEN
1812	RED
1813	BLUE
1814	PURPLE

4. Map of Walcheren, 1809.

5. The Walcheren Expedition, 1809.

6. Private, 42nd Foot

7. The Black Watch at Corunna, by Harry Payne.

Right: **8.** James Stirling Senior. (Reproduced by kind permission of the Black Watch Castle Archive – Reference BW141-2-1)

Below: **9.** The Black Watch in camp, 1815.

10. Colonel James Stirling's gravestone.

11. Captain James Stirling's Epitaph inscribed on the rear of his father's gravestone.

were followed up by Don Julian Sanchez's Spanish cavalry,[57] together with part of our hussars. Medina del Campo is a town celebrated for being the birthplace of many of the old kings of Spain and was formerly very rich, commercial and enjoyed great privileges. It is rather in a pretty situation, on the small River Zapardiel and in a country abounding in bread and wine. The church of Medina possesses singularities and the square had once a most superb fountain which is now completely demolished. The inhabitants were excessively civil and happy to see us, and when our camp ground on the 4 [July] instant was changed to nearer the town, we had flocks of beautiful Spanish '*Donnas*' in the bivouac, who with the greatest familiarity and naivette, danced on the turf with us until the curtain of heaven was drawn, then we accompanied them to town and kept it up in their houses, till bright Aurora spangled us on our return to camp, with her crispy dew.

[6 July] Yesterday some French dragoons were taken and all their army was across the Duero and had established themselves in Valladolid and Tordesillas. Our little dancing parties were kept up with a great deal of vivacity and we showed our gratitude by giving two grand balls in the town house.

On the 7 [July] a report was circulated on the authority of a Spanish colonel, that General Sir Rowland Hill,[58] in an attack on Soult, had defeated him with the loss of 4,000 men, but the veracity of this glorious news was but ill-founded and no credit was given to it.

On the 8 [July] an order to cook and be in readiness to march was received and it was supposed the enemy had retreated blowing up the bridge of Tordesillas and there was a rumour in

57 Don Julian Sanchez, also known as 'El Charro', was a renowned guerrilla leader.

58 Lieutenant General Sir Rowland Hill.

the morning that the Spaniards were in possession of Burgos. No orders to march were given until 10 o'clock in the evening, when the same order was repeated and ordering all baggage to the rear.

[9 July] In the morning we were still on the same ground, no further order arrived and we accounted for it by supposing the enemy showing a disposition to retreat, we should be in constant readiness to follow him up. Don Julian and the other chiefs of guerrilla parties kept crossing the river and were continually hovering round the flanks and taking small detachments of the enemy's cavalry.

On the 10 [July] no change had taken place and the acquaintance and familiarity we had gained with the inhabitants of this patriotic little town, made us still wish for a prolongment of our present quarters.

The weather during our stay was very sultry and hot, but the old houses of this ancient town, were cool and pleasant. Every window has iron railings and the shutters are like folding doors, so that a through draught of air is allowed to enter, while double sets of white curtains, prevents the sun from penetrating into the rooms.

At last on the 11 [July] our fate was decided and instead of the enemy retreating, they had been making a moment on the river to our left and at 5 o'clock we moved to a small village Valverde [Villaverde de Medina], about one league from Medina [del Campo], towards the left. As we had no other shade but what the houses afforded, as many of the division were quartered as possible and the remainder took shelter under the shade of the houses, the whole bivouacking at night. Next morning no movement having taken place, in order to get under cover during the heat of the day, our brigade were sent to a small village about a league off, called Campilao [El Campillo], where the Duc del Parque[59] was routed in the commencement of the Revolution. Our quarters were indeed wretched, but the country around was well cultivated and every field bore fine thriving crops of corn, wheat & rye. It was so very level, that with ease more than 25 villages could be counted at one view, but with the exception of a few vines and olive trees no verdure was to be seen.

On the evening of the 15 [July] as we were, as usual taking up our ground for the night, an order to proceed to Villa Nave del Rey [Nava del Rey] arrived & there halt until further orders. This we performed and reached our destination at about midnight and reposed on the fields till morning, when quarters in the town were provided for us, which were tolerably good. Villa Nave del Rey [Nava del Rey] is of considerable size, situated in an abundant country and has an excellent market. It contains a handsome church and some convents, one in particular of '*Religeuses*' which has a chapel remarkable for its neatness and superiority of its paintings which were esteemed very valuable.

[17 July] We again had to experience the inconvenience of a night march and at 1 o'clock [am] set off 'helter-skelter' with our cavalry leading the way, back to Alaejos, which we passed through at 2 o'clock in the morning and proceeded to Carnisal [Canizal], where we halted, fatigued and exhausted and bivouacked. It appeared now that the enemy had gained very considerable reinforcements and was endeavouring to [out]flank us and cut off our supplies and communication with the rear. Orders and counter-orders seemed to affirm that the direct movements of the enemy were not ascertained . . .

59 James is not correct. General Diego Portocarrero, 7th Duque del Parque, fought at the Battles of Tamames (victory) and Alba de Tormes (defeat) and the Battle of Carpio near Medina del Campo on 23 November 1809 which was a Spanish victory over General Kellerman's force, but he was then forced to retreat because of Spanish losses elsewhere.

[18 July] . . . but at 1 o'clock next morning we marched through the small village of Carnisal [Canizal] and proceeded to Obada [La Orbada], when after remaining one hour, we marched and took a 'detour' to our right, making a complete circle, we regained our old ground at Carnisal [Canizal] at 8 o'clock, cursing in our hearts the day we allowed those rascals to escape and now to cause us such trouble.

On the 18th, our cavalry was pretty roughly handled,[60] but after 'hard fighting' we made 150 prisoners and killed and wounded several. In the same evening our cavalry picquets having run in on the infantry, the enemy pushed on and crossing a small stream near Alaejos, the 4th Division being the rear guard, found itself obliged to attack the enemy and in gallant style defeat them, taking upwards of 400 prisoners. This little affair checked the advance of the enemy on that point, but turning to their left, they obliged us to move . . .

. . . on the 19 [July] and during that whole day marched in a parallel line with the enemy continually in sight, at last we came so close, that from the heights they were marching on, they amused themselves by throwing some shot and shell into us, but with very little execution. Having marched till 8 o'clock at night and outstripping the enemy we bivouacked and started [again] at daybreak next morning.

On the 21[July], we kept retiring in good order in three columns, the enemy not daring to press us hard, we reached the Tormes without molestation at midday and halted near the ford. The enemy still wished to shoulder us off, by turning our right and we found that on the 21st he forded the river higher up and was on the move down on the opposite side and which caused us to cross likewise in the evening.

60 The French cavalry attempted to capture two cannon; two squadrons were ordered up to protect them but due to some confusion they were driven off and the guns were temporarily in French hands. Wellington, Beresford and their Staff had to draw their swords to protect themselves and barely escaped.

Our direction was towards the two conical hills in front of Salamanca called the '*Arapiles*' and which are connected both by strong ground but are themselves separated. The enemy wishing to have the possession of both these points, in order to strengthen his own position and leave us no point of '*appui*',[61] but oblige us to retire, kept pushing on until he brought his army opposite ours, but he was disappointed in obtaining both of the heights. We on the 21st moved on towards our position in silence by columns of battalions and halted about 9 o'clock in the same order. All our baggage, tents &c were in the rear on the road to Ciudad Rodrigo while a most awful, tremendous storm of thunder, lightning and hail came on and made us the most wretched creatures on earth, drenching us to the skin, the sleet driving in our faces, with no fire, nothing to eat and resting our wearied bodies sitting on delightful couches of ploughed ground. A ball of fire broke amongst the horses of a squadron of our heavy cavalry and all would have gone over to the enemy, if not brought up by their being chained together and running against a brigade of guns. An instance of the vividness of the lightning is related of an officer who while pouring out some spirits from his flask into a cup, had the cup knocked out of his hand and the spirits in it blew up and the cup knocked out of his hand consumed by the electric fluid. Our cavalry was posted some on our left but principally on our right, in order to check any movement the enemy might be inclined to make on that quarter.

The Battle of Salamanca

Marshal Marmont's troops continued their manoeuvres in attempting to turn Wellington's right flank at pace and threaten his line of retreat into Portugal. In doing so, Marmont was guilty of allowing his troops to become strung

61 Point de appui – The rallying point or point of assembly.

out with large gaps developing between his different divisions. Wellington, who had an undeserved reputation as a 'defensive general', saw his opportunity and did not fail to take it. With his forces formed out of sight at the centre of the arc which the French were marching around, Wellington launched a devastating attack on the French centre and right wing. Being in the 1st Division of Major General Henry Campbell (Sir Thomas Graham having returned home with a serious eye problem), the 1/42nd saw little action, being on the left wing and suffered only three men wounded. What hurt more, was that when ordered to advance to complete the victory, their general demurred, to their intense anger. The 42nd was not awarded Salamanca as a Battle Honour.

> **The morning of the 22 July** broke fine and the sun seemed to shine on us, to recompense us for the night we had passed. All the brigades began now to deploy and in regular order by divisions the army seemed to take up a position, opposite that of the enemy and about ½ past 7 o'clock, Don Julian's cavalry and part of our German hussars, began to skirmish with those of the enemy. At 9 o'clock the enemy's infantry were perceived to be in movement and in pursuance of his former plan, showing an inclination to turn our right. Several of our divisions moved likewise to the right and at 12 o'clock the enemy endeavouring to occupy the other Arapiles, sharp skirmishing commenced & several pretty charges of cavalry were made, both sides alternately successful. The Light and 7th Divisions who had been left as a '*Corps d'Observation*' on the right bank of the river, crossed and the 7th went in support of the right. Lord Wellington had been all morning on the Arapiles with the skirmishers and at 1 o'clock finding the enemy had withdrawn almost the principal part of his forces to the left, ordered an attack on his centre by the 6th, 7th & 4th Divisions, while the 3rd, Spaniards and our heavy cavalry, should attack their left. The 5th Division was on the right likewise and the Light and 1st Division left to observe the right of the enemy. The battle began immediately by the 3rd and 5th Divisions, who in fine style and supported by

General Le Marchant's heavy cavalry[62] and some Portuguese Brigades, soon put the enemy to flight, when they were surrounded and many sabred by our cavalry. The 5th Division posted behind the Arapiles & the 6th & 7th Divisions now advanced on their centre under a very severe fire of cannon, but soon overcame all obstacles, although the 6th Division greatly suffered in this attack. The 4th Division and General Pack's Portuguese Brigade[63] attacked the Arapiles and heights possessed by the enemy and unsupported carried them in fine style, although the enemy made a most resolute stand, but gave way on seeing part of the 6th Division coming to the support of the 4th who ought to have been ably supported by the 1st Division in reserve, had the general in command, obeyed the repeated orders given him.[64] By this period everything had been effected to the satisfaction of our noble commander and the cavalry, 1st & Light Divisions were sent in pursuit. The battle as it ended was most decisive, but if the 1st Division who were in reserve, had acted in pursuance of Lord Wellington's orders sent by the Prince of Orange,[65] to Major General Campbell Bart immediately supporting the 4th Division and going to the left, endeavour to cut the enemy off in the rear; the issue would have been much more successful, but instead of that fine division being employed, a few light companies were sent to support the 4th Division and thus allowed the enemy to get clear off after nearly destroying the 4th Division. The Light Division moved down at sunset and considerably cut off the flight of the enemy towards Alba de

62 Major General John Gaspard Le Marchant, commanding the heavy cavalry, was killed.

63 Major General Denis Pack commanded Portuguese troops from 1810–13.

64 Fortescue agrees that Major General Henry Campbell was ordered to bring the 1st Division up and drive a wedge between General Foy's troops and the main body. However, Campbell did not follow the order, only deploying his skirmishers. No reason for this failure has ever emerged. It is interesting that James, as an officer in the division was aware of the order. Wellington wrote home in September 'I think also that General Campbell will not last long' and it is probably not coincidence that Campbell was superseded in the October.

65 Colonel Prince William of Orange served as an aide de camp to the Duke of Wellington.

Tormes. Marshal Marmont[66] was wounded by one of our shells early in the action, when on the hill of Arapiles and giving orders for the advance of his troops, to the left. The 2nd in command was likewise killed or wounded[67] and the command devolved on Bonet,[68] who although not acquainted with the designs of Marmont, conducted himself in a manner highly creditable to his talents as a general. They had one general killed, 4 wounded and 5,000 killed and wounded on the field, many officers of rank & between 6 or 7,000 men prisoners on the day of the 22nd. Several pieces of cannon were taken and two eagles[69] and some small colours. Our loss including Portuguese was 5,880 and several officers of rank were wounded, among them Field Marshal Beresford severely.[70]

66 Marshal Auguste de Marmont, Duke of Ragusa, had superseded Marshal Massena in command of the army.

67 General de Division Bertrand Clauzel.

68 General de Division Jean Pierre Bonet.

69 Somewhere between twelve and twenty cannon were captured (reports vary) and the eagles of the 22nd and 101st Ligne were captured. Rumours abound at the time that the 66th Ligne also lost their eagle, but is not recorded as captured.

70 Beresford was now Field Marshal, commanding the Portuguese Army.

The March to and Siege of Burgos: 23 July–25 October 1812

[23 July] Our army continued in pursuit and Baron Bock's German cavalry[1] coming up with them on the morning of the 23rd, broke their squares and took upwards of 1,700.[2] Lord Wellington who was present at this gallant charge, said it was the finest thing he ever witnessed. The 16th Dragoons likewise took upwards of 200 horsemen[3] and prisoners were every moment coming in. We marched all night and next morning in hopes of coming up with them at the fords, they were supposed obliged to cross; but to the great surprise and mortification of Lord Wellington the principal part had crossed at Alba de Tormes, where the Spanish garrison had fled from the fort covering the bridge and left it open to the flying enemy.[4] If it had been only defended for a few hours, there is no saying what might have happened, but it is probable that all their baggage, artillery &c would have been captured and not 10,000 been able to escape.

Through all the villages we passed, the people hailed us as their deliverers and assured us of the many French wounded, together with their wretched state, not having had provisions for many days. Some columns of the enemy had crossed the same fords as we had, to attract our attention from the main

1 Major General Baron Eberhardt von Bock commanded the Heavy Dragoon Brigade of the King's German Legion.

2 This was the Action of Garcia Hernandez.

3 It is often forgotten that Anson's cavalry brigade fought with the French cavalry whilst Bock's troops attacked the infantry squares.

4 General Carlos d'Espana was ordered to hold the important crossing at Alba de Tormes, but abandoned the post and withdrew without informing Wellington.

force and at 2 o'clock we came very close on them, but they retired in admirable order, in columns of battalions. Our artillery sometimes was brought to bear on them, but with little execution and with the exception of a few being taken by the Light Division, they retired without hurt, before the eyes of our insipid & spiritless commander. He contented himself with sending down two battalions of the Guards after them, to see if they would surrender, but the wary enemy continued his retreat in the coolest and most delightful manner, laughing no doubt at our inactivity. Having satisfied ourselves with a look at the steadiness of the enemy, our division halted at 1 o'clock, instead of giving our soldiers a ration of rum and continuing the pursuit to Penaranda [de Bracamonte], where we should have taken all their stores and wounded and the commander in chief [Marmont], who could not be removed until 6 o'clock in the evening, as we were afterwards informed, when we stopped at the small distance of a league from his house.

[24 July] Next day we marched to the before mentioned place [Penaranda de Bracamonte] and found the enemy had only quitted it the preceding night and were in the most dreadful state of misery and wretched starvation,[5] officers offering 4 and five dollars for a small loaf of bread. The division was hardly in quarters when a general joy seemed to be infused into the people and the bells ringing &c, when on enquiry they informed us our troops had taken General Bonet and almost all the French army, but it happened only to be a few deserters and prisoners, who with their usual gaiety and naivette, had made the poor peasants quite delighted by this hoax.

Lord Wellington was understood to have sent off his despatches from this and the bearer was Captain Lord Clinton, his aide de camp.[6] Penaranda is a tolerable large town, has

5 Wellington is often criticised for a lethargic pursuit after his victory at Salamanca, but his supply train had collapsed.

6 Captain Lord Robert Clinton, 60th Foot, aide de camp to the Duke of Wellington.

several churches, convents of nuns and friars, the latter however now no longer exists, being driven from their abodes by King Joseph [Bonaparte], or *Pepe Botella* [Grandfather Bottle] as the Spaniards name him, from his [alleged] addiction to the *l'eau de vie*. We remained at Penaranda on the 25th and found the inhabitants very attentive, grateful and patriotic.

On the 26 [July] we marched [a] further three leagues and we found on the road several *cadavours* [cadavers] of French soldiers who had died of their wounds and tumbled out of the carts. The great foresight of all the French generals, is most conspicuous, in providing transport for their wounded after an action and after that of the 22nd very few fell into our hands.

Cabessa de Possa [Cabeza de Alambre?] was our night's quarters and in the evening 700 prisoners passed through, who assured us 900 more had been taken and that their loss since the 21st instant exceeded 16,000 men.

[27 July] Next morning we marched to a good town Arevalo, when headquarters were likewise established and their entrance was welcomed by shouts of joy, firing of small arms and ringing of bells. In the evening our bands attracted numbers of the people to our parade, especially the fair sex, who assuming their wonted degage[7] manners, most familiarly danced on the sod with us till dark. The dress and appearance of the Spaniards in Old Castille is quite the same as Estremadura and Leon, but the language is purer and considered the best of Spain. Arevalo is an old town and is situated on a small river, which takes a circuit nearly round the town and formerly made it very strong and ruins of its former strength are still extant. Arevalo gives the title of Duke who possesses a handsome old castle in the town.[8] It contains several convents of nuns and other public edifices.

7 Degage – Easy, relaxed.

8 The Dukedom of Arevalo was first established in December 1469, but it was a title for life and reverted to the crown on the death of the first recipient Alvaro de Estuniga and Arevalo became Crown property. The Dukedom was reinstalled in 1907.

Peasant women near Madrid and others.

[28 July] Next morning, we marched and crossed the Adagio [Adaja], by the Valladolid road and it was supposed some part of the army should proceed to Madrid with headquarters. The face of the country here and as far as we could see towards the Duero, was thickly planted with pine trees that grew to a great height and bearing a sort of apple, out of which the inhabitants derive a small nut, eaten by them with great avidity. The corn had been mostly cut and got in and on the ground there was an excellent vintage.

We halted on the banks of the Adagio [Adaja], which is a slow, placid river, but its banks are steep and in winter not fordable. Our bivouac was a very fine one, but in most parts the ground was sandy.

The brigade of 18 pounders,[9] drawn each by 12 fine oxen, with regular setts [*sic*] of harness both for them and horses came up with us this evening and encamped near our ground.

On the 29 [July] instant we marched through a delightful & fertile country and bivouacked on the same river. Opposite to us was a small village named Portilla [La Pedraja de Portillo?], situated on a very commanding eminence and from whence the French picquets only withdrew this morning on the appearance of our cavalry.

The weather was excessively hot and oppressive and the dews that descended in the morning were heavy and very pernicious to the health of the soldiers, however the sickness was by no means what it might have been expected. The Spaniards gave us hopes that the '*Juramentados*', or those who had sworn allegiance to Joseph [Bonaparte], would all come over, the very first opportunity and the bodyguards of the '*Intrudo*', or King were 12,000 men, well clothed and disciplined.

[30 July] Next day we went on towards Valladolid, as far as the ford on the Duero, but here halted and bivouacked close to

9 Siege guns.

this noble river. The peasants reported Marmont's wound to have been very high up and that 8 French generals were carried through Valladolid on biers, besides many other officers of rank wounded. The French army had it was supposed, followed the line of the Duero & were to concentrate at Aranda de Duero with Joseph's '*Juramentados*'.

[31 July] We remained in our bivouac on the 31st and many officers obtained permission to go to Valladolid, which it seemed on [their] return did not correspond with the ideas they had formed of it. The Archbishop's palace had been prepared for the commander in chief, but he preferred fixing his headquarters at a small village in the rear. The Duero here was but narrow and very rapid and deep, so that several small mules crossing with cargoes were swept away with the stream.

It having been now ascertained that the enemy had withdrawn towards Penafiel on the Douro, we marched on the Segovia road and were put into quarters at the Arebaldes de Portilla [Arrabal de Portillo]. In good weather, was it not for the intense heat during the day, we preferred bivouacking to quarters, for the customs and habits of the people were so filthy and their houses quite obnoxious and generally their beds filled with all sorts of vermin and we conceived a soft turf under the shade of a good tree, preferable to choosing the softest plank or stone in their vile habitations. Above the suburb of Portilla stands the town, which is very old and is walled round and has a very old Moorish tower in the centre, together with other remains of antiquity. A very elegant house was here left in flames by the French, because the proprietor was a little too late in bringing in his contributions. We were allowed to remain one day at Portilla [Arrabal de Portillo] . . .

Wellington had marched with a great part of his army on Madrid, a political rather than a strategic decision. This move did force Marshal Soult to abandon the tortuous siege of Cadiz, but once combined with Joseph Bonaparte's forces, they would pose a serious threat from the south and east. The French Army of the North under General Clausel had fallen back beyond Burgos but was still dangerously isolated. Wellington initially positioned the 6th Division of Sir Henry Clinton to simply observe Clauzel and prevent him moving into the rear of the army. Later Wellington decided that this would be an opportune moment to capture the fortress of Burgos, which would keep Clausel at bay. The 42nd were transferred to Clinton's command and therefore missed the 'glory' of entering Madrid. It was soon to cost them dear.

> **[2 August]** and next morning marched and took up ground on the small River Ceja [Cega] and near the village of Cojeas [Cojeces del Monte]. Our disappointment at not being amongst the divisions on the road to Madrid, was doubled by an idea that as we seemed to be a Corps of Observation, the enemy would keep us constantly on the *qui vive*,[10] whilst the rest of the army were enjoying the greetings and gaiety of the capital. We remained in our present bivouac for several days and amused ourselves hunting and shooting, our encampment being in an immense forest, extending for upwards of 30 miles and here and there intersected by the Ceja [Cega River] and many villages. It was supposed Lord Wellington would meet with but little or no opposition in his road to Madrid and we hoped soon to have an order to join him.
>
> Lord March, son of the Duke of Richmond,[11] and one of the aide de camps of Lord W[ellington] passed our bivouac with duplicates of the [Salamanca] dispatches of the 22nd and said he left the army close to Segovia.

> **On the evening of the 4 July [August]**, the division received orders to move and the 1st Battalion of the 42nd to march in the morning to Cuellar and report themselves to Major General

10 *Qui Vive* – On the alert.

11 Lieutenant Charles Lennox, Earl of March, 13th Light Dragoons, was an extra aide de camp to the Duke of Wellington. He became a Captain in the 92nd Foot on 9 July 1812 as a reward.

Clinton,[12] commanding the 6th Division, for what purpose no one could understand.

[5 August] Next morning, we marched and arrived at Cuellar at 2 o'clock and quartered in an old convent, whilst the [1/]5th[13] & 82nd[14] Regiments, were in an old castle belonging to the Dukes of Albuquerque and afforded quarters for both men and officers. Those regiments above had lately arrived and were very sick, which was the cause they were sent to have some rest with the 6th Division, but no such could be assigned for the 42nd being ordered likewise, for we had but very few sick and the regiment was 950 men strong. A corps of the enemy was left near Penafiel and as the 6th Division in its reduced state after the battle of the 22nd was thought too small a force in case of attack, these 4 strong regiments were left to make up the deficiency. Cuellar is a tolerable town and during the period we remained there was a most excellent market and things pretty cheap. Our expectations of our seeing Madrid had now vanished and we had only to hope for the intelligence of the triumphal arrival of the army in that capital, without sharing in the glory. Those regiments who had come from other divisions were brigaded and put under the command of Colonel Stirling of the 42nd and Colonel Grant 82nd Regiment.[15]

On the 9 August it was reported [that] Lord Wellington was within 9 leagues of Madrid, where the enemy had left 4,000 men, in the fortifications of the Bueno Retiro[16] and

12 Major General Henry Clinton.

13 The 1/5th Regiment had arrived in May and joined 2/5th in the 3rd Division. Both battalions were at Salamanca, but afterwards all fit men in the 2nd Battalion were transferred to 1st Battalion and the cadre went home to recruit.

14 The 82nd Foot arrived from Gibraltar soon after the Battle of Salamanca.

15 Colonel William Grant, 82nd Foot.

16 The Retiro was a star-shaped field work constructed around an old Royal porcelain factory, with a weak outer wall. Two thousand men had been left as a garrison by Joseph Bonaparte under the command of General Lafon-Blaniac to protect the vast stores of armaments, supplies and booty.

the remainder had gone towards the Ebro. Although we had an order to march regularly by regiments and brigades into the country a distance of two leagues, in order to keep the men in practise, yet we had [an] immense number of men ill with swelled limbs, completely disabling them and even one or two died of this disease. It went through a great part of the regiment and we sent daily from two to three hundred out to bathe every morning and by taking moderate exercise they recovered considerably. The country round Cuellar was varied and interesting and the ground had just been cleared of its covering, which was very productive and of a good quality. The mode of threshing corn is different from that in England. Having collected all the corn and grain in a public space of ground (generally found in all the Spanish villages) the sheafs are laid together in a circle and a pair of mules, or horses drawing a sort of sledge pierced with sharp pieces of flint, pass over the straw and reduce it to the size of two or three inches in length, it is then sifted and the grain is collected on the ground, cleaned and afterwards taken into town. It is a most laborious proceeding and requires a number of hands. The women are generally employed at this and with great patience drive the mules round, sitting on a stool singing a fandango or love song. We endeavoured to have some dancing parties with the fair ones and we partly succeeded, but we had a most heterogenous crowd, composed of marquise, cabalero's [Spanish gentlemen], hairdressers, orange women & corn threshers, but notwithstanding we are at more liberty and the dance went on with great esprit. Great reinforcements were daily arriving from the rear and [the] hospitals, the wounded by the attention paid them in Salamanca [are] soon likely to recover.

On the 13 [August] we had fully ascertained that headquarters were in Madrid, although we had not received the particulars, and we knew Joseph had with his tattered few, taken the road to Toledo, a direction different to that we had assigned him, while the army of Marmont[17] was between Burgos and Aranda [de Duero].

On the 14 [August], General Clinton sent off his aide de camp[18] to Madrid, we having had intelligence that Marmont's army with some reinforcements was making a move towards Valladolid. Owing to the regularity of living and moderate exercise the men were getting all well and would be again soon effective. On the 16th it was believed the French army had again reached Valladolid and that the Spaniards left there, had retired towards Toro.

On the 17 [August] an officer of the Corps of Guides[19] arrived with orders from the marquis and communicated the intelligence of Lord Wellington's entrance into the Spanish capital, not only without opposition, but with the greatest eclat. That on our being summoned, the Buen Retiro surrendered, with 800 men, 200 pieces of cannon, 20,000 stand of arms, 1,000 barrels of powder, 50,000 fanegas[20] of wheat & a large depot of all sorts of army clothing.[21]

No period of the war had been so replete with success, for in two months from the commencement of the campaign, the allied army had quartered themselves in Madrid, driving without loss of men, the *Mock King* from his throne and dispersing one of the finest armies of France, under one of its most experienced marshals. The fruits of promptly following up a victory were now gleaned and the taking of Madrid and these valuable stores was equal to a second victory.

17 Marmont had retired to France to recuperate from his wounds and the army was commanded by General Clauzel.

18 Captain George Couper, 92nd Foot, was aide de camp to General Henry Clinton.

19 The Corps of Mounted Guides was established by Wellington in 1809, run by the Quarter Master General's department; in 1813 it numbered 12 officers and 193 men. They increasingly became tasked with the transmission of dispatches.

20 Fanegas – bushels.

21 Two French eagles were also captured at the Retiro, those of the 13th Dragoon Regiment and the 51st Line Regiment.

On the 17th, the order for the usual exercise was countermanded and to be in readiness to march. To cook and send off the sick to Salamanca.

James records the joy shown by the crowds of Madrid, with only the merest hint of jealousy!

General Clinton on the 18 [August] made a reconnaissance on the Duero and on his return an officer was sent off by post mules to headquarters. The movements of the enemy had excited alarm, but it was supposed it was only to draw our army from the capital and make a diversion in favour of Joseph.

The joy which pervaded through all ranks in Madrid was excessive and their gratitude unparalleled; the streets were covered with carpets for Lord Wellington and cloth put under his feet and the poor were in raptures if they only could touch his clothes. All the officers were billeted on the first families and the town was given up to three days complete joy and amusement. The attention of the fair sex was carried to an extreme and when the arm of an English officer could not be obtained, that of the private soldier and drum boy was taken with avidity and received their favours.

No movement had taken place on the 20 [August] and the enemy's division at Valladolid had made no move, although as suspicions were entertained that they might cross the Duero, our depots at Medina del Campo were sent on the southern road towards Arebalo [Arevalo]. Some vague reports of the taking of Guadalaxara and Toledo by the Spaniards were in circulation but not believed. The officer who was sent to Madrid, confirmed the former intelligence of the stores &c taken and that recruits and guerrillas were collecting in immense numbers and that the prospect of success in Madrid was quite exhilarating. He also brought accounts of two regiments of Portuguese cavalry with 3 pieces of cavalry [cannon] had been surprised and taken, but the truth was that the two Portuguese regiments the 11th and 12th, together with Captain McDonald's [Macdonald's] brigade of guns[22] were on the outposts, having driven back the enemy in the morning, they were enjoying themselves. The enemy's cavalry came on in the afternoon and General d'Urban[23] ordered the Portuguese to charge, but before they came up to them, the[y] took to flight and got as far as where the 1st & 2nd Regiments of the German cavalry were quartered. Captain McDonald [Macdonald] got his guns off as well as possible but lost three upset and several men and horses. The French cavalry pursued until the[y] came up with the gallant Germans who charged them and took many, the rest retracing their steps. The Germans took a good many men and the commanding officers of both brigades of cavalry were wounded & taken prisoners. The 3 pieces of artillery were re-captured and our army went on towards Madrid.[24]

On the 22 [August] we received an order to be ready to march to Manzanilla on the Madrid road, which afforded us no small degree of happiness, but pleasure is often changed to pain and with infinite regret our Route was changed to Olameda [Olmedo] on the Arebalo [Arevalo] road.

We were on the 23 [August] 18 days at Cuellar and the men were almost all recovered of the singular disease of the limbs. We proceeded through the villages of Torequiteras [Torregutierrez] & Mata [de Cuellar] and turning to the left we bivouacked in a thick wood of fir, on the banks of the Ceja [Cega] near the small village of Isca, which is not so much destroyed being out of the high road.

[24 August] Next morning we went through a pretty and very picturesque country, keeping the course of the river and

---

22 Captain Alexander Macdonald commanded D Troop Royal Horse Artillery.

23 Brigadier General Benjamin d'Urban commanded a brigade of Portuguese cavalry.

24 This describes the Action of Majadahonda.

> arrived at Olameda [Olmedo] at midday and were put into quarters. It is now greatly reduced, as it formerly had been a large place and contained fine convents of friars and two of nuns, besides churches and a college. It was a fortified town in the time of the Moors and the walls still remain and all the entrances are through arched gates. It is 8 leagues from Valladolid and 25 from Madrid.
>
> Near Olameda [Olmedo] is the Convent of Mojadores [Mejorada][25] formerly occupied by the richest friars of Castile and consisted of 30 noblemen or their sons. It was in a charming situation on the banks of the river, the ground for leagues around belonged to the convent and those lazy '*Religieux*' had every comfort and every luxury imaginable. The convent was a large square building, with piazzas inside and had two rooms of immense size, the cells branching off from them and spacious galleries and balconies. The abbot had separate & elegant apartments and an excellent library, but when we were there, it had been destroyed. The stables, gardens &c had been most magnificent and as the troops had every likelihood of remaining some days at Olemada [Olemedo], it was determined to send Colonel Stirling's Brigade to the convent.

Suddenly orders arrived, ordering the regiment to Madrid; the ad-hoc brigade was commanded by his father Brevet Colonel James Stirling.

> Every arrangement for this purpose was made to march there on the 26 [August], but an order came in the evening for the march of the 5th, 42nd & 82nd Regiments to Madrid, under the command of Colonel Stirling. Thus our hopes again were highly raised of having an opportunity to see Madrid, but our inconstant profession laid many doubts in our minds and it was impossible to affirm that we should be gratified until we beheld actually its lofty spires.

---

25 Convent de Santa Maria de Mejorada.

On the 26 [August] we marched to Arebalos [Arevalo] and were well accommodated in quarters. Some peasants gave a report that the French had crossed at Tordesillas and moved down as far as Villa Nave del Rey [Nava del Rey]. The guerrillas had taken upwards of fifty French prisoners and some Portuguese soldiers whom they had stripped of every article, being in the prison here in a most wretched state.

[27 August] Next morning at 3 o'clock we marched over a very flat country but on the high metropolitan road to a small village called San Cidrian [Sanchidrian], where we were quartered. The inhabitants spoke with the greatest enthusiasm of the conduct of the English troops and we here were styled '*Buenos mobos roxos mozos*', '*The good red lads*'. Every article of food had been monopolised by those '*red lads*' and we could only satisfy our *gout* with a little bad country wine and the *Esperance* [hope] of feeding better at the capital, whose enjoyments were constantly before our eyes. The high road was made by the Romans and was a concave of strong paved flint stone.

[28 August] Our next day's march was to St Castin [Villacastin] a pretty village, where the people were very civil and several good families whose superb edifices had been destroyed and pillaged. Several pretty girls were in a convent here, to see whom we went with an eccentric old woman, the *patrona* of our house. She gave me the same bed '*Napoleon*' 6 years ago had slept in and last year *Joseph* [Bonaparte], which did not serve to render my rest more profound or agreeable. The house was elegant and well-furnished and had suffered but little.

[29 August] The following day our Route was for Guadarama [Guadarrama], a village distant 5 leagues and so named from the famous pass near it. We found league stones more regular on the road and they were equal to 4½ miles and called the

Spanish statute leagues. The distance to march was conceived too far and it was proposed to bivouac this night and go as far as the Escurial [El Escorial] next day and thereby divide the distance. However as many of the designs and purposes of we mortals are frustrated, so ours were that we had formed, for when under the pass of Guadarama [Guadarrama] and looking out for ground, an order from headquarters to halt and wait at the village of Espinar, for the arrival of the 1st Division on the road to Arevalo.

Our fond & airy hopes were again blasted, but being only eleven leagues from the capital and in all probability never be again so near, I with the major[26] and two more, formed the resolution of asking leave and running all risks, proceed on, going first to breakfast at Espinar.

Permission was no sooner asked than granted and about 11 o'clock we set off and retraced our steps towards the pass of Guadarama [Guadarrama]. This is a most impenetrable defile, but the roads are good and well made, winding to the summit, from whence we had a most noble prospect. The ridge of hills run from east to west and are covered with immense dark forests of pine, intersected by deep ravines and sources of rivers running in all directions. Situated immediately below is the small village of Guadarama [Guadarrama] and farther on to the right appeared embossed in woods, the venerable spires of the Escurial [El Escorial]. Our anxiety to get on, prevented us going so far off the road as to examine this ancient and noble palace, but on our return proposed visiting it. The park of the Escurial [El Escorial] extends for more than two leagues on the right of the high road and seemed intended for the preservation of deer.

At a small village near the road and about 5 leagues from Madrid, we halted to feed our horses and we partook of a rustic feast of bread and wine, the only articles to be procured. The '*Buenos mozas*' [Good girls] seemed to be

26 Major (Lt Colonel in the Army) Robert Macara, 42nd Foot.

held in the same estimation here, as at every place, they had made their '*entrance*' and with difficulty the poor wretches were prevailed on to accept any remuneration for their wine &c. About 4 o'clock we came to the ground where the Germans had been engaged with the French cavalry and found still unburied several dead bodies, but whose appearance seemed rather French or Portuguese than English. Getting rather gloomy towards evening we erred from our proper road and instead of turning to the right, continued [on] the paved road and passed through immense avenues of tall poplar ties, which lead into town and made a round or detour of nearly 2 leagues. We passed through some beautiful triumphal arches and every noise or light that attracted our notice we conceived, told of our approach to the town. It was not until 10 o'clock we entered the streets, which were spacious and well lighted and on enquiring for the best posada, or hotel, a lady politely said she was going that way and should lead us to the '*Fontana de Oro*' [Fountain of Gold]. Both ourselves and animals arrived at last, mostly exhausted with fatigue and after a very good supper, brought up in the French style and a bottle of '*Villa de la pena*', we went to bed. An anecdote occurred which is worthy of notice. When we came off our horses and were walking into the inn, the major was addressed by a person in the habit of a priest, desiring to know if he should wish a '*moza*' [girl], but the major was a little more disposed for supper and repose. The hotel was not bad and the supper attendance & beds were tolerable. In a large oblong coffee room, sat multitudes of men and women promiscuously, a sight rather novel to an Englishmen. The '*Fontana de Oro*' is at the corner of the '*Placa de Oro*' [Gold Square] which is the commercial square and has a most superb fountain in the middle. After breakfast, next morning having procured a guide, we went to the Royal Palace, visiting on our way all the churches &c, which we found but little different to all the others we had seen.

One wing of the palace is only finished and part of it was occupied by Lord Wellington, the other part consisted of about twenty rooms and the audience room, most magnificently furnished, in the Grecian, Chinese, Turkish and modern tastes. The short space of time we had to examine it, hindered us from making any particular remarks, as the various articles of elegance, together with the most antique and valuable paintings, would have required our most minute attention for many days. most of the paintings were scriptural, but four in particular claimed our admiration and represented the four quarters of the day. *Daylight*, *Noon*, *Sunset* and *Night* and were most exquisitely finished. In one of the rooms is a most elegant painting of Bonaparte crossing the Alps and although there is a great deal of ingenious expression in his countenance and the painting beautifully executed, yet it is by no means a good resemblance and has rather the appearance of a youth of eighteen than a man of 40.[27] The Audience Room is a large stall of crimson velvet, containing some fine paintings and figures in bronze, two of which, *Wisdom* and *Justice*, support the throne, together with two noble lions with the globes under their feet. In our ideas altogether of the palace, we were not disappointed and the '*tout ensemble*' [all together] displayed great elegance & taste. The museum next claimed our attention possessing some very fine minerals and most precious stones. The Botanical Garden was likewise fine and the Academy built by Philip the 4th with the Foundling Hospitals, were all the public edifices worth attention. There are two theatres, but they are both small and the performers wretched except the ballet, which consists generally of boleros and fandangos. There are various fine markets, one in the Placa Mayor, not much inferior to that of Covent Garden, but the purchasers and venders have by no means that rude appearance of health and happy mien and countenances which is there to be met amongst the '*troupes*' of greengrocers. Indeed, the people of

27 Note added later – Buonaparte [was] scarcely more than 25 at that time.

Madrid, both the sexes are the most squalid, thin & diminutive wretches of Spain and although the air is esteemed very fine and salubrious, it is not at all difficult for the most common physionomist to discern in Madrid a man or woman lately arrived from the country. The dress of both sexes are the same as before mentioned, with this difference, that of the ladies is a great deal more Frenchified, though extremely graceful, when displayed on a good person, with an elegant deportment, for the Spanish females are taught from infancy, a certain walk or gait and to manoeuvre their '*evanicos*' or *fans*,[28] with grace and dexterity.

The streets of Madrid are spacious & clean, the houses well and regularly built, resembling greatly the new town of the capital of North Britain [Edinburgh]. There are in many streets, fine fountains and statues of marble particularly in the public promenade, which is near the Retiro and is a handsome walk of a quarter of a mile, shaded with poplar trees and cooled by handsome *jets d'eau* [water jets] and fountains. The appearance of the commander in chief, or '*Lorde*' attracted multitudes on Sunday to this promenade which towards dark exhibited a motley crew with dissipation, haughtiness and debauching most strongly depicted on their countenances and in their behaviour. The inhabitants still had the Allied army in great estimation and it was advertised to the people that there should be a grand 'bullfight' in the Royal Amphitheatre next day in honour of Lord Wellington and the British officers, for whom the balconies and boxes should be retained. This new performance caused us to encroach one day longer on the goodness of our commanding officer, being novel to most of us we could not bring ourselves to the resolution to leave Madrid without seeing it. There are numerous capital shops and manufactories, but it may be remarked that few houses in Madrid, have glass windows supplying them by lattices and Venetian blinds and the floors for coolness are of square tile

28 This actually translates from Portuguese as *evangelicals*.

and are washed and sprinkled three or four times daily with water or lavender. As the bullfight was to commence soon, we dined early and with difficulty obtained a seat at ½ past 4 o'clock. The commander in chief's box was in the centre and his entrance was long and heartily applauded with '*Viva el Lorde, Viva los Ingleses*' &c. After the circle was cleared of the mob, with some degree of ceremony by the Spanish military, the performers came in together and saluted Lord W[ellington] and the company.

They consisted of 9 or ten pedestrians and two men on horseback, in a sort of armour, the men on foot bearing cloaks of various colours on their arms and the horsemen were armed with a pike or spear and the others with darts. The trumpet sounded and the bull frantic with rage, having been previously teased and goaded, in his den or stable, dashed into the area scraping the ground with his feet. One of the horsemen was in readiness to receive him at the side of the gate, by which he entered, whilst the other placed himself in the centre of the circle. This animal was not reckoned by the people as a good one, however he made some charges on the horsemen, but did them no damage, having been received on their spears; the footmen employed themselves in taking off the animal's attention, by throwing their cloaks and darts at him and escaping his fury by vaulting over the fence of the area, a height of about 4 feet. Having annoyed the poor animal with these darts for about 10 minutes, the matador appeared with a long strait [*sic*] two-edged sword and in a neat dress, made his 'obeisance' to the people by whom he was greatly applauded. He then with his cloak and sword, advanced towards the animal and played with him a little, at last watching the opportunity, he endeavoured to plunge the sword into the spine behind the bull's head but failed and dexterously escaped over the railing. However, he again met his antagonist undaunted by his former failing and plunged the sword up to the hilt, the animal immediately fell dead at his feet; the people applauded in the most savage manner. The trumpets sounded; and three finely caparisoned mules entered and having fastened traces to the bull's horns, dragged him out, with a grand flourish of trumpets &c.

The second bull was a most fierce beast and at the first charge, gored one of the horses considerably and wounded the other so much that his entrails hung out, while the rider with the greatest apathy kept his seat. The bull considerably irritated by the '*Banderillas*' or darts, to which were attached crackers made with gunpowder, leaped over the first railing after one of the pedestrians twice, but did no harm and at last was killed in the same manner as the preceding one. During the attack, the horseman, whose horse was so dreadfully gored, endeavoured to draw the bull to attack him again and was hurrahed in the most lively manner both by the men and women present.

Indeed it was a most savage, brutal amusement (if we can so call it) and sincerely believe that there was not an Englishman present, that would so much hurt his feelings as to behold, or patronage such a horrid scene of brutality again. Nothing can be conceived more painful to the human feelings than to see these eight noble animals, when so cruelly violated & wounded, look round with an eye of solicitation (as it were) to the crowd gathered to witness their torments, to see if one single friend could be found, whom probably he had lately served with patience and fidelity, to relieve him from his sufferings, acknowledge him or endeavour to succour him from his cruel tormentors. The females seemed to enjoy to the utmost this horrid cruelty and loaded the performances with their favours, which were generally a dove or ribbon, which he showed with great exultation. We next day formed the resolution to depart, having seen everything attracting and made all our purchases. Our bill in the inn was very moderate, but although we had everything good, yet it wanted that attendance and *proprete* [cleanliness], which is found in England.

Our first day's ride was to the Escurial [El Escorial], which as a village is small, but has a very large monastery built by

Philip the 2nd, in 1563.[29] There was also a very fine library & a palace, or country residence of the Kings of Spain, but all were stripped of paintings, books &c and on our advance the edifice and church, served to quarter two or three of our divisions. The church is after the same style as St Peter's at Rome, has an extensive choir, three fine organs and below a vault for the kings, which is entirely built of Dutch marble, as also all the coffins of the kings, are of a peculiar sort of stone or marble, eight of which are yet empty. The vault is of the form of an octagon and each side contains two coffins, except one opposite the door, which is a small altar, which has been pillaged of all its costly ornaments and particularly a fine gold chandelier, which was constantly kept lighted before the altar.

[2 September] At 10 o'clock we set off next morning from the Escurial [El Escorial] and finding the headquarters at San Castin [Villa Castin],[30] we went on to San Cidrian [Sanchidrian] and from thence joined the regiment and division at Arebalo [Arevalo]. Although it had cost us a great deal of fatigue, yet it was gratifying to have seen the capital and particularly as the army had taken quite a different direction, we might not have seen it at all afterwards.

On the 4 September we were ordered to march and occupy the Convent of Majorada [Mejorada], together with the [1/]4th and [2/]38th Regiments[31] and there we halted on the 5th and the division moved to the left bank of the Adaja and in the direction of Valladolid. We found every convenience at the convent, but what must it have been when occupied by its devoted inhabitants.

29 It was begun in 1563 and finished in 1584.

30 Wellington wrote from Villa Castin only on one day, 2 September.

31 Both of these other regiments were allocated to the 5th Division, but in different brigades.

We marched on the 6 [September] from the convent and crossing the Adaja moved on to a small village called Villa de Hillas [Valdestillas].

[7 September] Next morning we continued our Route towards Valladolid and crossing the Adaja at another winding, we came to the Duero, which we forded and found very rapid and narrow, but not deep and we got over without experiencing any obstacles either from the enemy or river itself. The French had been hutted this morning close to the river, but on our advance returned to Valladolid, on which we kept moving, but found that after endeavouring to raise a contribution, they had retired on the Burgos road this morning at 9 o'clock. The 1st and 5th Divisions, went after the enemy to the right, but did not pursue them far and in the afternoon, bivouacked on the banks of the Pisuerga, a river which joins the Duero at Valladolid.

James does not mention it, but Major General William Wheatley, commanding the brigade, died of typhus fever at the Escurial Palace on 1 September 1812; giving James' father temporary command of the brigade.[32] James (Junior) was soon officially appointed aide de camp to his father.[33]

[8 September] The 4th, 42nd and 38th Regiments[34] under the command of Colonel Stirling, entered Valladolid and were received with every acclamation of joy and happiness, the women even taking the men and hailing them as their liberators and '*Bravas mozos*' [Brave young men], kissing and embracing them. The men were quartered in a large convent near the Bishop's palace, into which headquarters

32 This was announced in General Orders dated 11 September 1812.

33 Challis states that his appointment was confirmed in October 1812, however he is not mentioned in any General Order, perhaps because it was a temporary appointment until his father was succeeded.

34 This appears to be an ad hoc brigade, formed whilst on the march as mentioned previously in James's Journal of 5 August.

came this day. The officers were billeted on the inhabitants from whom they received every civility and attention. There was a report very current in the afternoon that Soult had raised the siege of Cadiz[35] and was endeavouring to form a junction with Suchet and afterwards to march on the capital in a parallel direction with General Hill and probably attempt to draw Lord Wellington off from attacking Burgos. Major General Maitland[36] who had landed with his Eastern army at Alicant [Alicante] and when on the advance into the interior, found himself obliged to retire, owing to the badness of his Commissariat and want of supplies.

Valladolid is an old, large, and one of the finest and most considerable towns of Spain in Old Castille [*sic*] with a Bishoprick and university established by Pope Clement the 6th.[37] The town is extensive, standing on a great deal of ground and is situated on the River Pisuerga and Herrera near the Duero. The houses are large and fine, the convents are numerous and almost all had fine churches attached to them which are now much destroyed. The Placa [Plaza] Mayor is a large square with piazzas and in the morning the market held there, is not inferior to Covent Garden. The palace is a fine building, but neither its architecture, nor equipment is to be held in comparison with that at Madrid. The situation of Valladolid is in a charming valley, a fertile and pretty country, watered by three noble rivers.[38] On the evening of our arrival, the theatre was open, which is but small, however the performers were by no means bad, especially the '*Corps de ballet*' were excellent. A Grand Ball was given by the inhabitants, in honour of the Allied army and was of course attended by Lord Wellington and the principal officers of the different regiments.

---

35 Marshal Soult raised the siege of Cadiz on 24 August.

36 Lieutenant General Frederick Maitland.

37 He is mistaken, Pope Clement VI was pontiff from 1342–52, whereas the University of Valladolid was established in 1241 which would be under Pope Celestine IV.

38 The Pisuerga, Duero and Esgueva Rivers join in this valley.

[9 September] At 4 o'clock next day the proclamation of Ferdinand the 7th to the throne, was read by four senators and the people swore allegiance to him. In the evening there was a *Grand Illumination* and the townhouse was neatly fitted up, decorated with crimson velvet and in the centre a portrait of Ferdinand, from whose side, rockets and fireworks were let off in profusion. The theatre was open and was attended by the Commander in Chief, who in his passage and entrance into the theatre, was saluted by hearty and continued vivas. There had been a report, that owing to the movements of the French army near Madrid, two of the divisions with headquarters, should move in that direction, but in the evening an order was received to march to Cigales on the Burgos road.

A splendid Ball was given this evening by His Excellency the Commander of the Forces, to all the nobility and gentry of Valladolid and every refreshment was provided and the dancing kept up till an early hour, although we were to march at 5 o'clock to Cigales.

On the 10 [September] the whole army was on the move, headquarters proceeding from Valladolid to Cigales. This night we were in quarters at Corios [Corcos], a small village, where General Boyer[39] commanding the French cavalry, had carried off all the mules and sheep he could find, the night previous.

[11 September] At Duenas the whole army was encamped on the Pisuerga and near the Carrion, which passing Palencia, 2 leagues north-east of Duenas, comes down and falls into the Pisuerga. Duenas is a town of a moderate size, but has been greatly destroyed by the French, particularly on this retreat where they took away more than 1,000 head of cattle, 12,000 sheep and all the grain they could find.

39 General de Division Pierre Boyer commanded a dragoon division in Spain, where he earned the sobriquet 'Pedro the Cruel'.

On the 12 [September] we were bivouacked near Magaz [de Pisuerga] and here it was expected the Spanish army would join us, consisting of upwards of 11,000 men, but they were in Palencia and once in a good town it was difficult to get them out of it. The French retired before us in great order and as slow as we advanced, being a little beyond Torquemada two leagues off. Some trifling skirmishing had taken place between the rearguards and our cavalry, but nothing of importance occurred. The country here was flat and arid, but at Torquemada it was fertile and pretty enough and the Pisuerga ran its course between two hills. The above place we found nearly ruined by the repeated visits of the enemy and their resistance to King Joseph made it receive worse treatment, than the other towns who acknowledged his usurpation.

[13 September] From Torquemada we moved on the right bank of the Arlanza [Arlanzon] River and headquarters were at [Blank-La Real], a small village on the river. We continued our march to Quintana del Puente and the army encamped on the right bank, in a thick cork wood. This was a most miserable little place, nearly laid in ashes and the enemy had attempted to blow up the second arch of the bridge but were too hurried to effect it.

Our situation in bivouac was rendered very disagreeable by a very heavy fall of rain and . . .

. . . next morning [14–15 September] we pursued our Route to Pampliega,[40] but the enemy had formed his forces in position, with their left on the Arlanzon and their right on a strong ridge of hills and we halted between the two villages of Villa Mune [Villaldemiro] and Villazopeque. From the heights of Pampliega we could discern the position of the enemy perfectly and although he had concealed his columns behind

40 Pampliega was a two-day march and they would most likely have stopped near Vilodrigo.

the hills yet as a retreating army should show all their force, we supposed his not [to] be more than 20,000.

The Spanish army at last joined under the command of Castanos[41] and the appearance and discipline of their cavalry and artillery, even exceeded our expectations. The infantry also were fine looking men, but were very badly officered and worse clothed. As the enemy at 9 o'clock at night was still in his position, orders were given to the army to attack him next morning, by turning his right flank towards the hills and endeavour to get on the high road to Burgos, whilst the rest of the army should manoeuvre in his front; . . .

[16–17 September] . . . however very prudently he withdrew his troops at 2 o'clock in the morning and only left some cavalry as a rear guard. It was briskly followed up, by our cavalry and with that of Don Julian, skirmished a good deal and sustained little or no loss. Again, the enemy finding himself harassed, drew up his force on the heights to the right of the road, but in the afternoon retired towards Burgos and we were quartered in a small but pretty village called Bunell [Buniel].[42]

On the 18 September we were in sight of Burgos and we bivouacked about three miles from it, the cavalry patrols pushing up to the town. It was understood the enemy had retired, leaving a certain garrison in the outworks and castle. Burgos appeared to be an irregular town and is situated on a declivity, on the River Arlanzon over which there are three handsome stone bridges. On the brow of the hill is the castle & is an old lofty square building, surrounded with walls, double walls, ditches and other strong works and bastions made by the French. Near the castle is a convent, which was strongly fortified and beyond on an opposite hill, called

41 Spanish General Francisco Castanos, 1st Duke of Bailen.

42 This again was a two-day march; the site of their encampment on the 16th was likely to have been in the vicinity of Esteparo.

> St Michael's, is a strong hornwork, partly commanding the castle. The commander was reported to be a famous engineer and had solicited to be appointed governor[43] and no doubt but he would hold out well, the place being of great importance to us.

Storming the St Michael Hornwork

On 19 September, Wellington ordered the army to move forward in two columns, passing left and right of Burgos castle to completely surround it. The French had a garrison numbering some 2,000 men to defend it.

As the left column marched around St Michael's mount, the light companies were ordered forward, to drive in the string of voltigeurs that circled the base of the mount and push them back into the redoubt. The memoir of *A Private Soldier* states that the light company of the 42nd lost some twenty men killed and wounded in this operation.

The main attack was planned for eight o'clock that night, when the Hornwork of St Michael was to be stormed. The stated plan of this attack and what actually happened differ in a number of instances and it would be useful to investigate this attack in detail, in which James and the 42nd were fully involved.

Sir John Jones in his *Journal of the Sieges in Spain* states that two storming parties had been organised, to attack the demi-bastions to the right and left of the Hornwork. Their advance to the assault was to be covered by a 'firing party' of 150 men, who would advance in the centre, to the very edge of the ditch, where they were keep up a heavy fire on the defenders. A third storming party under Major Edward Cocks, 79th Foot, would move around to the rear of the Hornwork and attempt to enter here. Portuguese troops were allocated the task of escalading the left bastion, preceded by a party of the 42nd (led by Lieutenant Pitts of the Royal Engineers) carrying the ladders. The attack on the right bastion would again be Portuguese, led by the 42nd ladder party.

---

43 General de Brigade Jean-Louis Dubreton commanded. He had an infantry background rather than that of an engineer.

However, Lieutenant Donald Mackenzie of the 42nd, supports James' assertions that the attack consisted of one captain, two subalterns and 100 men of the 42nd with each wing attack (Makenzie was in the right attack with Captain Menzies and Lieutenant Gregerson), each attack column carrying seven ladders with them, supported by the Portuguese troops who followed them. He also states that the rest of the regiment (eight companies) were in the centre attack, not 150 men as stated by Jones. Unfortunately however, the ladders that were not damaged by enemy fire (Mackenzie states that four of the seven with the right attack were broken before they got to the bastion). A number of the 42nd managed to get into the Hornwork, *A Private Soldier* stating that a narrow pass was discovered, through which the regiment crowded through at the point of the bayonet.

Cocks of the 79th commanded a light battalion which attacked the rear of the Hornwork, the men getting over the palisades on the shoulders of each other, the first man in being Sergeant John McKenzie of the 79th. The French garrison, realising that the Hornwork was lost, attacked on mass, overwhelming those of the 79th at the palisade and most succeeded in escaping to the main fortress.

The 42nd and 79th both believed that they had succeeded pretty much alone; it was probably a combination of both, although the actions of the 79th certainly were the more decisive.

> **On the 19 [September]** we made a long detour and coming near the outworks, our light infantry companies made a lodgement under them and in the afternoon succeeded in taking two fieldworks close to the redoubt, or hornwork on St Michaels [hill]. The division halted and bivouacked and orders were received for the 42nd Regiment of Colonel Stirling's Brigade, with the light infantry and part of Major General Pack's Brigade of Portuguese, to attack and storm the hornwork at 8 o'clock in the evening. The whole moved off at 7 o'clock, one captain, 2 subalterns and 100 men [forming] the storming party on the right, the same strength on the left, and the battalion to attack the centre supported by the Portuguese.

At 8 o'clock the attack was commenced and although the ladders were too short, the work was taken instantly and the regiment put under cover of the parapet from the musquetry and cannon shot, from the castle. At daybreak the regiment was relieved and our loss ascertained to be as following viz.

	Captain	Subaltern	Sergeant	Drummer	Rank & File
Killed	-	2[44]	1	-	32
Wounded	3[45]	2[46]	10	1	152

A partial failing on account of the shortness of the ladders and their scarcity, caused a greater loss and it was much stronger than at first supposed, as the whole time our men were under the fire from the castle. No stores were taken, only two small six pounders[47] and about 80 prisoners.

On the 20 [September] we broke ground to the right and the engineers began a battery in order to breach the outer wall. The castle was invested on the other size by the 6th Division who was to take a share in the siege.

The French army was at Briviesca, a walled town, about six leagues from Burgos and our army was encamped on the hills and in the villages betwixt us and the enemy.

[21 September] Our division was bivouacked as close as possible, but finding on the 21st that several shot and shell fell amongst our men, our ground was changed further to the right.

---

44 Lieutenants Dugald Gregorson and Peter Milne were killed.

45 Captains Donald Williamson and George Davidson were slightly wounded, Captain Archibald Menzies was severely wounded.

46 Lieutenant Hugh Fraser was severely wounded and Lieutenant James Stewart slightly. The history of the regiment also states Lieutenant Robert Macintosh was wounded, but he was in the 4th Foot.

47 Jones records the capture of seven pieces of field artillery.

On the night of the 21st, the guns were put in the batteries, consisting only of three 24-pounders and a howitzer and next day we made a breach in the exterior wall.

Lord Wellington therefore on the 22 [September] ordered a Portuguese Brigade of the 6th Division to storm the wall on the flank, while a party of 400 men under Major Lawrie of the 79th Regiment[48] should escalade in front. The Portuguese attack from some unforeseen cause failed and the party in front, although on the ladders were obliged to abandon the attempt, when Major Lawrie was unfortunately killed and a Captain Fraser of the Guards[49] together with other officers and men wounded. The French army was at Pancorbo and Miranda [de Ebro]. General Hill was reported to be at Oropesa and Soult had gone into Valencia.

In breaking new ground on the 24 [September] we lost several men and a young and most amiable officer Ensign Cullen was killed[50] and Captain Williamson wounded,[51] both of the 42nd Regiment.

On the 25 [September] our loss was severe and an officer of the 24th was killed[52] in coming out of the trenches, passing the 'Lazy corner', or where the enemy pointed his guns at the detachments coming in and out, being entirely exposed. On the 26th and 27th there were but few casualties and several mines and other batteries were in a state of forwardness.

48 Major Andrew Lawrie, 79th Foot.

49 Captain Charles Mackenzie Fraser, Coldstream Guards, lost a leg at Burgos.

50 Ensign David Cullen, 42nd Foot.

51 Captain William Donaldson, 42nd Foot, was severely wounded on 24 September and died of his wounds on 2 October 1812. On 8 October he was posthumously promoted to Brevet Major in the *London Gazette*. His letters will soon be published by the editor in *Napoleonic Archive* No. 16, by Ken Trotman Publishing.

52 Lieutenant Richard Walton, 24th Foot, was severely wounded and died soon after.

On the 29 [September] all the mines were ready, one below the exterior wall and another more to the right; and at midnight both were exploded and the wall was stormed, but owing to the darkness of the night, it failed and . . .

. . . the batteries were opened on the 30 [September] in order to keep the breach open, which was made by the first explosion. We succeeded in dismounting one of the enemy's howitzers, but our batteries always from their great inferiority, were very soon silenced.

Colonel Stirling's Brigade still suffering from the shot from the castle, was removed to a park nearer the high road, to Pancorbo [Pancorvo], completely out of all reach.

The arrival of Sir Edward Paget was daily expected, to take the command of the 1st Division and also the 1st Brigade of Guards who had landed at Corunna.

On the 1 October, our batteries were removed and all was ready, but we here waiting the effects of a new mine which was to be sprung on the 4th. The enemy having discovered our battery, succeeded in dismounting one of our few cannon, called the '*Thunderer*', each having their appelations, being only three in number.

At noon on the 4 [October] the 24th Regiment was ordered into the trenches and at 5 o'clock in the evening the mine was sprung and the gallant little 24th stormed it in style and with but trifling loss. The castle sustained a most tremendous cannonade and our solitary guns returned the compliment as well as possible.

When the mine was sprung, the French soldiers were amusing themselves on the top with cards and several were seen on the ground, laying dead with them in their hands and the officers on guard, were at their dinner. The 24th were relieved at night, but on the 5th the enemy made a most resolute sortie, with upwards of 700 men and succeeded in driving our men from their trenches and taking all the working tools, however our troops on rallying retook the trenches at the point of the bayonet, but not without sustaining a considerable loss. With the loss of the 24th Regiment the night preceding, the brigade had suffered more than 170 men.

On the 7 [October] the covering parties were furnished by entire regiments of the division alternately, which was the best and most regular method of carrying on the siege.

On the morning of the 8 [October] our parties of work being well advanced, close up to the interior wall of the convent and a mine just about to be commenced, at 4 o'clock the enemy made a sortie, drove our working parties past the breach and kept possession of it for nearly half of an hour, when the 1st Regiment of King's Germans then in the trenches and the working parties under the command of Major the Honourable C[harles] Cocks 79th Regiment, stormed with the bayonet and although with considerable loss, established themselves in their old ground. We had to regret the loss of Major Cocks, an officer of the greatest talents, abilities and most amiable good heart and temper. The Germans lost five officers killed and wounded[53] and many good men. Our battery now consisted of one gun, the '*Nelson*', the others having been disabled and we had no hopes of soon getting any from Santander.

53 Captain William von Saffe, 1st Line Battalion (Beamish 978), was killed; Lieutenant Augustus Winckler, 5th Line Battalion (Beamish 575) was taken prisoner and Captain Frederick Lodders, 5th Line Battalion (Beamish 1184) and Lieutenant Ernst Wyneken, 2nd Line Battalion (Beamish 429) were severely wounded, along with forty-six men killed and sixty-three wounded from the KGL.

[13 October] Sir Edward Paget having arrived, he inspected the division on the 13th and General Campbell proceeded for England.[54]

The enemy had made no movement up to this time to obstruct our operations but on the 13th the whole of the sick and wounded were ordered to the rear, which gave rise to a suspicion, that they were making some forward movements. On this day we had a report that there had been a good deal of skirmishing with our cavalry and that Lieutenant Colonel Ponsonby of the 12th Dragoons was severely wounded.[55]

The town of Burgos although besieged was crowded with everything and the people seemed to care very little who was in possession of the castle. The Cathedral of Burgos is very finely ornamented, but heavily; and has a very sombre appearance being situated immediately under the hill on which stands the castle.

Nothing of any importance occurred until the 18 [October]; when our mines under the Convent of St Roman [San Roman] being finished and our battery keeping open the breach in the second line, Lord Wellington determined on pushing the troops on, at the convent whilst they should also escalade the second line. The mine succeeded and some Portuguese of the 6th Division succeeded in getting into the convent and a detachment of the King's German Legion, together with some of the Guards, under Major Wurmb[56] carried the breach but owing to their inferiority of numbers and the immense fire brought on them from the castle itself, obliged them to fall back and not without considerable loss.

The gallantry of the brave Germans and Guards was unequalled, but the superiority of forces and want of support,

54 Sir Edward Paget took command of the 1st Division, succeeding Major General Henry Campbell.

55 Lieutenant Colonel the Honourable Frederick Ponsonby, 12th Light Dragoons. He was wounded at Monasterio on 13 October.

56 Major Adolphus von Wurmb, 2nd KGL Line Battalion (No. 973 in Beamish), was killed.

was the consequence of their relinquishing what they had so dearly gained. The Convent of St Roman [San Roman] remained in our possession and it was supposed Lord Wellington would now send off for more guns.

On the same night 150 men of the 58th Regiment received an order to occupy the trenches and the remainder of the brigade to be in readiness to march at the shortest notice. This of course led us to imagine the enemy was advancing and that Lord Wellington would leave a number of men, sufficient to maintain the siege and with the rest, join his army in position at Majardas [Las Mijardas] and the neighbouring villages.

Our supposition was next morning [19 October] confirmed and we received orders to march to Villa Mar [Villimar], leaving the 24th & 58th Regiments,[57] General Bingham's Brigade Sixth Division[58] and a Portuguese Brigade,[59] all under the command of Brigadier General Pack. For some time past the weather had been very bad and the consumption of fuel had been so great, that the wood was nearly cut down, so that altogether we were very happy to be relieved from the duties of a siege, which did not promise much reward for our labours. When marching on the road to Villa Mar [Villimar], we received orders from one of the Commander in Chief's aides de camp, to march on Villa Fria [Villafria] and at midday we took up a strong position above the village of Orones [Hurones]. The roads were in a dreadful state and hardly recollect having had a worse day's march than

57 The 2/24th and 2/58th were formed into the 3rd Provisional Battalion in December 1812 as their numbers were so low.

58 Major General Richard Hulse, commanding the 1st Brigade of the 6th Division, had transferred to the command of a brigade in the 5th Division on 31 July 1812, leaving Lieutenant Colonel George Bingham, 53rd Foot, in command.

59 Eben's Portuguese Brigade was now commanded by the Conde de Rezende in the 6th Division.

this. The enemy's army had assembled near the village of Monasterio [de Rodilla], about a league and a half from our position and we were ordered to be on the alert.

At ½ past 4 o'clock [20 October] we heard on all sides '*Turn Out*', '*Under Arms*', which we found to be the enemy advancing in force on our outposts, who were already engaged. In ten minutes the division was formed, the baggage sent off and we marched, after forming on the hill towards the enemy. The outposts had retired and the enemy still advancing, we formed in line of battle, loaded and moved on the enemy's right flank and at 7 o'clock in the evening coming very close to him, he principally retired and our outposts were again established in Quintana Valla [Quintanapalla].The enemy had not more than 12,000 men and this was a movement merely to see our force and engage our attentions from the castle.

On the 22 [21 October] all was quiet until about 2 o'clock, when we received orders to send off all our baggage &c to the rear, by the left of Orones [Hurones] and at 6 o'clock we commenced our march in the direction of Burgos.

It was now conjectured the enemy had sent a force round our right and accounts were received of Sir Rowland Hill being obliged to fall back in front of Soult, he having been joined by Joseph in Valencia and having an army of nearly 80,000 men. Our movements had therefore to be guided by his and Lord Wellington saw himself obliged most reluctantly to raise the siege.

Everything had been done to attain this object in the power of our brave men and officers, but adequate means were wanting for its accomplishment. Although the division commenced its march at 6 o'clock we did not get on the high road until 11, where we were kept stirring for orders, always the attendants of a retreat.

[22 October] At midnight we were under the guns of the castle and although it was clear moonlight, we passed through the town, crossed the bridge and the enemy seemingly having only a very slight idea of our being so much under their power, fired only two or three round shots and we passed in the greatest silence and unhurt. Our horses awakened our fears passing, but they likewise had the good fortune to escape. We carried off all our engineer stores &c from the castle, except poor '*Nelson*' the only remaining gun[60] and the 24th and 58th Regiments blowing up the hornwork, came away at 2 o'clock in the morning and joined us on the road.

We halted at daylight near Bunell [Buniel] and continued our retreat to Celada del Camino and after a dreadful long march of nearly fifty miles, we crossed the Pisuerga and bivouacked there.

60 The gun barrels were buried and their carriages burnt.

Retreat to Portugal

Failure to take Burgos, combined with forward movements by superior French forces against General Hill's troops covering Madrid, forced the Duke of Wellington to order a retreat, with the aim of re-combining his army in the vicinity of Salamanca. The retreat initially was measured, with Wellington defending the major river lines and a number of serious actions occurred on the retreat as the French sought to gain the advantage.

> **[23 October]** The enemy was not long in following our movement and being very strong in cavalry they were very bold and pushed our cavalry very much. Colonel Halkett with the two battalions of Light Germans were in support of the cavalry and Don Julian with his guerrillas, were on the hills to the left of our rear guard.
>
> General Anson's cavalry[1] charged twice with great effect and the rearguard fell back in good order, until the guerrillas giving way, some squadrons of the enemy darted in upon the 16th Dragoons and causing some confusion, Colonel Pelly commanding officer, was taken[2] and several officers and men wounded.[3] The enemy towards the midday brought up all their cavalry and they were charged twice by General Anson's

1 General George Anson's Brigade consisted of the 14th and 16th Light Dragoons.

2 Lieutenant Colonel Raymond Pelly, 16th Light Dragoons, had only arrived with the regiment the day before. He was captured and remained a prisoner of war until the end of the war in 1814.

3 The 16th Light Dragoons lost eight men and thirty-eight horses killed, two officers (Captain George Murray and Lieutenant William Lockhart), thirty-nine men and twenty-four horses were wounded. Lieutenant Colonel Pelly, Lieutenant George Baker, eleven men and five horses were captured. Lockhart died of his wounds in November 1812.

& General Bock's Brigades, but to very little effect and our rearguard was pretty hardly pushed.[4]

At last the enemy finding Colonel Halkett had formed his two battalions in squares, charged them, but they were received by two most steady and well directed volleys, which checked their progress and they lost upwards of 150 men. Our cavalry and Germans retired in good order in the evening on the main of our army at Torquemada.

There all the divisions had nearly been concentrated and as it was pitch dark when we bivouacked, there was the greatest confusion. All were mixed and many officers lost their portmanteaus from under their heads.

[24 October] To increase the confusion the soldiers had found out the wine vaults[5] and we found many next morning in such a horrid state of bestiality, as cannot be well described. This obliged us to leave behind after all our exertions, upwards of 300 men completely senseless; and it was an unpardonable neglect in the Staff department not to have had them secured by strong guards.

[25 October] The enemy still pressed very hard, although they received a temporary check in the morning at the bridge of Torquemada from the 6th Division. We took up a position on the Carrion with our right on Duenas and left at Villa Muriel [Villamuriel de Cerrato], all the bridges being secured and ready to blow up. In the morning the Guards joined from Coruna[6] and here placed in a cut field with us, which did not seem so much to their *gout*[7] as mounting guard in London. We marched from Duenas to the heights over Villa Muriel [Villamuriel de Cerrato] and to the support of the 5th Division.

---

4 This action took place at Venta del Pozo near Celada del Camino.

5 In the villages around Torquemada.

6 The 1st Battalion 1st Foot Guards, some 1,100 men strong, arrived as reinforcements.

7 '*Gout*' – French for 'taste'.

In the afternoon the enemy came across the Carrion to the number of some thousands and were driven back by the 5th Division and some Spaniards, who on this occasion behaved with great coolness and gallantry and mixed with the enemy's tirailleurs, who found themselves obliged to ford the river up to their necks. We suffered a good deal on this occasion and Lord Wellington finding that a number of their troops had crossed at Palencia on our left, ordered the troops to return to Duenas and cook.

Next day [26 October] we commenced our march to Cabecon [Cabezon de Pisuerga] and marched across the plain in beautiful order, ready to form squares, the heavy cavalry in three columns in our rear and last the light dragoons.

Retiring in this order to near the bridge of Cabecon [Cabezon de Pisuerga] we halted and drew up in line towards the enemy and seeing all clear past, we crossed and took up a bivouac near or behind the small village of Cabecon [Cabezon de Pisuerga].

The bridge was mined and a traverse of carts, planks &c was thrown up on the outside of the bridge and three pieces of artillery above on the heights.

James describes the French attempts on the Bridge of Cabezon de Pisuerga as happening over two days, whereas it all happened on a single day.

[27 October] The enemy had halted at Duenas and did not make his appearance until next morning, when he formed his army in front of us on the plain and extended his light infantry close up to the bridge, where they remained all day. We had an opportunity of seeing all their army this day and they had certainly received very strong reinforcements both of cavalry and infantry. Towards evening they were filing their columns towards Valladolid and Tordesillas and at night they made an attempt on the bridge at Cabecon [Cabezon de Pisuerga] but were repulsed with the loss of one officer taken and several men killed and wounded.

On the 28 [27 October] we still halted here and at noon, a flag of truce was brought in with women who had got drunk and fallen behind.[8] They were awful objects, seemingly half-drunk still and most of them more than half-naked. This event collecting a great number of officers and men towards the bridge, no sooner had our officers and women returned, than they [the French] brought up some guns and howitzers and sent a shower of shot and shell amongst the spectators at the bridge making us scamper off in all directions.

However, our artillery on the heights retaliated immediately and losing some men and horses, they made off in great haste. Lieutenant Colonel Robe of our artillery was severely wounded by a cannon ball.[9]

[28 October] The enemy attempted the bridge at Simancas and Valladolid, at both of which places they were defeated with loss, by Colonel Halkett at Simancas and the Earl of Dalhousie[10] and his division at the latter place. Both bridges were blown up and the enemy was seen drawing all his forces towards Tordesillas, therefore Lord Wellington crossed the Douro with his army and . . .

We left Cabecon [Cabezon de Pisuerga] at 10 o'clock on the **29 [October]** and blew up the bridge. The state of Valladolid was distressing and we saw with infinite regret the principal families, moving off with their movables, jackasses, cars &c, leaving their homes to be plundered by those rapacious robbers.

On the 30 [October] in consequence of intelligence that the Regiment of Brunswick Oels had been obliged to abandon the

8 At Torquemada.

9 Lieutenant Colonel William Robe was wounded on 27 October.

10 Major General George Dalhousie commanded the 7th Division.

bridge at Tordesillas,[11] we marched and crossing the Adaja encamped opposite the enemy at that place. Our cavalry and light infantry picquets were close up to the bridge . . .

. . . and we remained here until the 3 [November] without the enemy making any attempt to cross. Headquarters were at Rueda and Sir Rowland Hill with his army and the Spaniards were expected daily to join us. At the bridge of Puente Largo,[12] the mine having failed, the enemy in large numbers attacked the 47th Regiment, but were repulsed with great loss and our army moved afterwards without molestation.

The capital was again in the hands of the enemy, having then [renewed] their advance on the 1 November.

[5 November] The weather had greatly favoured us and we remained in bivouac until the 5th instant, when at midnight we had orders to be under arms at 3 o'clock in the morning, but the baggage not to be packed or sent off. The latter part of this order appeared rather strange and we supposed an attack was to be made on the bridge and [to] drive in their picquets.

However, it was different and we had orders to march and relieve the 5th Division who had been employed constructing some field works in our front and were changing their position. The enemy line extended from Valladolid to Toro, at which place the bridge having been repaired, we marched and continued our retreat to Salamanca, where joining General Hill it was probable Lord Wellington would wait the enemy and give him battle on the old ground. This we trusted should

11 On 29 October, Captain Guingret of the 6th Légère, collected a party of volunteers from his regiment. Early that morning, they swam across the ice-cold river stark naked, pushing a raft containing their arms and ammunition. They attacked the Brunswick troops still naked and forced them to abandon their post.

12 During General Hill's retreat from Madrid, Skerrett's Brigade held the Puente Largo, a long bridge over the River Jarama. British engineers only partially succeeded in blowing up the bridge, one parapet and part of the roadway remaining. Marshal Soult launched two successive assaults on the bridge om 30 October, which failed with loss, but Skerrett retired in the night.

be the ultimatum, as we began already to feel the bad effects of a retreat and laying out under rain and [the] very inclemency of [the] weather, the brigade of Guards having upwards of 300 men sick.

On the 7 [November] General Hill's army was bivouacked on the same river and had orders to cross the Tormes at Alba [de Tormes], Soult with 40,000 men having left Madrid on the Arebalo [Arevalo] and Ariba [Avila] roads.

We continued our retreat at the rate of 8 leagues a day until we reached the heights of San Christoval [San Cristobal de la Cuesta], one league from Salamanca and for the first time for six weeks had a roof over our heads. Our division was cantoned in the different villages on the Zamora and Toro roads and had orders to fortify them and keep strong out-picquets. The enemy since Valladolid, had not at all pressed us and we had hopes of remaining here some days.

[10 November] The poor people of Salamanca were in the greatest anxiety, shutting their shops and begging us to remain and fight for them again and we were sure of victory. The enemy's principal force being on our right, he attacked General Long's cavalry in front of Alba [de Tormes] and in the evening brought up his whole force opposite our army on the Tormes. On the same day they attacked Sir R[owland] Hill's troops in Alba [de Tormes], with 20 pieces of cannon[13] and infantry, but they made no impression on our steady fellows and they retreated at night. Our villages were all fortified with fieldworks and we had an alarm of a French column of cavalry being seen on the Toro road, we occupied our little forts and awaited them. But they were no longer heard of and we returned to our cantonments, turning out daily at daybreak under arms and thus remaining one hour.

13 Fortescue states eighteen cannon.

By a General Order on the 12 [November] Colonel Stirling's Brigade was removed from the 1st to the 6th Division, a change which was universally regretted, although the division was as good as another.[14]

On the 14 [November] the enemy forded the Tormes in three places above Alba [de Tormes] . . .

. . . and on the 15 [November] the army moved from San Christoval [San Cristobal de la Cuesta] to the old heights of Arapiles leaving our division at Salamanca, on the Zamora and Toro roads. Lord Wellington finding the enemy in position at Mozarches [Mozarbes], drew the whole of his forces from Alba [de Tormes], to the Arapiles . . .

Wellington offered battle on the same position that the Battle of Salamanca had been fought four months previously.

. . . and at 2 o'clock on the 16 [November] we crossed the bridge at Salamanca and halted near the 1st Division at Aldea Tejada [Aldeatejada] who had been left in reserve, whilst Lord Wellington was employed with the 2nd Division and cavalry in reconnoitring the enemy's movements and position. Towards evening we were ordered to cook, the enemy all day showing no inclination to fight a general action and detaching columns towards their left, to intercept our communications, should we remain in [this] position. They were therefore supposed too strong and too well posted for us to attempt attacking them and our army re-commenced its retreat towards the Agueda in three columns under Sir Rowland Hill, Sir Edward Paget and the Spaniards on the right. Some skirmishing with the cavalry took place in the evening, but of no consequence. The weather was most tempestuous, the roads bad and we had but little or nothing to eat. At midnight most dreadfully harassed and

14 The General Order was actually dated Salamanca, 11 November.

fatigued, we halted in a wood near the village of Munilia [Matilla de los Canos del Rio] and not being able to procure any comfort for ourselves, lay down in our cloaks.

With the French seeking to turn his flank, Wellington ordered the retreat to continue to the Portuguese border. The weather turning very inclement and the Commissary being poorly directed led to the troops virtually starving. These few days were remembered by the soldiers as the worst days ever.

[17 November] Nearly at daylight we continued our retreat, raining torrents, roads knee deep, women and children on asses, laying half choaked [*sic*] in the roads and smart firing of musquetry on our flanks. Owing to the continuation of the firing an officer and party was sent out to reconnoitre and ascertained that it was some straggling soldiers shooting pigs let loose to feed on the acorns, which fall from the dwarf oak[15] and are most excellent food and when boiled are but little inferior to chestnuts. We continued our retreat unmolested until the 17th when at noon the enemy pushed their cavalry close to our flanks.

At first it [the firing] was supposed to be the usual custom of pig killing, but some of the men who had escaped from them gave the first real intelligence. We were marching through a very thick woody country and by divisions. At 2 o'clock many of our sick and stragglers fell into the hands of the enemy and Sir Edward Paget commanding the centre column, finding that owing to the state of the roads there was an interval between the 5th and 7th Divisions, rode alone to the rear and a French cavalry patrole [*sic*] took him. Sir Edward being very short sighted and having neither aide de camp or dragoons with him, allowed the French to seize him by the collar ere he perceived them.

Crossing the Huebra, a small river at San Munoz, we bivouacked in an adjacent wood. There the enemy having

15 The Spanish or Pin Oak (Quercus Palustris) is a small tree, but not dwarf.

advantageous ground, commenced a smart cannonade on us and attempted to annoy the passage of the Light Division, who they attacked but were repulsed with loss. The 43rd Regiment had suffered most and to be out of reach of the cannon we retired some distance into the wood and passed a most miserable night. The baggage of every officer had been sent off, the torrents of rain still fell and we were up to the knees in mud and water, rendering it impossible to lay down or even kindle a fire. Having however towards midnight succeeded in lighting a fire, we had some beef piggled on a stick on the fire, without bread or salt and we commenced our fatigues at daylight.

[18 November] The distressing objects that presented themselves on this retreat were almost equal to that of Sir John Moore's and at every step were dead men, horses, mules, asses, oxen and women and children starving.[16] For three days our poor horses had subsisted on the leaves of the oak and ourselves on the acorns and when we arrived at the heights of Tenabron [Tenebron], a piece of coarse bread was eat [*sic*] with the greatest avidity. However, as Ciudad Rodrigo was not far off, a deputation was sent to procure bread and corn for our animals. At the sight of the corn, they seemed to forget it and looking at us, to say '*we were joking*', however when they had regaled themselves with the smell of it, all was bolted in an instant.

[19 November] The enemy had not followed us and on the 19th the army passed the Agueda except the 5th and 6th Divisions . . .

. . . who waited until the 20 [November] to cover the bridge and on that day we left the garrison to its fate and bivouacked

16 Many state that the lack of supplies made this retreat infinitely worse than that to Corunna. There is some suspicion that James fared better because of his father.

near Gallegos [de Arganan] between Ciudad [Rodrigo] and Almeida.

The army finally settled into winter quarters, the troops being very sick, but with improved supplies and dry quarters, the sickness abated and morale improved.

[21 November] Cantonments on the Coa were allotted for the army and next morning the division broke up and marched to their separate villages. They were indeed miserable and everyone worse than another, the only thing [of] worth they contained was hay and dry grass for our horses. As to eatables, our rations were our only stand by and even at Almeida there was but little of anything except salt fish and oil.

Headquarters of the army were established at Freineda on the Coa and it was supposed the army should not remain long in their present cantonments but go farther to the rear. Our village called Junca, was only one league from Almeida, a frontier and fortified town of the province of Tra los [Tras os] Montes. It [Almeida] has sustained several sieges by the Spaniards and has a commanding situation on the Spanish side of the Coa. The works were strong but of late greatly neglected, however the parts finished since the last siege, are well built and capable of resistance. The town of itself is nearly in ruins but is daily improving. The weather became very cold and frosty and our dwellings were but little calculated to secure us from its inclemency.

On the 25 [November] instant we received orders to march to Azinhal and cross the Coa at Castelo Bom, a very intricate and bad passage. As the order to march came late in the day, it was with great difficulty we reached Azinhal at 10 o'clock and the 24th Regiment owing to the extreme darkness found itself obliged to bivouac. The situation of Castelo Bom is singular and romantic, standing on a high prominence on the Coa, encircled by, but separated from other mountains by deep vallies [*sic*] covered with the oak and olive trees, the road very bad, winding to the summit, where there is an old Moorish castle, with a few white-washed houses.

Next morning the 26 [November], we marched to Freixedas, which was a village that had once been good, but now nearly depopulated. The country to this from the Coa is wild and rugged and here and there is to be seen a patch of vine planting or an olive tree.

On the 27 [November] we marched in front of the Sierra d'Estrella and were quartered in the small but pretty village of Meningual [Minhocal?], one league from Celorico [da Beira]. A further continuation of our Route had not arrived, but Cea [Seia] was imagined to be our winter quarters.

Remaining two days at Meningual [Minhocal?], the division marched to Moimenta da Serra and on St Andrew's Day were in their winter quarters and although by no means elegant or comfortable, the people were civil, happy to see us and their habitations afforded us shelter from the weather. It was at first intended by the general of division to stow the 42nd and 79th Regiments here together, but they barely found cover for the 42nd Regiment and the 79th Regiment was in small villages in the valley.[17]

Here for a while, we ended our toils and campaigns which had begun with so many glorious events and ended so very disastrously. But Lord Wellington knew the immense strength the enemy had formed against him on the Tormes, which was not to be computed at less than 90,000 men, of which nearly 10,000 were cavalry and a large artillery. It therefore would have been ill judged to have remained in opposition against so powerful a force in winter and an attack or attempt at a general action would have been overrating the physical powers of the soldiers. Be it as it may, we were glad to find ourselves

17 The 79th were quartered at Vodra.

again under cover, and although not quite so comfortable as at home, yet everything was put in train to be so, such as erecting chimnies [*sic*], laying in a stock of beef and tongues to cure and establishing a card club.

Cea [Seia] was formerly the see of a bishop and a place of note in the history of Portugal but is now reduced to a small village. Its situation is beautiful, on the brow of one of the hills of the Sierra d'Estrella and would have made a charming summer residence, but the houses being thin, the thought of winter made us frigid and the snow lay deep on the top of the sierra.

Our luxuries were but few, however in a few days after our arrival, we could boast of having good wine, butter, cheese, rice, sugar, fowls and eggs in plenty and not extravagant.

The ladies were at first very diffident and very shy, from their customs of coolness to strangers, but finding some of the officers '*muito politico*' [very polite], they gradually came round & we had a few '*conversations*' and singing in the evenings. My good fortune led me to a house, where there were two genteel & well-bred young women, but I was a week in the home before more than a distant bow was passed between us. However, they surprised me one night, sitting reading in my '*bedgown*' and from that time our acquaintance became familiar.

All our earnest solicitations could not prevail on the *Duenas* [owners] to allow their children to shake the '*fantastic toe*' [dance] and all our hopes of Balls were at once dissipated. Little dinner parties, where we devoted ourselves freely to the pleasures of the bottle, whilst at night and sauntering in the square during day, or by taking a short ride to prevent our horses getting 'grease from laziness',[18] made up all our amusements and with them we were to pass a long and tedious winter.

18 Greasy heel is an inflammatory dermatitis of the lower limbs, which often develops if horses stand in muddy or wet conditions.

Routes and Distances marched from 21 April to 1 December 1812

Names of Places	Leagues	Miles	Remarks
To Campo d'Ourique Lisbon	¾	3	Through Lisbon
Sacavem	2	8	Road paved
Villa Franca [Vila Franca de Xira]	4	16	Road paved
Azambujio [Azambuja]	3	12	Sandy roads
Santarem	4	16	Hilly country
Golegao [Golega]	4	16	Deep sand
Punhete[19]	3	12	Close to Tagus
Abrantes	2	8	Bad roads
Gavaio [Gaviao]	4	16	Deep road
Gafete	4	16	Good road
Total	**30¾**	**123**	
To Castello [Castelo] de Vide	3	12	Indifferent roads
On Spanish frontier	1½	6	Indifferent roads
Gafete	3	12	Indifferent roads
Nisa	2½	10	Good roads
Sobral [Cebolais] do Cima	5½	22	Rocky country
Castelo Branco	2½	10	Good roads
Lardosa	3	12	Good roads
Camphina [Capinha]	3½	14	Indifferent roads
Carzalhao [Castelheiro?]	3	12	Bad roads
Agoas Villas [Aguas Belas]	3½	14	Bad roads
Camp near Aruda [Renda]	2	8	Bad roads
Bismula	2	8	Bad roads
Bivouac near Fuenteguinaldo	2½	10	Good roads
Bivouac near Pistores [Pastores]	3½	14	Good roads
Bivouac near Tomabron [Tenebron]	3	12	Good roads
Bivouac near Tamames	2½	10	Good roads
Bivouac near Matilla [de los Canos de Rio]	3	12	Good roads
Total	**78¼**	**321**	

19 Modern-day Constancia.

Names of Places	Leagues	Miles	Remarks
Bivouac near a small village	2	8	Good roads
Crossed Tormes at St Martin [Santa Marta de Tormes]	2½	10	Fine roads
Heights of San Christoval	1	4	Fine roads
To ford of St Martin [Santa Marta de Tormes]	1	4	Ploughed fields
Manoeuvred and recrossed	3	12	Ploughed fields
To bivouac on road to Valladolid	3	12	Good roads
Bivouac near a small village	3½	14	Good roads
Near Alaejos	3	12	Good roads
Medina del Campo	2½	10	Good roads
Change ground	1	3	Good roads
Zalende [Zahere?]	1½	4½	Good roads
Campilao [El Campillo]	1	3	Good roads
Villa Mure [Nave] del Rey	2½	8	Good roads
Carnizal [Canizal]	6	19	Bad roads
To Obada [La Orbada] and back to Carnizal [Canizal]	5½	19	Bad roads
To near a small village	3	12	Bad roads
To bivouac	3	12	Good roads
Salamanca	2½	10	Crossed Tormes
Total	**125**	**497**	
To position on the Arapiles	3	9	Good roads
After action of Salamanca	5	15	Good roads
To Penaranda [de Bracamonte]	2½	7½	Good roads
Cabeca de Possa [Cabeza de Alambre?]	3½	11½	Good roads
Arebalo [Arevalo]	3	9	Good roads
Wood on the River Adajio [Adaja]	4	12	Through fields
Wood on the River Adajio [Adaja]	3	9	Sandy country
Wood on the Duero	2	6	Through fields
Arebaldes de Portilla [Arrabal de Portillo]	2	6	Good road
Wood on the Ceja [Cega]	2	6	Good road
To Cuellar	3½	7½	Good road

Names of Places	Leagues	Miles	Remarks
Marching out of Cuellar	3	9	Good road
Iscar	3½	11½	Sandy country
Alameda [Olmedo]	3½	11½	Sandy country
Arebalo [Arevalo]	4½	13½	Good road
San Cidrian [Sanchidrian]	4	16	High road
St Casten [Villacastin]	3	12	High road
[El] Espinar	3	12	High road
To Madrid	11	44	High road
Total	**184**	**725**	
From Madrid to Arebalo [Arevalo]	21	84	Good road
Convent Majareda [Mejorada]	5	15	Bad roads
Valdesillas [Valdestillas]	3	9	Bad roads
Valladolid	4½	13½	Good road
Coreas [Corcos]	2½	7½	Good road
Duenas	2½	7½	Good road
Mazas [Magaz de Pisuerga]	2	6	Good road
Torquemada	2	6	Good road
Quintana del Puente	2	6	Good road
Pampliega	2	6	Good road
Bunell [Buniel]	2½	9½	Good road
To within 3 miles of Burgos	1	3	Good road
To South East of Burgos	1½	4½	Bad cross road
Change of ground	½	1½	Bad cross road
Orones [Hurones]	2	6	Bad cross road
March on the enemy	2	6	Bad cross road
Bunell [Buniel] by Burgos	3	9	Good road
To Torquemada	8½	25½	Good road
Total	**251½**	**948½**	
Duenas	5	15	Good roads
Cabezon [de Pisuerga]	4	12	Good roads
Puente de Douro	4	12	Good roads
Tordesillas	4	12	Bad roads
Castrejon [de Trabancos]	7	21	Bad roads

Names of Places	Leagues	Miles	Remarks
Pitsuerga [Pitiegua?]	6	18	Bad roads
Aldea Seca [Aldearrubia]	5	15	Deep roads
San Christoval [San Cristobal de la Cuesta]	1	3	Deep roads
Salamanca	1	3	Deep roads
To Ciudad Rodrigo	17	51	Deep roads
Rodrigo to Junca	4½	18	Deep roads
Azinhal	3	12	Bad roads
Freixedas	4	16	Bad roads
Muriqual [Minhocal?]	3	12	Bad roads
Celorico [da Beira]	2	8	High road to Lisbon
Linhares	2	8	High road to Lisbon
Moimenta da Serra	3	12	High road to Lisbon
Cea [Seia] Winter quarters	1½	5½	High road to Lisbon
Final Total	**328½**	**1252**	

Winter Quarters and Spring 1813

The army had suffered enormously in the few days of retreat from Salamanca to the Portuguese border, due both to the inclement weather and the lack of supplies. Their mood was not improved by the publication of a critical memorandum which Wellington had sent to senior officers for private consumption. However, a few months in winter quarters quickly improved the men's health. Wellington knew that Napoleon was withdrawing significant numbers of experienced troops from the Peninsula following his disastrous campaign in Russia. By the spring, the army was raring to take the fight to the French, confident in victory, but they were delayed by poor weather and a late start to the growing season for forage.

Cea [Seia] Portugal

By our own exertions and cordiality our winter quarters were daily improving and our little dinner parties were kept up with a great deal of vivacity. A card club was soon established, more for the purpose of bringing us together to enjoy society and a sober glass, than for gaming. A reading room was also nominated, where all the papers from England and Army lists were sent and on no reason whatever were allowed to be taken out of the room.

Every mail brought more glorious news than the last, of the successes of our allies in the north and we could do nothing less in the spring than pass the Pyrenees and enter France. A very severe circular was sent to the several divisions by Lord Wellington pointing out the great want of order & discipline in the retreat of the army from Burgos and calling on the general officers commanding divisions and brigades to exert themselves in again re-establishing that discipline so necessary for the future good conduct of the army.

The brigades were ordered to march twice a week the distance of two leagues for exercise, but notwithstanding this good precaution, the men were fast getting sick. Two month's pay in English guineas were issued to the army and this, owing to the cheapness of the new made wine, greatly increased the fever and dysentery amongst the men.

On the 11 January 1813, the brigade acquired the addition of a very fine & strong regiment, the 91st from England; after a most tedious march from Corunna across the country, often being very ill supplied with provisions and the soldiers arriving nearly barefoot. The 24th and 58th Regiments at this period were made a Provisional Battalion and their headquarters were sent to England and the battalion went to the 7th Division.[1]

The Commander in Chief had set off for Cadiz with very few attendants and the command of the army was left with General Sir Rowland Hill, whose quarters were at Placentia [Plasencia].

Our advances with the families and the fair inhabitants of Cea [Seia] were but very slow, they still keeping themselves very much reserved and formal and at their tea parties, or '*conversazziones*' we generally engrossed their greatest attention and we found they possessed but little or no information of anything past the boundaries of their little village or at most of their province. Their great wish was to convince us of their ancient lineage, rich and noble connections and of their own former opulence before the ravages committed by war on their '*Terras*' [lands]. Their anxiety to appear polite was carried to an extreme, but they had customs very hostile to real good breeding and in their persons were very careless and even dirty. The very idea of a young, well dressed (and in their idea)

1 The 1st Brigade in Lieutenant General Henry Clinton's 6th Division, then commanded by Lieutenant Colonel Stirling, consisted of 1/42nd, 1/79th and 1/91st.

polite female rising from a meal, consisting of garlic, oil and French beans and in her first essay to speak, precede it with a hideous belch and a mass of matter collected from the ill savoured ingredients of her stomach thrown on the ground, was sufficient to shock the politeness of the lowest fair-one in Billingsgate.[2] In justice to my fair hostesses, they had tasted a little more of genteel breeding than their neighbours and what with a good example, which is better than precept[3] were the admiration of the officers.

General Clinton had received the leave of the Commander in Chief to proceed to England and Major General the Honourable Edward Pakenham[4] was expected to command our division. The weather although bad had not prevented many of the officers from tasting the healthy amusement of shooting and owing to the abundance of game they were generally well repaid for their labour. In the sierra the quantity of rabbits were immense and it was by no means uncommon to see two Portuguese set out with a weasel and a few dogs and return with a mule load of fine fat rabbits.

Fairs at Cea [Seia] were held once every month, when jewellery, crockery, garlic and salt fish were the principal articles of commerce. It was always held on a Sunday and the 'Manuels & Marias' ere attend in their best, but simple apparel.

Fresh arrivals [news] from home assured us of the successes of the Russians and also of our arms in America and pamphlets of them were written in Spanish, Portuguese and English and sent to the different provinces.

The weather had become fair and frosty and the whole sierra was 'capped' in snow. Many officers had solicited and obtained leave of absence and very few general officers were at present with the army. The sickness among the men

2 Billingsgate was the main fish market of London.

3 Precept – regulated behaviour.

4 Pakenham was actually a Lieutenant General from June 1811. He commanded the 6th Division from 26 January to 25 June 1813, when Clinton returned.

was daily increasing and our brigade had not lost less than 150 men, since arriving in winter quarters. It was a sort of Remitting Fever,[5] which generally succeeded in carrying them off after a relapse.[6] Every precaution was taken and several of the regiment's quarters were changed and found beneficial.

Lord Wellington had arrived at Lisbon after having it was said, accomplished everything he wished for the ensuing campaign with the Cortes of Cadiz. Up to the 15 February, nothing particular had occurred, but every packet brought us intelligence most interesting of the various successes in the north.

During the fine weather we took several rambles up the sierra, to the different '*povos*' [people] or small villages[7] and regaled ourselves with goat milk and cheese, with the coarse bread of the country. The scenery above all was wild and romantic and the situation of the villages was generally in the deep gullies between the hills, which were covered with the finest pine tree and wild lily. The roads were only passable for men and mules, over many rapid streams; and many families during the retreat of Massena took refuge in these inaccessible mountains, enduring for many days the most severe weather with only the shelter of the walls. The green forage round Cea [Seia] was now nearly consumed and our animals were obliged to ascend the sierra to procure Indian corn straw.

General Pakenham had arrived and taken the command of the division and was highly respected for his polite and affable manners. By the able dispositions of the Major [Lieutenant] General, the cantonments of the division were changed much for the better and the men made more comfortable, the sickness not yet abating but the mortality far less frequent.[8]

---

5 Remitting fever is one of the four main types of fever. In this case the patient's temperature fluctuates, but never drops to 'normal' temperature.

6 Regimental records show that the battalion suffered 21 deaths in December 1812; 79 deaths in January 1813 and 49 deaths in February 1813. Effective numbers in the ranks fell from 1,007 to 872 in the same period.

7 The Portuguese for small village is *Vila Pequena.*

8 By March the number of monthly deaths was below 20.

> The inhabitants of every village were very civil and attentive, particularly those of Cea [Seia] and they claimed our warmest thanks and gratitude. But although we were fortunate enough to find many very respectable families in Cea [Seia], yet all our entreaties to have a ball, or any public assemblies were of no effect, indeed dancing seems to have been given up completely and made room for singing duets or with the guitar, an instrument much used both in Spain and Portugal. But few excel in singing, but they display great taste and even the common class of women, when employed in washing or beating the dirt out of their clothes at the stream, will hum over a little love duet with a sweetness peculiar to themselves and quite foreign to English ballad singing.

Strangely, Stirling completely ignores a major and very unfortunate incident in the regiment at this time. On 22 March 1813, Corporal Michael Macmorran shot Lieutenant Alexander Dickenson and killed him at the village of Aldea de Ceira near Seia. A General Court Martial formed on 23 March found Macmorran guilty and he was hanged on 28 March. This incident is recorded by virtually all memoirs of the 42nd, but perhaps Stirling found it an embarrassment to his regiment. It is recorded in great detail by the anonymous *Narrative of a Private Soldier* but some of his statements are at variance to the known facts.

> The only change in the general cantonments of the army were towards the middle of March, when the 4th Division moved from St Jean de Pesquera [Sao Joao da Pesqueira], to cantonments between the Coa and Agueda, in order to protect the construction of magazines at Almeida and Ciudad Rodrigo, where a large proportion of the bricklayers, carpenters and masons were ordered to assemble.
>
> The means of procuring forage now became very interesting and it could only be got with money and a strong guard to enforce the peasants in the sierra to sell it. We had hoped that by the 1 of April, there should have been plenty of green barley

or grass, but the rainy season had hardly begun and the ground was dry and parched.

Horse races were now held every Wednesday and Saturday by the 6th and 7th Divisions and afforded great amusement, principally to the inhabitants, but who were cautious of entering the lists. The horse races were very poor, but the mule, pony and jackass heats were quite diverting and several sack and pig races afforded great mirth.

Cea [Seia] visibly was becoming every day more beautiful and the broad leafed chestnuts, the evergreen bay and the lively blossoms of the cherry tree, were blended with the smiling verdure of the sloping fields and budding vineyards.

Finally at the end of April the orders to advance arrived.

On the 28 April we received orders to march to Midones [Midoes] and Ervidal [Ervedal da Beira], in order to give the cantonments up to the cavalry on their route from Lisbon and the Tagus. To leave Cea [Seia] where we lived in the greatest harmony for 5 months and where everyone endeavoured to show most their kindness, cost us no small share of regret and we embraced each other with mutual protestations of friendship and cordiality. Nothing could exceed the regret that was shown on this occasion by the worthy family with whom I lived and I parted with giving the most faithful promises, never to forget them or their kindness and to muster up all my abilities in the language to write them.

[29 April] We marched for Midones [Midoes] on the 29th and had a very tempestuous, rainy morning, the roads very bad and streams running across them like rivers. We were greeted at Midones [Midoes] by our landlord with every mark of attention, who was one of the richest men in the province. Midones [Midoes] is a poor village but is prettily situated on a small river whose banks were covered with lofty pine trees.

The villages wherein the brigade were cantoned were very distant and principally situated on the Mondego, which here is narrow, but very deep. The regiments had again got strong and the sickness had nearly subsided, so that we had every expectation of entering Spain in good order.

[6 May] General Pakenham inspected the brigade on the 6 May and was invited to a grand dinner given by our wealthy landlord. The party consisted of upwards of thirty people, amongst them several very pretty and genteel looking women. As they were all from the country, they arrived early and before dinner the ladies sung to the guitar and the gentlemen played at whist, at which several were equal to Hoyle[9] and played very high. Dinner was announced at 2 o'clock and the landlord ordered everyone to his post. Everything had got perfectly cold and no one was allowed to carve but the landlord and his brother. There were in the first course, two dishes containing each - four roast pigs, besides stews of garlic, oil and all the various boiled or roast dishes were done to threads. The wines were good and the Portuguese during the repast, drank of them profusely. The desert was immense and not an inch of the surface of the table could be seen, it consisted of all sorts of sweetmeats of rice, honey, eggs, milk and jellies. It remained on the table and the ladies took their departure and something in the English style, the gentlemen remained and drank the health of their respective sovereigns and commanders. The same amusements occupied the hours after dinner as in the forenoon and several cousins or nieces, slept all night in the town.

At last our final orders for a campaign arrived and tents were given to the men with a mule per company to carry

9 Edmund Hoyle (1672–1769) became a tutor to members of high society in whist. Hoyle then published *A Short Treatise on the Game of Whist* in 1742 which rapidly went into a number of editions. These rules became the authoritative version until 1864.

them, a measure it was hoped would be of the most beneficial consequence to the soldiers.[10]

[14 May] Having everything arranged, we marched to Moimenta de Sierra [Moimenta da Serra] and although the weather was not settled, we reached it without rain.

[15 May] Next day we continued our route to Celerico [da Beira] and there encamped a sight quite novel and had an appearance of comfort different to that of laying under a tree or wall. We hitherto had imagined that our line [of march] was by Ciudad Rodrigo, on the old road and were most agreeably disappointed to learn that it was by Tra[s] os Montes and Benevente [Benavente].

On the 16 [May] we marched to Trancoso, which is a very old walled town and stands on a very high ridge of hills. The country here appeared mountainous, but fertile and well cultivated. In Trancoso are several good houses and a convent of nuns, containing about 30 old women.

[17 May] Marialava [Marialva] our next march was like Trancoso, of great antiquity and being on a commanding situation, was surrounded by Moorish fortifications. The castle is a very old structure built by Adrian [Hadrian] and the residence of the chief justice, or *Juiz de Fora*, is built within its walls. The troops now were regularly encamped, which they preferred infinitely to being crowded in filthy quarters.

[18 May] Over hill and valley, we continued our march to Villa Nova de Foscoa [Vila Nova de Foz Coa], the mountains were excessively steep and perfectly barren and one near Villa

10 The mules previously allocated to the large iron camp kettles of the company were re-allocated to carrying bell tents when the soldiers were issued smaller and lighter individual cooking implements.

Nova [Vila Nova] was so long, that three companies of the brigade were left to assist the guns. The town is situated in a plain on the summit of this hill and is famous for its excellent wine and bread. The inhabitants here were very civil, but they were very cautious of the soldiery whom they had not seen before and conceived that we might be a humble imitation of 'French fraternity'.

[19 May] Having the Douro to pass next day, we rose long before daylight and travelled hills leagues high but found the roads good. Arriving at sun rising at the summit of a stupendous hill, a scene equally novel and interesting to us and suitable either to the imagination of the poet, or painter opened on our view. At the foot of the mountain ran a pretty and broad tributary stream of the Douro, on whose banks were encamped the 4th Division in a thick wood of olive and chestnut tree. Down the luxuriant valley the river winding often, ran its course and as far [as] we could see, the smoke was rising from the foliage of the woods. The highlanders, artillery and soldiers in the foreground, following the zigzag path of the rugged mountain, whilst the grey sombre tint of the distant hills, bounding the view, were subjects highly interesting for the pencil.

Towards the Douro the country was rugged and wild and its bed was narrow and banks steep and barren. After considerable difficulty, the brigade passed in about an hour in boats and marched on to Toro de Moncorvo [Torre de Moncorvo], where we encamped about two miles from town. It is rather a large town, possesses a fine church, many excellent houses and has been little destroyed. Sir T[homas] Graham was expected to take the command of the troops on the right bank of the Douro.

On the 20 [May] we entered the town [Torre de Moncorvo] and halted. The inhabitants from not being accustomed to see so many troops, showed but little disposition to sell anything until the second day when eggs and mutton with wine and other articles, were had in abundance.

[22 May] The country was only cultivated with rye and vines and the roads to Fornos, our next march were very bad, although we had passed the greatest mountains. Fornos bore a great resemblance to a little Highland or Irish village and was embossed in lofty chestnut and the fields near it produced the finest forage. In our worthy host, a civil honest cure, we found a person possessing the greatest esteem and respect of his poor parishioners and seemed more contented and happy in his little village than the Archbishop of Canterbury.

The manner and appearance of the people here was not altered, although on the frontiers of Spain, but the language of the lower class, has a mixture of Spanish and Portuguese hardly intelligible.

[23 May] We found agriculture more studied in our next day's march than any part of Portugal or Spain heretofore and Villa Della [Vila de Ala], the village nearest our camp, had excellent courtyards & stabling to every house. This small village was most charmingly situated in a rural '*baranco*'[11] or glen, with a small streamlet running through the luxuriant fields and gardens and the village church proudly towering over the lofty and broad chestnut and oak trees. General Graham had passed on to Miranda do Douro, where it was supposed the column would concentrate.

On the 24 [May] we marched and halted near a small village called Cercio,[12] but General Sir Thomas Graham's orders came in sufficient time, to cause us to march a league further and encamp on the right of the 7th Division near the miserable little village of Malhada [Malhadas]. The divisions were on a barren mountain of furze and thick underwood and the soldiers had to descend it to get water. The two divisions were inspected by Sir Thomas, Lord Dalhousie, General Pakenham and a numerous Staff.

11 He means *barranco* or ravine.

12 Cercio is 3km south-west of Miranda do Douro.

We remained on this mountain on the 25 [May] and expected to wait the arrival of our great commander with the hussars, as with this exception every equipment for the army to make a decided move were in readiness & the pontoons, heavy artillery and stores were across the Duero.[13]

On the 27 [May] the heavy artillery, cars with the pontoons and the hussars marched towards the Esla and orders were sent to the divisions to send off the sick to Miranda [do Douro].

The weather was very fine and we on the 29 [May] continued on through a very pretty diversified country and after a pleasant short march of two leagues, we encamped on a high mountain covered with heath and the neighbouring views were most romantic and picturesque.[14]

[30 May] Next day's march brought us within ½ a league of the Esla, near a considerable village called Caravajales [Carbajales de Alba] and encamped with the 4th and 7th Divisions. About a ½ a league from the village of Muga [de Alba], we forded the deep and narrow little river Alista [Aliste] and when within ½ a league of our camp, we heard several guns in the direction of the Esla, which afterwards proved to be General Pack's Brigade of Portuguese with some artillery, driving the enemy's picquets across the river on their main body, said to be 10,000 men.

We halted at Caravajales [Carbajales de Alba] on the 30th [31 May] which was a pleasant circumstance not only for our own good, but for that of our animals, having a fine situation, plenty of excellent forage, wood and water requisites very necessary to make a camp agreeable. An

13 Stirling is inconsistent in his spelling of this river; it is correctly the Douro in Portugal and Duero in Spain.

14 In the list of encampments at the end of this section, James states that they stopped at Paradela this night.

account, equally agreeable as authentic, reached us this day of the two heavy brigades of cavalry under Major Generals Fane and Alten having fallen in with the rear guard of the enemy at Salamanca, the whole being put to the rout and 500 men killed and wounded, together with three pieces of artillery taken.[15]

Wellington's main thrust in 1813 was led by Sir Thomas Graham, crossing from northern Portugal into Spain and keeping north of the Douro River, the army neatly side-stepping the French prepared defences on the various rivers running north to south. The French were manoeuvred out of their defences and streamed back towards Burgos and Vitoria on the main road to France.

[1 June] Next morning, we were under arms at an hour before daylight, our baggage packed but not loaded and marching through Caravajales [Carbajales de Alba] arrived at the river at 10 o'clock, over which the pontoons were placed with but little opposition.

The 7th Division in fording, lost a few men drowned owing to the rapidity of the stream, otherwise no obstacle opposed our operations. The pontoons were principally made of tin, broad at both ends and flat bottomed. They are fixed by two anchors at stem and stern, the whole supported by cables on the opposite sides and rafts and thick planks are laid across and form the bridge. An officer and 30 men of the enemy's cavalry remaining rather too long, were surprised and taken.

After crossing the river we marched on to Palaceos [Palacios del Pan], a small village, where General Ponsonby's and General Anson's brigades of cavalry were bivouacked round the village. The language of the people now was pure Spanish, their dress that of Galicia, the women wearing a green bodied gown, a yellow petticoat and red stockings finely

15 This refers to the Action of Aldea Lengua. The Allied cavalry could not break the French squares and the French losses were largely caused by the attached horse artillery. A few hundred were killed and wounded, but the rearguard escaped intact. There is no mention of French guns being captured in Wellington's report, only caissons.

Gallicians.

brought about the ankles & the higher sort still having the black fringed gowns. The men wore cowls, or a sort of peaked cap of black velvet and a short jacket and breeches of brown Spanish cloth and gaiters of leather, or stockings and sandals.

On the 2 June we passed through Andarius [Andavias] and Zavrieta [La Hiniestra], two small villages and encamped on a lovely piece of ground close to a purling stream of the Douro and a mile from Zamora. At noon Lord Wellington entered Zamora amidst reiterated acclamations of joy, ringing of bells, fireworks &c. The bishop, justices and the most respectable people accompanied him to the town hall, where he was long and loudly viva'd as the '*Liberator de Espana*', '*Nuestro Lorde*' and from them he moved uncovered, through crowds of men and females, throwing velvet cloths under his feet, to his quarters, preceded by a couple of state trumpeters, surrounded by his Staff and principal inhabitants; the Spanish beauties from the windows and balconies, throwing rose and pink leaves on them as they passed. A Grand Ball was given by His Excellency in the evening and the theatre was open.

Zamora is a considerable, well built and pretty town, although from the constant residence of a French garrison it has greatly been destroyed. It is prettily situated on the right bank of the Duero, over which it has an excellent stone bridge. In the town all sorts of merchandise was to be obtained and the neighbouring country supplied every necessary of life.

[3 June] We had hoped for a halting day here, but marched over immense plains waving with fertile crops of grain to Tagara Buena [Tagarabuena], a small village close to Toro. The roads were excellent and our merry soldiers got on very fast, being on our ground at 10 o'clock before the heat of the day began. All the country from Zamora to Toro was perfectly flat until coming to the hill on which the latter town is situated. Toro is an irregular large town, but bears no comparison at all to Zamora, either in regularity of building nor accommodation. The castle had been fortified to resist the attacks of the guerrillas, as almost in every village or town, the church or a convent were barricaded and loopholed. The Light Division crossed the bridge at Toro and we marched on the 3rd to Morailes [Morales de Toro], to allow that division [to] occupy our camp ground at Tagara Buena [Tagarabuena].

On the 2 [June] a sharp affair took place here, between our hussars and the enemy's cavalry. The enemy had been endeavouring to collect a contribution previous to their taking 'farewell' and gave our cavalry time to advance from Toro and meet them a little beyond Morailes [Morales de Toro], 350 of the cavalry were killed and wounded and 400 horses taken. We lost one captain taken, 1 lieutenant killed and six men, together with some hundred belonging to the 10th or Prince's Royal Hussars under the command of Major Robarts.[16] The French soldiers taken were of the 16th Dragoons and were good looking fellows, but their horses were in a miserable state of starvation.[17]

On the 3rd before we halted at Morailes [Morales de Toro] the 6th and 7th Divisions were drawn out in line on a fine flat and were inspected and passed by the Commander in Chief, who was very much gratified at their strength and good appearance.

16 Major George Robarts, 10th Light Dragoons, was made a brevet Lieutenant Colonel for Morales.

17 James' account is a little confused regarding British losses. General Didgeon's Brigade of French cavalry were not aware that Wellington's troops were nearby on the same side of the River Esla. Grant's Hussar Brigade advanced immediately on discovering them; the French 16th and 21st Dragoons forming line to the west of Morales de Toro. The 10th and 15th Hussars attacked them frontally while the 18th Hussars attacked their flank. The French cavalry broke and fled until they reached the safety of General Darricau's infantry and guns. French losses numbered 2 officers and 208 men wounded and prisoners, while another 1 officer and 70 men were wounded but not captured; Don Julian Sanchez killed or captured 50 more the following day; virtually annihilating the 16th Dragoons. The British lost Lieutenant John Cottin, 10th Hussars, killed, 2 officers wounded (Captain James Lloyd, 10th Hussars, was wounded and made a prisoner; Captain James Grant, 18th Hussars, was wounded and Lieutenant James Morris, 18th Hussars, was made a prisoner), with 18 men being killed, wounded or prisoner.

The habitations in these small villages were something like our farmhouses, clean, white-washed inside and out and floors being within laid of tile, or pounded clay, they were very cool. They were low, only being one flat, generally consisting of a visiting parlour, with two recess beds, a room sufficiently large to allow all the family to sleep in and entrance where they dine and commonly sit in all the day, it being coolest and a large kitchen. Almost all the houses had excellent courtyards, stables and straw houses.

Unmentioned by James; General Orders of 3 June 1813 appointed Major General Pack to command the brigade, his father returning to command of the regiment.

[4 June] From Morailes [Morales de Toro] we marched on the 4th instant to a small village to the left of Tordesillas, called St Salvador [San Salvador de Hornija]. From all reports almost all the enemy had left Valladolid and we heard of that vigilant partisan Don Julian Sanchez having surprised and taken 60 of their cavalry.

We were encamped in the most luxurious pasture and our poor animals fared in the most sumptuous style, a circumstance looked to sooner than almost any other on a campaign.

[5 June] In the morning we were under arms to march at daylight, but owing to some delay of the advance of General Hill's column, we did not move until light. On our march we passed through Villa de Baton [Torrelobaton], a small village but having a very handsome old quadrangular Moorish castle, beautifully situated on the back of the village and commanding an extensive and abundant valley, the fields covered with fine crops of wheat, rye and meadow grass. The country was completely divested of any sort of wood and it was only by making application to the Alcalde or head magistrate, of the villages that the soldiers got fuel to cook with. The soil of these flats is of clay mixed with chalk and in wet weather makes the roads very deep and almost impassable. Our two divisions proceeded to ground near Penaflor [de Hornija] whilst General Hill's corps rested at Villa de Baton [Torrelobaton]. Penaflor [de Hornija] could boast of but one or two good houses and a fountain of capital water.

The divisions were encamped in ploughed ground and the rain caused the camp to be a dreadful puddle. Forage and wood was scarcely to be procured and shows what diversity of fortune an army is exposed to in more points than fighting or manoeuvring.

On the 6 [June] we marched to Villa Abla [Villalba de los Alcores], an ancient town surrounded by Moorish castles and walls. The country still was destitute of wood, but the valleys contained good forage.

On the 7 June we were on the banks of the rapid Carrion at a small village Morailes [Los Olmillos?], about half a league from Palencia. General Sir T[homas] Graham had got a division of Spaniards and with some English corps was marching on the road of Reynosa near the source of the Ebro. General Hill was on the Burgos high road and we were under Lord Dalhousie as a centre column and moving through Palencia, cross the Ebro at some point between Miranda [de Ebro] & Reynosa [Reinosa]. The enemy's cavalry left our village at 6 o'clock in the morning and King Joseph's headquarters were in Palencia last night at 11 o'clock.

Morailes [Los Olmillos] was rather a pretty little Spanish village, had a good bridge of three arches and an excellent road to Palencia.

[8 June] Next day we arrived at Palencia at 8 o'clock on our road to Villa Gimene [Villajimena]. It is a fine town, well built and on the Carrion, over which there is a good modern stone bridge. The streets are capacious, but mostly all are very filthy in the '*Calle Grande*.' are a few tolerable shops. There is a good vegetable and pork market held in the square, a place but very little desiring of notice. It had many convents until abolished most prudently by Joseph and a cathedral built by King Sanchus the Great,[18] one of the handsomest and most opulent of Spain. The exterior (although by no means such as Salamanca) is still handsome and round the building is a broad pavement, secured from the street by stone pillars & chains. There are four grand entrances into the body of the cathedral, which contains the altar and choir, divided by iron railings. The altar is handsome enough and in the passage round the church are small, but magnificently adorned chapels, dedicated to holidays, saints and other particular days in the year. Several of the figures in the niches, were well executed and the paintings were also of the first artists, but the appearance of the cathedral altogether is heavier and has not that airy elegance of that at Salamanca.

The weather had been very rainy and rendered our encampment at Gimene [Villajimena] & our next day's march to Samara [Tamara de Campos] very disagreeable and the roads bad and deep. The latter place is rather a good village but of no magnitude, however it possesses one of the handsomest village churches of any seen yet in Spain.

[9 June] Next morning expecting no march, as the Route had not been sent the preceding night, we were enjoying a comfortable nap, when to our great regret, orders for an immediate turnout made us jump and with difficulty had sufficient time to swallow a little breakfast. Our march was for Hera de la Vega [Itero de la Vega], a small village on the Pisuerga, on which nearly all the army was that day encamped.

[10 June] Here we had a halting day and after such rapid strides was very necessary and for an encampment our situation was

18 King Sancho III of Pamplona (996?–1035) re-founded the Diocese of Palencia in the year of his death, but the cathedral was not started until over 100 years later.

delightful, being close to the river in a fine thick wood and plenty of forage and grazing for the live cattle. The country here was uncommonly fertile producing the most luxuriant crops of corn, but the Spaniards appeared very indifferent as to our success, being with difficulty they would allow us [to] enter their houses.

Our cavalry had been pushed as far on as Castellanos [de Castro] five leagues from Burgos, which it was generally supposed Lord Wellington would pass, leaving a blockading force and push on to the Ebro, in hopes of bringing the enemy to a general action. Sir Thomas Graham by last accounts was with his column only two leagues from the Ebro and we had every reason to think he by this time was either on it or across it. At Reynosa [Reinosa] from whence it had its source in the mountains of Santillana,[19] it is a mere rivulet and little or no time would be lost in crossing.

On the 12 [June] our march was as cool and pleasant as it was short and although for some distance after leaving Hera [Itero de la Vega], the country was rather barren, yet in our halting place Villa Silos [Villasilos], we found a pretty little encamp ground and the people totally different to those we had met before. About a mile from the village we were met by the poor but happy inhabitants of all ages and were greeted by them in the most grateful manner, accompanying us with tambourines and songs until we reached our ground, where they danced whilst the columns were forming.

The old donna of my house was very attentive and kind and seated by her at the kitchen fire at night she give [*sic*] me her whole history. She had two '*Guapos Mozos*' [handsome young men] in the corps of guerrillas and from whom it was a long time she [had] heard; and with great composure, supposed they had both been killed by the barbarous French.

19 The Ebro starts near Fontibre.

Our march had been so rapid that the supplies principally of bread was getting deficient and although the country abounded in grain, we had not time to prepare it and our men were reduced to ¾ of a pound per day.

[13 June] The march next day although rather long was very agreeable and diversified and we encamped near Villa Mure del Puerta [Villanueva de Puerta], a small, isolated village, but the country affording [an] abundance of wood, water and forage, which always made up for a poor village.

[14 June] We have heard a great deal of the mountain or pass, called La Puenta [La Piedra] which we crossed in our next day's march & entered a country totally different to any we had yet met. The mountain itself is of hard slate stone and the roads were very bad and even dangerous. After ascending this hill we had nothing but a series of rugged steep rocks and the face of the hills formed into a regular strata of slate stone. The scenery at once became mild and extraordinary as if by magic and we came into a most romantic little valley, hemmed in by high cold ridges of hills, covered with nothing but a few herbs and underwood, on which were feeding numerous flocks of goats. At the extremity of this sequestered vale stood the little village of Fasovilla [Basconcillos del Tozo?], completely enclosed by overhanging cliffs and mountains, on one of the prominences or peaks, was an old chapel where pilgrims were wont to confess their faults and ascend the rugged steps on their knees. The scenery was uncommon and afforded scope for the curious artist not under the rigour of martial law. No sooner had we with considerable danger top[p]ed one hill, than we found ourselves again enveloped in others, whose sides from the top to the bottom were carved into precipices and covered with overhanging shrubs and heath.

The artillery came on with the greatest difficulty and at one of these tremendous ascents a regiment remained and cleared the roads. We now had gone over a track of the most singular and sterile country and only a poor deserted village appearing to gladden the prospect here and there in the intervening valleys.

Our march had been very tedious and we had no idea where we could halt as there was no appearance of water, wood or forage near. Continuing our march, we came most suddenly to a most enchanting diversity of prospect and stood on the brink of a precipice overlooking a most delightful valley, through which ran the Ebro.

Nothing could surpass our astonishment on this very precipitate change and during the time some men were employed in clearing the road down this stupendous mountain for the cavalry and artillery, we lay on the summit, enjoying this rude but charming scene of nature. The valley was rich, covered with the most luxuriant crops of wheat, Indian corn and green meadows, the numerous little village churches rising their humble spires above the foliage of the oak and chestnut and the Ebro, although very small, placidly running its varied course down this lovely country. The cavalry going down very slow, the general marked a small village, St Martin [San Martin de Elines] for the rendezvous of the regiments and allowed everyone to follow his own path and reach the foot, the best manner they could. In an instant the whole mountain appeared in motion and presented a most lively prospect, for in less than half an hour the whole formed at St Martin [San Martin de Elines] and at 6 o'clock encamped about two miles up the valley. Fires were kindled, but we had little hope of seeing our baggage before 10 o'clock. However our pious host, the padre of a little village, or few houses, presented us with a neat repast of fine bread, goat milk cheese and some excellent wine, which taking the keen edge off our appetites, invited us to seek repose after a tedious march of six most harassing leagues.

[15 June] Next morning, at 6 o'clock, we crossed the Ebro, once the height of all our wishes, but now we entertained the hopes of even crossing the inseparable barrier of the Pyrenees. This river is one of the largest and most celebrated rivers of Spain and taking its source in the confines of Old Castile in the mountains of Santillan, runs through Aragon and Catalonia & debouches itself into the Mediterranean a little below Tortosa. There it was very narrow and rapid, its banks not steep, but the neighbouring scenery the most rugged conceivable. It commences to be navigable at or near Tudela, a fine town of Navarre.

The bridge at St Martin [San Martin de Elines] had been destroyed at some period but had been sufficiently repaired by the peasants to admit of our cavalry and artillery to pass. Our route was for Villalcayo [Villarcayo], along the banks of the river, the cavalry and 3rd Division going on a road to the left.

[16 June] On our march this day, the country was possessed of the same singularity of nature and about three leagues from Villalcayo [Villarcayo], we encountered another road, leading over a precipice and shelves of rock and the scenery below was even more rich and possessed more singularity than that at the Ebro.

The ridges of uncommon rocks, crowned with lofty trees, ran in cross lines round the valley and bounded it on all sides, whilst a majestic eminence, thickly covered with the oak, elm and chestnut trees and cultivated partly, rose in the centre, more fanciful even than the imagery of a theatre. Although the road was very bad, nay even dangerous, from the hard-edged stones in shelves, everyone was charmed with the novel beauty and wildness of the country and every step presented us new scenes and curiosities of wanton nature, blended with richness and fertility. The little vales which were alternately between the hills, abounded in all sort of grain, plentifully watered by little purling streams and the villages situated in the recesses of the hills shaded by the venerable oak and broad spreading elm, were uncommonly pretty and drew a wish from the heart of many a tired & worn out soldier, to there make his abode and spend the remainder of a life already burthensome.

Friar at Valladolid.

It had been the intention to have gone on to Villalcayo [Villarcayo], but the distance still being great, the roads bad, together with the consideration that the men had little or no bread, caused us to encamp on the banks of the river, near the little secluded village of Mandanessa [Manzanedo].

[17 June] Next morning we had gone but a few yards, when we met a most enchanting prospect along the river of a lofty convent rising above the road and the cliff overhanging the river and a distant view of Villalcayo [Villarcayo] and other villages about 3 leagues off.

On our approach to Villalcayo [Villarcayo] we lost the mountain scenery and the town was situated in an extensive plain, which contained many other villages of less note. Villalcayo [Villarcayo] is a pretty clean village and possesses several good houses and shops and a spacious square.

[18 June] We had confidently expected a halt here, but on the 18th we had a short march to Medina del Pomar, a village about a league from Villalcayo [Villarcayo] and more considerable.

A column of the enemy was at Frias and the 7th Division went on three leagues in that direction in order to watch their movements.

[19 June] We remained here on the 19th for the same purpose and the report was that 16,000 men were intercepted from joining the main army at Vitoria, where General Graham's column was fast approaching.

[20 June] However our column at Frias had escaped and we marched from Medina [de Pomar] to Quincoces [de Yuso], a distance of four leagues. This as well as all the other villages here very miserable and most of their inhabitants having deserted them, nothing remained but poverty and wretchedness. The poor people seemed to have not sufficient to support life and fed their children on a potage of boiled herbs eaten with mouldy coarse bread. Often from these scenes of misery, were we led to contemplate the lot of happy Britain, whose sacred territory never felt the ravages of war and whose inhabitants regaled themselves in the lap of plenty and luxuriousness.

The Battle of Vitoria

The 42nd were not present at the Battle of Vitoria, marching hard to get there but still being some 23km from Vitoria on the evening of the battle. However, James records what he heard of the battle, presumably from others who were present.

> **[21 June]** We were drawing very near to Vitoria, where it was said Joseph intended to give battle and our march was prolonged to Anda, instead of halting at Barbarena [Berberana].
>
> This was the 21 June and about 11 o'clock, being at the distance of four leagues from Vitoria, we distinctly heard the firing of cannon and musketry and having towards noon increased, put it almost beyond all doubt, that a general action had commenced near Vitoria.
>
> From the distance we had already marched, the badness of the crossroads and the artillery not having yet joined, gave us but little hope of sharing in the glories of this action. Having arrived near Anda, we were halted in a field for upwards of three hours, in the uncertainty whither to proceed or not; at last General Pakenham determined on encamping here. In the evening an officer of dragoons brought us the welcome intelligence of the total defeat of the French army under Joseph in person and Marshal Jourdan by Lord Wellington.
>
> The enemy occupied a strong position in front of Vitoria, with their left on a high ridge of hills, their centre '*appuyed*' [supported] by some small rising conical hills strongly fortified with artillery and their right on the high road to Bayonne, resting on some fortified villages. Joseph was so confident of success and of the superiority of his cannon and numbers,[20] that his whole court and baggage remained in Vitoria, when he drew out his army in position.

20 The French army could boast 153 cannon against Wellington's 96; however, the number of French troops present was around 58,000 against 85,000 Allied troops.

On the morning of the 21st, General Hill began the attack on the enemy's left and although well contested, soon turned their flank and gained the [Puebla] heights. General Graham attacked and routed those on the Bayonne road, cutting off all retreat but by Pamplona. Lord Wellington with the 3rd, 4th and 7th Divisions attacked the centre and very soon Joseph and his whole army ran off, leaving their artillery and baggage in the most dire confusion.

The artillery that the enemy had posted on the different heights, got all in confusion when they entered together on the road from the fields and thus were taken. The confusion that took place in the town was inconceivable, chariots, Royal carriages, tumbrils, waggons, cannon, money chests, mules ladened & with no attendants, Joseph's ladies of the court and courtiers making their escape on foot, on mule or horseback, leaving their wealthy baggage in the hands of our soldiers. From the plunder left in sight of our soldiers, it was with some difficulty Lord Wellington could push on the cavalry, particularly some regiment of hussars, who was roughly handled in orders afterwards.[21] An immense quantity of money was found by the soldiers, several individuals bearing off, upwards of £3,000 in gold and valuables,[22] men wearing apparel, ladies dresses, cloths of every description was laying untouched on [the] ground and the quantity of books & paper was immense. A great stock of provisions, artillery and engineer stores of every description was likewise taken and individuals of the town came out to the roads and chose their '*equipages*'.

The ground on which the battle was fought was very much intersected by ditches and enclosures, circumstances highly favourable to the enemy, for our men could not come so well to the charge and our cavalry were completely useless. Our

21 The 18th Hussars were severely criticised, Wellington threatening to send them home in disgrace.

22 Equivalent to some £170,000 today.

loss in killed and wounded was in every respect equal to that of the enemy, but as yet no certain account was heard of it.[23] Few superior officers were killed except Colonel [the] Honourable Cadogan,[24] commanding the 71st Regiment, who fell gallantly charging the enemy.

On the 22 [June] we marched across the field of battle, to a small village on the Bayonne road, about a mile from Vitoria.[25] In every field were strewed cannon, tumbrils and ammunition waggons, in many were found large sums of money, buried under horse nails or shoes. Individuals found even money laying on the ground and mules and horses were selling in Vitoria for a mere '*sans*' [nothing].

In the evening Clausel[26] who had been ordered to join with about 10,000 men under his command, came to the hills near Vitoria, but hearing the tidings of his master's defeat and seeing the tents of the English below, made off and General Clinton who had just arrived from England, would not follow him with the division, although solicited by General Pakenham.[27]

The cannon when collected near the town, were upwards of 'two hundred and fifty'[28] with tumbrils and ammunition cars innumerable and proud proofs of one of the most decisive battles ever gained.

Vitoria is a large and considerable town of Biscay and is the capital of the province of Alava. The streets are long and narrow, numbered according to the profession of those who inhabit them. As the '*Calle de Gapateria*'[29] or 'Shoemakers

23 The numbers killed and wounded on each side were around 5,000; however, the French also lost some 3,000 men prisoners.

24 Lieutenant Colonel the Honourable Henry Cadogan, 71st Foot, was killed at Vitoria.

25 This almost certainly refers to the village of Durana.

26 General de Division Bertrand Clauzel.

27 This is an unfounded criticism on Clinton. Clauzel's troops did not approach closer than Trevino, some 19km south of Vitoria, and hurried away, having been apprised of the recent defeat. Clinton's troops were not ordered to pursue him.

28 An exaggeration, although 151 guns out of the 153 French guns present were captured.

29 Now Zapatari Kalea. The roads of Vitoria arced around the city walls.

Street' where leather &c is sold. '*Silleria*' or 'saddlery', '*herreria*' or hand made goods. The square[30] is very regular and particularly handsome, with good cloth and jewellers shops, under the lofty piazzas. In it are the best houses, but they have no stabling and the town hall is in the centre of one [of] the squares. On the north-east side of the square there is a street built on a terrace[31] at one end of it, is the principal church,[32] but has nothing remarkable. Joseph had a palace here, but it has more the appearance of a rich gentleman's town house in England.[33] There are some fine promenades in the town shaded by trees, a boulevard, some good inns & coffee houses. The French had been quartered here for 6 years, consequently left behind a number of friends, but amongst the lower classes (who by their own account had been treated like dogs) by them, were rejoiced at their defeat, those of the higher sort appeared discontented and if they had dared expressed their feeling, would have wished their friends back. Vitoria has its entrances by gates and the French had fortified it very strongly and with a garrison of 10,000 men might have resisted a considerable time.[34]

There are two excellent shops in the square, one kept by a German and the other a Frenchman, both having resided a long time in Vitoria, are very rich and they have their commodities from all quarters and of the most curious and best sorts.

A Private of the 42nd records that they remained in the vicinity of the battlefield for three days and a number of men discovered great riches still lying about.

---

30 The Plaza Espana.

31 The Paseo de los Arquillos.

32 The Iglesia de San Miguel.

33 The Montehermoso Palace was actually owned by the family of Joseph's mistress in Vitoria. It is now an art centre.

34 This is an exaggeration: the old medieval walls could not have withstood modern artillery for long.

On the 24 [June] we remained in the same camp and were waiting orders from the Commander in Chief. It was understood that of all the money captured, only sixty thousand pounds were sent to our Treasury or Paymaster General's Office at Vitoria, although some officers were known to have secured upwards of £10,000.[35]

On the 25 [June] we marched on the Bayonne road, which is capital, well paved with a sort of limestone and admitted [us] to march in subdivisions. The country was mountainous but well cultivated where it was practical and the road kept winding prettily round the hills, until we arrived at an extraordinary village called Salivas [Salinas de Leniz/Leintz Gatzaga]. This village was seen from the summit of the hill and seemed buried in immense mountains & which were covered with the dwarf oak and elm trees and at their feet ran a beautiful stream through a narrow but pretty valley.

At our approach the inhabitants all turned out and saluted us with the most lively effusions of joy and gratitude and the honest peasants and fair Biscayans had many a conjecture at seeing the highlanders and echoed forth acclamations of astonishment and doubting wonder. After winding to the bottom of this mountain we came into the valley and the roads being good and the weather fine, we had a most pleasant journey to [Arrasate o] Mondragon, after passing the clean little village of Anchalabeta [Aretxabaleta] about ½ a league from the former place.

On the road likewise we saw two very strong blockhouses erected by the enemy and also one at [Arrasate o] Mondragon, from whence the garrisons had been withdrawn, but several guns been left. The division was closely encamped or bivouacked in a thick wood near [Arrasate o] Mondragon and

35 It is estimated that there was treasure worth £1 million in the French baggage train (some £100 million today). Certainly little of this coin reached the Treasury and a few individuals made huge fortunes.

the ground was so slanted that the tents could not be pitched and all the fields were sown with Indian corn, or some other grain. The people of [Arrasate o] Mondragon were very much elated and gratified at our appearance, receiving us kindly and showing the greatest confidence in disposing everything for sale.

The manners, dress and even language was changed and the race of people altogether was very far superior to what we had seen in Spain. The young men were tall, active and robust,

Biscayans.

with countenances more open and frank than the Castillian and wore short coats or jackets, necks bare, short breeches loose at the knee and many only sandals on their legs and feet. The women were very fair and possessed a great deal of life and animation, almost all wearing their hair plaited long down to the waist, tyed [*sic*] nicely with a black, red or green ribbon and with a good figure and their majestic gait was pretty & graceful. They wore their petticoats loose and very short and their well-made ankles were bound with ribbon as sandals.

Almost all the middling class spoke Spanish, but this province of Guipuscoa & almost throughout Biscay, has a language completely peculiar to themselves. There is in it no similarity to the Spanish or French or any known language ever heard.[36] [Arrasate o] Mondragon is a compact, clean little village and we found everything very moderate, particularly wine, the claret being 2s/6d [£8 today] and Frontenac 3s/6d a bottle [£11 today].

The French had had a garrison here for a long time and made themselves liked, but for the contributions of money and rations they levied. The Governor and Intendant General had resided here in comfort for 4 years and is trusted; and the latter a few days ago carried away by force, one of the prettiest girls in town with him '*offering marriage in France*'.

Some suspicions still remaining of the retreat of Clausel's column, a company of the 91st Regiment with a party of dragoons were sent back on the road to Archabatela [Aretxabaleta] in order to forward any intelligence of the enemy in that quarter.

On the 26 [June] we had every hope and belief that we should halt here for some days and many of the girls of the place were all alive at the thoughts of a Ball in the evening and we were sitting quietly enjoying our glass of claret after dinner

36 He describes the Basque language, which is unique in having no origin from any other language.

when that bane of a soldier, 'the Route' to march immediately opened our door and issued his provoking mandates.

As we never had the privilege of ordering, we could only have the satisfaction of 'growling' to ourselves and only showing our teeth, but not able to bite and although such a sudden order caused a little confusion in clearing plates, packing wet clothes, pans [panniers] &c and saddling & loading our mules, yet practise made us so careful, that at six o'clock, ½ an hour after receiving the order, we were on the road with the regret, but good wishes of the honest peasants of [Arrasate o] Mondragon who wished us well '*Hasta la vuelta*' or '*until our return*'.

The reason for this retrograde movement was in order to join the 5th Division and the Life Guards [at] Vitoria and proceed in pursuit of Clausel.

[27 June] The night was fine and not dark, the roads in excellent order & our men got on very fast. We passed through Salinas at 12 o'clock, when every animal was hushed to rest and enjoying the balmy slumbers of the rude and healthy peasant.

At ½ past 2 o'clock we halted on ground about a mile from Vitoria, to kill and cook and again in readiness to march at 9 o'clock. The column of the enemy was heard of last at Logrono on the Ebro and had a force of 12,000 men in infantry and cavalry. At 10 o'clock on the 27th we marched through Vitoria and passing to the east, got on the high road to Logrono.

Soon after we met the brigade of Life Guards and Blues, who were on the Route to Penacerrada [or Urizaharra], where our division was also ordered and there to meet the 5th Division. We encamped near that place at 6 o'clock very much fatigued, having marched nearly 12 Spanish leagues in 24 hours. It is a tolerable village and held the Staff of the two divisions with ease.

It was said there had been a skirmish at Tolosa and that Pamplona was invested on the 28th at 3 o'clock pm, there was no order for marching. In an hour after when at dinner, orders came for the 6th Division to march towards Logrono, by Laguardia and the 5th Division to return to Vitoria, leaving with us their artillery and the brigade of Heavy cavalry.

The road from Penacerrada [or Urizaharra] soon after leaving it, winds up a pretty hill enriched with pasture and all kinds of arborage [*sic*] and at its summit discloses to the beholder, a most glowing and beautiful prospect. The vast extense [*sic*] of plain below, was as far as the eye could reach & its rich and luxurious appearance from the height gave us great hopes of arriving in a most plentiful country. Laguardia, which is an old fortified town, situated in the middle of the plain on a towering eminence, had the most rare and commanding appearance imaginable, its lofty turrets and wall, looking boldly over the wide expense of territory below & numerous villages were scattered in this vast circuit and here and there we had a view of the Ebro.

The peasants from the villages came running in all directions to the road and welcomed us with greetings of joy, seemingly the most sincere and at Laguardia, which is a large, ill built old town, the inhabitants were quite frantic, turning out on the walls, roads &c waving their handkerchiefs, ringing of bells, firing small arms and the crowd and noise was so extraordinary, that with difficulty the horses of General Clinton and Staff would be brought to pass. The country about Laguardia was very pretty and abounding in corn and wine. About 12 o'clock at night, the troops encamped by the side of the road in some orchards, ¾ of a league from Logrono. We were greatly tired and we were at too great a distance to go to a play and Ball given by the people of that good town and contented ourselves with the society of an honest gentleman and family, who had some years back retired from Logrono and had an excellent comfortable house on the road. When we entered, the whole family were ready to receive us, consisting of the old patriotic gentleman, three merry daughters and a very pretty young grandchild, full of animation and naivette.

They apologised for want of the accommodation that was their wish to entertain their liberators, but in a very short time, sat a most sumptuous supper on the table and we found the view of Navarre so excellent, that we did not once think of our long march we had undergone and the one we was about to begin at daylight.

James received an offer from Marianna, one of the daughters, to throw in her luck with him and accompany him on the march.

[28 June] However the order for marching was prolonged until 8 o'clock and we betook ourselves with our clothes on, to that sweet power which '*seldom visits sorrow, when it doth, it is a comforter*'.[37] The hospitality of our landlord had produced for us at 7 o'clock an excellent breakfast and the cheerful, young Marianna secretly offered to accompany war's dreadful clangour, if I would but allow her to see her '*madre*' [mother] at Laguardia. Such is the animation of Spanish girls, who with the greatest spirit and heedlessness, would have deserted her family, with one of a day's acquaintance.

After taking a grateful leave of our kind host and family, we were soon at Logrono, which was as deserted as Laguardia of its inhabitants and [who] crowded the bridge and sides of the road. Stopping here for some time to receive provisions, I took the opportunity of riding through the town, which is large, well built and the streets paved. It is prettily situated on the Ebro, in Old Castile and the country round is beautiful and abounding in excellent wine, grain & exquisite fruits. It has a good bridge over the river, which is about 200 yards broad, with its banks low and shaded by lofty poplars and fruit trees. A handsome promenade goes round the town, which has a fine cathedral, marketplace, amphitheatre for bull fights and a Royal palace, but it is only a common, well-furnished dralling [*sic*] house. The females testified the greatest surprise and joy

37 From Shakespeare's *The Tempest*.

at the highland corps and in themselves hazarded many a droll conjecture.[38]

[29 June] At Logrono we learnt the enemy had gone down the Ebro, towards Tudela & Zaragossa [Zaragoza] and from the direction we marched this day, had given up the pursuit and turned towards Pamplona. After an excessive long and tedious march, over an undulating but best cultivated country, we encamped at Ladosa [Lodosa], a distance of seven leagues from Logrono and found it a tolerable village.

On the 1 July we were at a small village on a rapid River Yeglea [Ega] called Levin [Lerin] and where the gallant Mina is adored and the town is a great rendezvous for him and his followers. We passed some fields on the road to Levin [Lerin], where their invincible Mina attacked a column of the enemy about 4 months ago, taking and killing upwards of 1,400, permitting only a colonel and a few men to escape. The killed patriots were all collected and interred, but the bones of the French were bleached white on the spot they fell. The people here gave great proofs of their patriotism and boasted of having sons in the ranks of their favourite chief and of having had him in their houses. Our patron was a venerable old priest and although we held out for a long time against his remonstrances of cooking our own dinner, he insisted on us dining with him, when all the municipality of the town came and paid us their respects.

[2 July] Next morning we marched to Puente de la Reyna [Puente la Reina], a pretty little village and where the people equally showed their patriotism as at Levin [Lerin] and insisted on us eating & living with them. To indulge their kind offers once, was all we could do, for their time and manner of living was quite different to ours, but generally their little presents

38 Presumably as to what lay beneath the kilt!

of fruit and wine we could not dispense with. The town has been considerably damaged by the guerrillas and French, but it is still a pretty clean little village and had a most abundant market. We halted here on the 3rd and 4th and having the advantage of very good weather, we enjoyed the company of the fair '*Espanolitas*' [Spanish women] every evening on the promenade.

On the 4 [July] or the '*Virgins day*' there was grand processions and ceremonies performed in church and they were attended by our Portuguese troops and bands of music. The devotions in church continued almost all day, but really they seemed to worship (especially the females) the creator in the creature & kneeling were ogling the Portuguese officers and tittering to each other as if confessing their sins. We had whilst here some very pleasant dancing parties, of which amusement the people are very fond and seem as if they could never wear out, dancing boleros, fandangos, waltzes and country dances incessantly.

On the 5 [July] we marched at 5 o'clock and turning a ridge of hills came in sight of Pamplona, which was invested on all sides by the 3rd, 4th and part of General Hill's Divisions. It lay very low, seemed a large town, the country round it appeared for upwards of a league as one corn field, here and there interspersed with small villages. The hills near seemed too far off to be of any great assistance in a siege, or in commanding the castle.

Our position in the blockade did not seem exactly known and after turning to our left through the village of Astrain, we marched to Azarmior [Zizur Mayor] and there took up ground on the heights. A battalion of each brigade was sent down to relieve the picquets of the 4th Division, who were on the opposite side and when dark came on, our sentries and videttes were pushed on to within 400 yards of the walls.

Redoubts at equal distances had [been] begun all round the town, about within range of their guns and it was supposed that when completed, General O'Donnel[39] and Don Carlos D'Espagna,[40] with their Spaniards would blockade it and the army continue on to the frontiers.

General Sir T[homas] Graham was on the high road to St Sebastian [San Sebastian], General Hill on the road to the Pass of Roncesvalles and our cavalry were sent off to villages in the rear, being of little use in such a mountainous country. Pamplona is the capital of Navarre and it is said was built by Pompey.[41] It is situated in a plain surrounded by hills at the distance of a league and to the north-east, rises in rapid succession, the hoary heads of the Pyrenees. The Arga, a small river runs through it and by it garrison is supplied with wood, floated down from the mountains in bars or logs. It is the residence of a viceroy and its cathedral, squares and shops are reported to be very fine. An old extraordinary windmill has been turned into a very strong tower in the citadel, which is likewise very strong and has ravelins and other works thrown out to the eastward, with double ditches, once supposed to be a wet one. The gate on the road near our encampment was protected by a strong half-moon battery and the ramparts were strong and seemed crowded with troops. It had been mentioned that from our rapid advance they had not sufficiently supplied it with provisions and that Joseph in his retreat had not had time to give orders for its supply.

The poor intrusive king at Salvatiera [Salvatierra/Agurain] had not a knife to eat his dinner and took a handkerchief from his landlady's neck, whose lovely little daughter of about 13 years old, he most brutally violated, in the hearing of her distressed parent and this only about six hours after losing the Battle of Vitoria and his 'kingdom'.

39 General Enrique O'Donnell, Conde de La Bisbal, was of Irish descent.

40 General Carlos de Espana, 1st Conde de Espana.

41 Roman General Gnaeus Pompeius Magnus (106–48 BC).

[6 July] The enemy on the 6th pushed out a strong foraging party towards our picquets, protected by a squadron of cavalry, but on their approach, were briskly received by our advance and obliged to retire.

The redoubts were carrying on without the least annoyance and indeed the orders expressed a wish that they might be finished with as little delay as possible, in order that we might be more actively employed in the field. When our works were above the ground, the enemy attempted to disturb us by firing some shot and shell, but fortunately did little or no harm. In the manner or dress of the people in the villages here, there was no apparent difference, except that a great portion of them spoke Bascuenssa [Basque].

[8 July] The weather was very warm and on the 8th we had a severe thunder-storm, accompanied by gusts of wind that blew down several of the tents. Lord Wellington was supposed to be at Beurneta [Berroeta][42] in the Pyrenees about 10 leagues distant from Pamplona.

On the 9 [July] our redoubts were fast improving and only now and then annoyed by a shot or shell, but in the evening a foraging party came out a considerable distance on the high road, but were quickly drove back by our cacadores.

On the 11 [July] they again attempted to forage too close to our lines and after some smart skirmishing were obliged to retire without effecting that purpose. The Spanish Army under O'Donnell had arrived at Puente de la Reyna [Puente la Reina] and we hoped we should soon be relieved.

Siege had been laid to St [San] Sebastian by the 5th and 1st Divisions and it was reported that Foy[43] with the army, had retired to France, followed by General Hill and the 7th Division.

---

42 The Duke was at Irurita at this time

43 General de Division Maximilien Foy commanded a force of about 20,000 men, which was not present at Vitoria. He was pushed back by Thomas Graham's troops and crossed into France from Irun.

The enemy having been disappointed in his first attempt to forage in the morning, he came out in strength in the evening at sunset and drove back our videttes and sentries, but being instantly reinforced by the cacadores and 60th company of Riflemen, with two field pieces, smart skirmishing took place and the enemy again retired without his forage and with some loss. Our loss was 10 killed and wounded, but it would it was hoped, be a caution to them, ere they came out again.

On the 12 [July] the enemy kept snug within their walls and instead of skirmishing, amused us with their fine bands playing on the ramparts.

In the evening we received an order, as agreeable as unexpected, to be in readiness to march next morning, the picquets to be relieved by the 3rd and 4th Divisions.

[13 July] Everyone seemed happy once more to be on the move and we passed through Villa Abba [Villava], where we had a most distinct view of the works, which were far stronger than we had imagined. We left those two corps at Pamplona, only until the Spaniards should arrive and [with] this day's march, we fairly were in the Pyrenees.

The Pyrenees are a grand chain of mountains separating Spain from France and extends from the Atlantic or Bay of Biscay to the Mediterranean sea; a distance of 85 leagues.[44] They are covered with forests and possesses mines of different metals and several rivers have here their sources. The hills are covered with good pasture and the intervening valleys produce excellent wines and Indian corn. They are divided into three parts, Lower, Higher and Eastern Pyrenees and after them are named 3 Departments,[45] situated all under their different divisions.

44 The Pyrenees extend for 500km or 310 miles.

45 They are split into the French departments of Pyrenees Atlantiques, Hautes Pyrenees and Pyrenees Orientales.

We marched to within a mile of a little village called Ostitz, which consisted of large buildings built of wood and seemed intended for inns or catering houses. The valleys were pretty and well tilled and produced excellent crops of Indian corn, wheat, turnips and peas and beans. All the houses had very snug little gardens and in their orchards were beautiful fruit trees, which bore delicious fruit.

[14 July] Next day we marched to Lanz [Lantz] a village, the same sort of construction as Ostitz, but the houses larger and better. They informed us, contrary to our ideas, that at Christmas it was the custom for their friends to entertain each other in their houses for weeks together and that it was the reason of the houses being so large and long tables and benches in them. Very few spoke Spanish here and their dress was but little different to that of other parts of Navarre.

'For as refinement stops from sire to son, unaltered, unimproved their manners run'.[46]

They however were rather diminutive but very active in their domestic affairs and the men were tall, well made, hardy and industrious. They wore their necks and breasts bare and their breeches at the knees were always open & sometimes without stockings.

Nothing was to be procured here but pork and vegetables and we had nearly to depend on 'king's own'.[47]

[15 July] We had expectations of a halt here, but we had an order next morning to march to San Estevan [Sanesteban/Doneztebe] and Colonel Stirling was ordered to report to headquarters,[48] the rest of the division remaining at Lanz

46 From Oliver Goldsmith's *The Traveller.*

47 Army rations only.

48 On 15 July Wellington was at Lesaka.

[Lantz]. The roads from Pamplona to Lanz [Lantz] had been very bad and narrow, but this day we experienced roads (if they be so called) hardly practicable for goats.

On leaving Lanz [Lantz] we ascended a steep mountain and continued for upwards of two leagues without seeing a single habitation, turning and winding round stupendous mountains covered with towering oak and elm trees and below us deep gullies and ravines, through which ran streams, which joining, formed the waters of many a river. The scenes were grand and majestic but too wild, until we arrived at a pretty little village called Mandares [Almandoz], situated on a small stream and enveloped by mountains covered with wood.

There the people had shut up all their houses, but were happy to see us and presented roast chestnuts and cherries and seemed

'To love their mountains and enjoy their storms
And ask no more than simple nature gives'.[49]

The roads in some places were paved, but so very steep and narrow in others, that they presented insuperable obstacles to artillery ever attempting to pass on them. The country still continued most wild and picturesque, especially near Bermuta [Berroeta], a pretty small village situated on a rising hill in the valley and was strongly fortified by the French against the attacks of Mina and his guerrillas.

Proceeding from Bermuta [Berroeta] we got into a most intricate country covered with underwood and for upwards of an hour lost our road and probably should have been obliged to bivouac all night, had we not by fortune stumbled on the humble but pretty cottage of a worthy Bask [Basque], who ordered his son to be our guide and retracing our steps, we got upon a sort of road or bypath. His mazes were on the banks

49 A distorted version of Henry Longfellow's *Lapland.*

of a charming little streamlet and we were alternately riding through orchards of the most luxuriant plum trees, apples and pears hanging in clusters. Near a little sequestered heap of houses in a vale close to the rivulet we met strings of women bleaching clothes and hitching their petticoats up to the hind leg, showed their rude state of health, in the firm texture of their limbs and their happiness by singing simple Bascayen [Basque] duets.

After a most interesting but tedious journey we came into the luxuriant valley at the extremity of which is St Estevan [San Esteban/Doneztebe] and is watered by a rapid river, which joining with another near the latter place, falls into the Bidassoa, the boundary river of France and Spain.

The weather being very fine and the roads good, we soon crossed the river by a bridge which was very strongly fortified by a strong barrier gate, thick walls at one end loop-holed and a gentleman's house on the same side turned into a barrack and loop-holed in the same manner.

The road led down the valley, winding with the turns of the river and all along the country presented the highest cultivation and beauty. The houses were large & commodious and generally white-washed, giving an air of cleanliness and comfort to the eye. We passed some enchanting little spots and formed a striking contrast between the industrious, homely inhabitants of those Alpine districts and of the proud indolent Spaniards. Indeed, a better character of the vain Castillian, cannot be better given than in the words of Goldsmith when speaking of the Italians:

'Contrasted faults through all their manners reign
Though poor, luxurious, though submissive, vain;
Though grave, yet trifling, zealous yet untrue,
And ev'n in penance, planning sins anew'.[50]

50 From Oliver Goldsmith's *The Traveller.*

> Under towering mountains we beheld St Estevan [San Esteban/Doneztebe], which we found by far the best of any of the villages we had yet seen in the Pyrenees. The French had possession of it for years and it was so strongly fortified that it was only to be taken by cannon, which from the impracticability of the roads could never be brought against it and therefore was a very safe stronghold of the invaders.
>
> The town consisted of a square and two long streets and the houses were good and commodious and a good market, especially of the most enticing fruit.

James here gives a fascinating insight into the daily ritual of establishing a camp after a long march.

> From the idea that headquarters were to be here, the brigade was encamped across the river in orchards on the brow of the hill and the tents and smoke arising out of the foliage of the trees had a novel appearance, but looking like the camp of a band of wandering gypsies in England. Indeed a better conception of the term 'bivouac' cannot be, than to suppose a camp of pedlars near a village in England, who tying their donkies [*sic*] to trees, light their fires under the hedge, get out their pots and pickings of the day or 'night' and cook their rustic, but ill got fare. They then pitch two blankets on poles and surrounded by their children and bags, calmly lay down to sleep. In encamping, ground near a village was generally preferred and near wood and water. The brigade were usually drawn up facing the enemy, in contiguous columns of battalions at quarter distance, or if the ground admitted at ½ distance. The rolls of the companies being called to ascertain those who might have fallen out of the ranks on the march, they piled arms and the guards, picquets, watering and wood parties were called out. The tents are pitched in rows of three to each company, those of the officers in any spot in the rear or flanks. A subaltern officer took charge of the wood and watering parties, who were regularly marched, in

order to prevent plundering or straggling. The beef is killed in advance & the soldiers were allowed one pound of beef, one pound [&] ½ of bread & ¼ of a pint of rum. As soon as we came on the ground, we chose the situation of our tents and sort wood to boil our kettles, tea being a beverage the most refreshing after a march. In half an hour after coming to the ground, we had our breakfast, our horses out for forage and our goats at grass, in fact a most complete little colony was soon established. Our next consideration was for ourselves and we strolled to the village in search of any extra comfort it might afford and principally wine. It was indeed wonderful how well in the worst of weather we had our little fare cooked and even gave snug dinner parties for necessity like:

'Misery acquaints us with strange bed fellows'.[51]

Our cattle were generally fixed to trees or stakes drove in the ground near to our own tents, our goats lay round their shepherd, a little Portuguese boy; and the servants were couched to leeward of our tents, as thick and close as a basket of figs, better securing them from the weather. When we had any idea of a short stay in any place, huts of branches were erected for our horses, bowers for cooks and a small parterre and ditch round our canvas palace. In bivouac, the men lay more connected & near their arms, without any covering and the officers if possible sheltered themselves by a tree and lay in their clothes. We were here so encircled by mountains that we had but little idea what part we were acting in the great game of chess, nor did we hear even where the noble conductor had his headquarters.

We heard distinctly the firing at San Sebastian and had every reason to suppose that its outer works and convent had fallen and that our battering guns were up and all ready to commence operations.

51 From Shakespeare's *The Tempest*.

Our amusements here were but very limited and but few females showed themselves on the promenade in the evening. The men here wore bonnets similar to those worn by the peasants of the highlands of Scotland and having attracted our notice, they soon became the undress cap of all the officers. Several of the women here were comely and very fair, but many had those extraordinary and disgusting tumours called '*goitres*' in their throats, excrescences which grow from the[m] drinking the snow water.[52] It is a curious fact that those with these enormous swellings, are happy and really considered as beauties and an old lady, the '*patrona*' of our house, wore her neck & bosom bare, on which hung one of these shocking protuberances.

We had the pleasure in the midst of our recesses to receive a mail from England, bringing us not only intelligence from our friends, but thanks from the Prince Regent and Parliament for our conduct at the Battle of Vitoria.

On the 23 [July] we received a Route to march to Sumbillo [Sunbilla], a little village on the same river, distant about ½ a league. All the ground round was so completely sown with wheat and Indian corn, that it was with great difficulty sufficient ground could be found to encamp the brigade. At this little village the scenery was very pretty and it had a neat and simple bridge over the river, which abounded with fine trout and salmon. The peasants fished here with landing nets and wading through the water, got on the stones, which they struck violently with a large wooden mallet and the fish beneath and all round, stunned by the frequent concussing, came up stupefied to the surface of the water and [were] caught in the landing nets.

There were here several amusements, a good billiard table and boulcvard and although many had the goitres, they seemed

52 Goitres are actually caused either by inflammation of the thyroid gland or iodine deficiency.

happy & content with their lot, signifying what a beautiful writer says in comparing nations:

'And yet perhaps, if countries we compare,
And estimate the blessings which they share,
Though patriots flatter, yet shall wisdom find
An equal portion dealt to all mankind.
As different good by art, or nature given
So different nations make their blessings even'.[53]

On the 24 [25 July] we heard a severe firing from San Sebastian and we soon learnt it had been stormed by a party of the 5th Division but the attempt had unfortunately failed, owing it was supposed to want of support.[54]

Sumbillo [Sunbilla] afforded us excellent fish, mutton and vegetables and we were sorry at an order arriving, to be in readiness to depart from our comfortable seclusion amongst the hills.

Marshal Soult had been appointed to the command of the French army [of Spain], under the title of Lieutenant of France and on arriving had made a declaration to recover the late misfortunes of his army.

On the 26 [July] we had orders to march immediately to St Estevan [San Esteban/Doneztebe], as it was certain Soult had or was endeavouring to turn our right, thereby obliging us to abandon the siege of San Sebastian and make an attempt to relieve or throw supplies into Pamplona.

A light brigade of horse artillery came into Sumbillo [Sunbilla] before we had left it and had lost (although the roads had been repaired) two of its guns, by inadvertently

53 From *The Traveller, or a Prospect of Society* by Oliver Goldsmith.

54 A mine was exploded on 25 July and storming parties attacked the two nearby breaches too early, whilst still dark, preventing the artillery from supporting them. They failed to break in, the Allies losing 700 killed and wounded and 300 prisoners.

going too near the edge of the precipice and fell over, but most miraculously the drivers escaped unhurt.

We reached San Estevan [San Esteban/Doneztebe] at 11 o'clock and were ordered to cover the town, whilst the two other brigades went up the river towards Lassea [Legasa] to communicate with Sir R[owland] Hill, who had been obliged to fall back from his position at and near Maya.

About midday Lord Wellington and his whole Staff came into the village bedaubed with dirt and mud and after remaining a few hours, set off in great haste for Almonda [Almandoz] on the road to Lanz [Lantz].

We remained in bivouac all day, with restrictions not to unpack our baggage, but be ready to start at a moment's notice.

[27 July] However, no Route came until next morning, when we perceived by the direction, that the army was retiring and Soult had so far succeeded as to force the 3rd and 4th Divisions on the Pamplona road. An incessant fire of cannon and musquetry was heard all day on that road, supposed to be the 3rd & 4th Divisions gradually retiring before the enemy. At 10 o'clock after a long fatiguing march of 4 leagues, we halted in a pretty wood and [were] desired to cook with all haste and [be] ready to march again at 4 o'clock. The firing was getting closer to Pamplona and considerable fears were entertained for the safety of our two little divisions who had been fighting and retiring in admirable order so long a time in the face of an army of 36,000 men, which Soult had attacked Sir Rowland [Hill] with. The brigade of Sir R[owland] Hill consisting of the 50th, 71st and 92nd Regiment[55] were stationed at the Pass of Maya and the enemy receiving information of their force by a deserter of the 71st Regiment of the particular hour the mules went for forage, and on Sunday [25 July] when the

55 Sir Rowland Hill commanded 2nd Division, and Lieutenant Colonel John Cameron of the 92nd Foot commanded the 1st Brigade as detailed above. James omits any mention of the other two brigades of the Division, who also fought there.

brigade were at Divine Service without arms, this shame to his country and name, led a strong column up the pass, who attacking the brigade unprepared, caused them to retire, taking the tents and officers' baggage. However, after several charges and expending all their ammunition, they were supported by the 6th and 82nd Regiments of the 7th Division and Sir Rowland retired in the night in good order.[56]

We resumed our labours and did not halt until dark, when we bivouacked in a thick cork wood near Lassea [Latasa], two leagues from Ostitz. The night came on extremely bad and the thunder and lightning were terrific, accompanied with severe falls of sleet and rain. Our poor bodies were in a hopeful way, drenched to the skin, no baggage, nearly tired and exhausted, no prospects of anything to eat, but the night augured hopes of a battle next day, which would set us to rights again.

The First Battle of Sorauren

[28 July] This dreadful weather continued until next morning when we set off to battle at Pamplona with well washed faces, but very empty stomachs.

At 10 o'clock we turned to the left near the village of Benefilado [Berrioplano] and coming near a hill in which the enemy were posted, the 11th Regiments and Cacadores were ordered to attack and carried it with but little loss, the Portuguese Brigade keeping possession of it all day afterwards.

We now had the pleasing sight of our two brave little corps posted on a strong position opposite the enemy between the villages of Lahuerta [Huarte] and Sorauren, into the latter below in the valley, the enemy had thrown some strong columns, being on the high Pamplona road.

56 Although the 7th Division arrived in the late afternoon and retook most of the heights in the Maya Pass, news that the troops at Roncesvalles Pass had retired persuaded Hill that his troops must also retire.

We advanced and intercepted this high road running down the valley from Sorauren and had hardly halted, when Soult directed several columns on the road, hoping to force us to give way and thereby turn the *flank* of the position chosen by General Picton and gain the high road. But he was disappointed for perceiving immediately his attention [intention], General Pack formed our division in line and the columns still advancing, gave them some well-directed fire & sent our light infantry companies down, to line the different hedges. The enemy were very bold but paid dearly for it and soon retired. They again advanced but were well received and on the arrival of a howitzer and nine pounder of ours, they scampered off, leaving the road and fields strewed with dead. The arrival of our division was of the greatest consequence, for in the morning Soult finding his progress not obstructed on the high road would have soon obliged the army to retire either to Pamplona or probably past it.

The enemy had no cannon, but Soult was determined to make another grand attempt before other reinforcements could arrive. Forming his solid columns, he charged the 4th Division in their position six different times and was as often most gallantly repulsed. Once he so far succeeded as to drive some Spaniards and Portuguese off the summit, but our troops coming immediately to their support, charged and caused dreadful slaughter. Our troops made some most beautiful and very regular charges and Soult finding all his efforts vain, gave up the contest at about 3 o'clock, confining it merely to a fire of skirmishers.

An order arrived for our brigade to march up the valley and storm the village of Sorauren, supported by the Light Brigade,[57] accordingly we advanced until we came nearly within musket shot of the enemy, who seemed fully prepared to give us a warm reception. At this moment counter orders

57 He means the light companies, as the Light Brigade/Division were not present at the battle.

were issued and we covered the men from the fire of the enemy under some banks of stones and gravel, collected in the fields. Sharp skirmishing continued until dark, when all was hushed and the scene above exhibited the appearance of a brilliant illumination and apparently the two armies, although only a hundred yards distant, had but very little dread of each other.

The enemy was very strongly posted in there in the village and had columns innumerable concealed behind the houses and churches. The hill behind was likewise lined with troops and had there been artillery, it would have been hard work to drive him from such a hold.

Collecting a little pease straw, after a frugal repast of fried stakes [*sic*], we threw ourselves down to such repose, our horses close to us.

The 1/42nd only had losses of three men killed and nineteen men wounded.

[29 July] We had every expectation of a serious attack next morning, but the thoughts of it did not hinder us napping profoundly until an hour before daylight, when we stood to our arms. At the same time the French bands and trumpets struck up and played some charming music, which being a certain signal of peace, we retired at daylight to our various places of shelter.

The morning was fine, no movement, or firing whatever was heard, the Frenchmen came out to the neutral ground to pick pease and the 29th was a day of idleness. It was not however so, with some of our comrades, for the 7th Division on their Route to join us, were ordered back to support Sir Rowland Hill, who had been attacked by very superior forces.

Our loss [in the Brigade] on the 28th exceeded one hundred and 60 men,[58] but the enemy on the 29th on the road lay in dozens, huddled one over the other, most of them in a horrid

58 Most of these casualties were suffered by the 91st Foot.

state of nudity, committed by the hordes of women following the army.

The enemy being so very pacific on the 29th and the weather cold, we threw on some more straw on our couch, got an extra blanket and even took the saddles off our horses, placing them as pillows under our heads. Everyone was confident that on a moment's alarm, he could find his things ready and about one o'clock at night we had occasion to put it in practise.

Some horses in our first line getting loose gave the picquets an alarm and were immediately fired on and the alarm instantly communicated to the whole line. The enemy's picquets and advanced post supposing likewise that they were attacked, gave a dreadful yell '*Aux Armes*' and all their lines beat to arms. In an instant our men were at their posts, but on recovering a little from our first sensations, we found some had forgot their horse's blanket, others their holsters and some riding with the pommel of their saddles unused. The Spaniards from the heights on our right began to fire and in the obscurity wounded some of our men. The enemy soon perceiving that it was a false alarm, gave up firing & he laughed most heartily at the ridiculous style some had sallied out of their coverts to the attack.

The Second Battle of Sorauren

Having been prevented from relieving Pamplona, Soult now sought to march westward to break the siege of San Sebastian, but Wellington attacked the French centre and rear, forcing them to retreat; the rear via Roncesvalles, while the advance guard and centre, having passed the bridge of Sorauren, retreated via Bera.

[30 July] The morning dawned and the enemy manifested no signs of attack, indeed he had detached some of his force to the attack of Sir Rowlands corps and seemed only to wait its result.

We received some supplies of provisions from our baggage and could have wished the protection of our tents and comfort of a clean shirt, but the proximity to our adversaries denied us having these luxuries.

Our attention was directed towards the enemy who was making several movements, some indicative of an attack, others of retreat. At 6 o'clock the skirmishing became general and the enemy seemed jealous of his right and there detached several strong columns. Our 7th Division was seen taking possession of the heights to our left and which in some degree flanked the enemy. The firing about 9 o'clock became very brisk and our artillery being ordered up, threw some shot and shell into the enemy's columns with most admirable effect.

About 11 o'clock the firing became very sharp and General Pack commanding our division was wounded severely and several other officers. The artillery continued and the principal attack began by the 3rd Division turning the left of the enemy, assisted by the 4th Division; the enemy now retired towards their centre, but columns were seen running off in all directions and our picquets and light companies supported by the brigade, attacked and soon carried the village of Sorauren. The enemy in his retreat lost many prisoners and killed and wounded, in all of which our number were inconsiderable. Nothing could be more judicious and finer than Lord Wellington's manoeuvres this day, nor could a victory be more complete, considering the strength of the enemy and the almost impracticable position he held.

General Pakenham succeeded General Pack and after giving the men a ration of spirits, we pursued the enemy and took the whole 34th French Regiment and many other men who were straggling in the mountains. The officers and men taken, complained of the want of sustenance and mentioned their having lost upwards of twenty men a company, on the 28th instant. Altogether we had diminished Soult's force to less than 22,000 men, having crossed the [Pyrenean] passes with 35,000. Their principal columns had retired by Lanz [Lantz] and Burguete [-Auritz] & many were making their retreat in the woods by unknown roads.

They had time however in the afternoon of the 30th to plunder and pillage several villages in their Route and at one we passed, all the furniture of the houses were in the fields and the poor peasants bewailing their losses were engaged in collecting mattresses, sheets, chairs, table &c and most of which were wantonly tore or broken.

Our baggage still remained behind & we slept another night in our cloaks, smothered in delectable filth and dirtiness, some of us not having had a change of linen since the 25th instant.

At the Second Battle of Sorauren the 1/42nd had one man killed and 7 men wounded. It is a remarkable fact that the entire 6th Division suffered across the two Battles of Sorauren, 42 men killed and 22 officers and 396 men wounded, but not one officer fatality.

Next morning, the 31 [July] we continued our pursuit through an uncommon wild and mountainous country, with here and there a pretty retired valley, watered by innumerable streams falling from the hills and generally a snug little village and its tapering spire, were seen peeping out of the trees at its extremity.

The roads were very bad and our men had to ford several rapid rivulets, that ran across them, which with the varied steepness & declivity of the country began to fatigue our soldiers. At 10 o'clock we halted at a small village called Iguia [Egui], where we halted for 3 hours and getting under a roof, we cleaned our heavy frames and once more got a little comfortable. At ½ past 4 o'clock very considerably refreshed, we plodded on through labyrinths of hill and dale and just as sun was setting, we suddenly came to Lasones [Lintzoain], a most enchanting little group of cottages and reminded us of those sylvan hamlets so often described as being the habitations of the happy peasants of the Alps.

In this lovely spot the 2nd & Portuguese Brigades halted and we continued our march in the dark to Burguite [Burguete-Auritz], which we found a pretty village, but completely ransacked by the enemy. The houses here being very large, the soldiers were put into quarters and overcome with fatigue threw themselves on the floor to seek refreshing sleep.

On the 31st General Hill had fallen in with the enemy near Lassea [Lizaso] and drove them from their position, taking many prisoners.

Back to the Mountain Tops

Despite their fervent hopes for a rest, the regiment was ordered to the Roncesvalles Pass.

> **[1 August]** Next morning, bringing no orders, we had a hope of rest, but 'none to the wicked' is the proverb and we marched to Burguite [Burguete-Auritz] and arrived on our ground at midday and made themselves so far comfortable. Here we were under the famous Pass of Roncesvalles and far to the east were seen the snowy tops of the high Pyrenees.
>
> 'Eternal snows the growing mass supply,
> Till the bright mountain, prop the incumbent sky,
> As atlas fixed, each hoary pile appears
> And gathered winter of a thousand years'.[1]
>
> The bright luminary shone full on our little encampment, the men had begun to cook their scanty fare and the officers were in the village, or strolling (unfatigued by their short march) on the banks of a fine river which meandered close to our ground, enjoying the delights of a wash in the limpid stream.
>
> When things were in this comparatively happy state, a precipitate order came for our brigade immediately to march and occupy the Pass of Roncesvalles. 'Curse to the woeful, inconstant life of a soldier!! I'd be rather a cobbler at his awl, or a scavenger in the streets of St Giles,[2] than an officer!!' Were

1 From *The Temple of Fame: A Vision*, by Alexander Pope.

2 The St Giles district (now part of Camden) had seen a great influx of poor people as vagrants expelled from the City of London sought an area with more generous charitable relief.

in the mouths of everyone. In rage and cruel disappointment, our 'luxurious' pots of soup, were consigned to mother earth, our lofty tents in the wood taken down and in hurry we began our march.

Our vehemence of passion far from being cooled by a hard and plenteous thunder shower, which to crown our miseries, fell just as we bent our breasts to the tremendous hill, rather served to increase it, until completely drenched and blown by the excessive steepness of the road, we could no longer vent them, but inwardly digested at every blast of sleet until we reached the summit.

The name of the pass is taken from the valley and village of Roncesvalles, between the village of Burguite [Burguete-Aurritz] and St Jean Pied de Port, the first town of France, about three leagues from the village of Roncesvalles. The road was good but the ascent great to 4 miles and when we arrived at our position on the hill of Altabascar [Altobiscar] at 7 o'clock, we were completely enveloped in thick, dense, mist or cloud, which by no means rendered our situation agreeable, not being able to ascertain our proper position or to see three yards before us.

In the best manner possible we disposed the brigade in line, defending the road by several advance picquets and two grenadier companies in support of the first line. We found on the ridge a very old line of circumvallation and two redoubts which nearly flanked our line.

Thus situated, not aware but the enemy might be within a few hundred yards of us, we pitched our tents, but with infinite danger, for the ground behind the ridge of the hill was very rugged…

[2 August] . . . and next morning at 10 o'clock, when the mist cleared a little, we found our tent standing close to a precipice of 40 feet and our horse's feet close to another. In this transient glimpse of daylight, we shifted our position and so far bettered our arrangements in case of attack.

The day even became worse than when we ascended and attended with a sort of sleet or rain and rendered it impossible to stir out of our tents. Our situation was horrid to a degree and it became more and more bleak and the mist impenetrable.

The men became badly off for provisions and our horses for forage and we almost imagined our bones bleaching on these bleak inhospitable regions of the clouds. On our right, about a league off, our right brigade were posted and the brigade of Portuguese were at the Friary of Roncesvalles near the middle of the hill, in readiness to support either brigade.

The morning of the 3 [August], the wind had changed and brought us better hopes, the sun already making many efforts to dispel our enemy and finally succeeding, we hailed him as the Greenlanders.

'The welcome sun, returns again
And brings us weather fair and fine.'[3]

As a sort of consolation for our being banished from the world, we had a most uncommon prospect and saw over upwards of thirty leagues whilst seas of mist rolled in the valleys below. We could perceive nothing of our enemy's position and some of us moved out to the front to the adjacent hills but finding out nothing except large droves of wild horses, the return of the mist compelled us to retire to our dreary shades of canvas and heath.

The sound of freedom from his chains to the ears of the prisoner, could not be more welcome, than orders for us to march next morning and with infinite satisfaction we quaffed an extra glass of grog, wishing better weather to those that bad luck brought to succeed us.

3 The song of the ancient Sun Feast, as recorded in *The History of Greenland*, published by David Crantz, London 1767.

The 4 August we rose with the sun, whose bright radiance illumined one of the most uncommon and perhaps among the most superb and sublime prospects of genuine nature. The top of our Altabascar [Altobiscar] serenity itself, the crispy dew lay in drops on the heath, whose fragrance, a soft breeze around us in wanton profusion. The whole expanse below us on all sides, where millions were laying in profound and sweet repose, appeared as a complete sea of white mist, laid on in irregular but magnificent masses over each other, whilst the brilliant luminary of the day, was breaking the ague clouds in the east, in grand refulgence [radiance]. Indeed such a splendid spectacle of nature, can hardly be described and is but rarely seen, being to us almost a compensation for climbing such a height and passing three days of penance in the clouds.

We reached the foot of the mountain at about ½ past 5 o'clock and took the road to the valley of Los Alduides [Aldudes]. The road (or footpath rather) ran through thick woods of oak, elm and beech trees, affording us now and then, some wild and picturesque scenes and a cool and refreshing shade. We met several deep ravines or gulleys, broke by the torrents in winter, which were soon placid little rivulets and watered the fertile valleys everywhere found in the Pyrenees.

The valley of Los Alduides [Aldudes] opened on us at once and was most beautiful, with the village at the upper end, enclosed by high mountains. The two passes lay on the mountains at about a mile distant from the village and we were posted with orders to defend them to the last.

We might now say we had transgressed on the sacred territory of France and we had very strict orders in no manner whatever to molest the inhabitants, who had shown so much confidence in us as to remain.

On the 5 [August] we changed our position, to the opposite ravine, by very dangerous and intricate footpaths over rocks and crags nearly impassable.

> **On the 6 [August]** the peasantry up the valley took some soldiers who had been out plundering and the armed peasantry had fortified as strongly as circumstances would admit of, a little detached rock opposite the pass of Los Alduides [Aldudes].

Another long winding march through the mountains would take them to Maya Pass.

> **[7 August]** General Hill's Division being ordered to occupy these passes, we marched on the 7th instant towards Maya, leaving a regiment to give up the posts to General Campbell's Brigade of Portuguese. Passing through the village, we ascended a steep hill, but which through the industry of the Basks [Basques], was cultivated to the summits.
>
> Here we halted and a handsome brigade of Spaniards of Don Murillos Corps,[4] passed on to join Sir Rowland Hill. The country until we reached the hills over the valley of Maya, was very barren and wild, and the roads by no means good. Elizondo a pretty village lay in a valley which we passed on our left and proceeded to near Maya, where we encamped. The houses near our ground were large and had been nearly entirely sacrificed by their 'brethren' the French troops, who it seems all expressed great happiness, that we had drove them out of Spain.

> **[8 August]** Next day we passed through Maya, a long straggling, ill built village, the cure's house being the only decent one in the whole village. Traversing thick woods and ravines up the valley from Maya about two miles, we encamped in a very bad piece of ground, with the stumps of trees remaining that had been cut down by some other brigades. Distant however about a quarter of a mile, we found a sweet little spot, close to a purling stream which ran through our copse & fell into

4 Spanish General Don Pablo Morill, Comte de Cartagena.

the neighbouring river, our three tents, horses, goats and domestics, making a separate colony and all enclosed in a spot of ground of one acre.

The other brigades had already ascended the hill towards the passes and we also . . .

James leaves a harrowing description of the battlefield of Maya Pass. It would seem that the 2nd Division who had fought here so hard and had now returned, had no inclination to clear the debris, which was left to James and his men.

. . . next morning the 9 [August] proceeding by a good road made by the 2nd Division & relieved the 34th and 39th Regiments, attended by our old friend the mist, though by no means so dense.

On this very ground the enemy had made his attack on the brigade of the 2nd Division and the slaughter had been immense for the ground lay yet covered with the sad remains of many a gallant fellow and highland bonnets, kilts and hose were strewed in every direction. In the afternoon, detachments from the different regiments of the brigade performed the last duties of humanity and laid their fallen countrymen underground.

The language here was Bascueisa [Basque] & but few spoke good French and almost none Spanish. The men were stout, tall & very muscular, wearing their breeches open and no stockings, but the women were exclusively plain and their dress by no means improved their appearance. The inhabitants of the farmhouses were very domesticated and happy, with their families and servants cultivating with great industry their portions of the valley in winter and driving their flocks of sheep in the mountains in the summer season.

From the heights on the 10 [August] we had a clear and distinct view of the interior of France, as far as thirty leagues with a good spyglass and could discern the streets of Bayonne, in whose harbour lay a fine frigate. The country appeared most luxuriant, well cultivated and possessed an agreeable variety of landscape, three considerable rivers running through it from east to west.

The enemy was in possession of two strong rocks and a ridge of hill in our front about a mile and a half from our lines and which they seemed to be strongly fortifying. Their huts which were capital, extended in different lines to our left and opposite Echalar [Etxalar], the position of our 7th Division. On our right was a very high hill and between us and it, lay a deep gulley and the head of it was observed by a subaltern's picquet. On the right of our position, or ridge of hills we had to defend, was a rock nearly opposite and similar to that possessed by the enemy and being the key to our stronghold, it was garrisoned by two companies of the 79th Regiment who had their ground on the ridge immediately below. Altogether our position was formidable, but the numerous ravines and by-paths with which the enemy were well acquainted, made the greatest caution necessary . . .

. . . and on the 12 [August] strong looking parties from the division began to throw up redoubts & breastworks, throwing down abattis and strengthening the rock and commanding heights of the position. Several detachments of the enemy had been observed going round to our right and from their frequent drilling, we supposed few were in our front, but conscripts.

The weather had been very fine and clear & with this exception, that until the 13th our poor men were on low rations, we were pretty well off.

The hills on which we were, produced nothing but fern and although in our front there were some valleys of Indian corn, (it was dangerous not knowing the dens and gullies of the ravines to go there without a regular party), which was sent and brought back excellent forage.

It was rumoured that a principal part of the enemy's force was going to our right in order again to gain admittance into

Spain by Oleron [Oloron-Sainte-Marie], as the Pass of Jaca and is the high road to Zaragoza, when they might join Suchet's Corps and advance on Pamplona. This movement might make our army fall back but would neither oblige us to abandon the siege of St [San] Sebastian nor the blockade of Pamplona.

On the 16 [August] the firing at St [San] Sebastian still was unceasing, but we had no accounts of the results. The weather this day being very clear, a party was formed consisting of some officers and eight light infantrymen, to ascend the high mountain on our right[5] and reconnoitre the position of the enemy and in what point it might have connection with our own.

Mounting our mules and taking two led ones with the intention of bringing home some sheep, we commenced our journey and about 11 o'clock began to wind round the point of the hill in front, gradually ascending by a sort of footpath, which our mules carried us over, not without running considerable risk of falling over the precipices into the deep gullies on our left side of the path. However at 10 o'clock having weathered the point of the hill, we cautiously advanced and stood on a high crag, over-topping gullies unfathomable and commanding a view of the French position to the left.

Retracing our steps along the declivity of this advanced point, we suddenly were surprised at the sight of three peasants who had come out of the wood below and who on perceiving us instantly disappeared. We now began to ascend the mountain from its point, which bore most excellent pasture. In the woods below us, on every side we heard the tinkling of sheep bells and we dispatched the servant with the mules & escort to try to purchase some sheep, while we proceeded on to the summit of the mountain.

Not a speck dimmed the brightness of the atmosphere and we lay on the grass for upwards of an hour, enjoying the most delightful prospect. We beheld at one *coup d'oeil* the

5 This would appear to refer to the Baztan Mountain.

country from near Bordeaux to St [San] Sebastian, Bayonne, St Jean de Luz, the rivers Adour, Nive and Nivelle. Our own formidable position from the cloudy Roncesvalles to Fontarabia [Fuenterrabia],[6] St Jean Pied de Port and the whole French encampment from right to left. The happy and beautiful appearance of the interior of France inspired us with ideas of our own lovely spot, but yet not to be put in comparison with it when described by the poet.

'A fairer isle than Britain, never seen,
Viewed in his wide career! A lovely spot
For all that life can ask! Salubrious! Mild!
It hills are green! Its woods and prospects fair!
Its meadows fertile! And to crown the whole,
In one delightful word. It is our home.
Our native isle.'[7]

We almost found ourselves rivetted to this charming scene, but it was getting late and after having partook of some bread and cheese, we came back and endeavoured for a while to follow the path of the sheep, down the east face of the mountain, which was covered with the most delightful bilberries and immense flocks of sheep and goats browsing, seemingly unheeded by any person. On our appearance they [the shepherds] probably had left their flocks and disappeared. Our sheep path narrowed at every step and we became involved in insuperable difficulties. Each side of the path was so *escarpe* [steep], that our horses could not turn without falling down the precipice, no path in our front was now discoverable and we had to clamber over immense stones and rocks, where if our animal had stumbled, they must have been precipitated into the gulley. Nothing was left but to proceed and we most fortunately came to plain ground at the foot of the mountain,

6 Modern-day Hondarribia.

7 From a poem entitled *Alfred* by Joseph Cottle.

without the least accident happening either to man or mule. The mules and sheep had luckily followed a more secure path and got to camp long before us and where we soon arrived, delighted with our day's excursion.

By the 18 August our works, from the regularity carried on and continuation of fine weather were well advanced and our rock had become a Gibraltar in miniature.

A flag of truce had been sent into the Count d'Erlon,[8] commanding the French lines opposite carrying letters from General Hill and Castanos and bringing back the joyful intelligence that peace was soon expected by the whole French army.[9]

Several reinforcements for the army was [*sic*] daily arriving at the port of Passages [Pasaia] and the fine brigade of Guards from Oporto, had joined the 1st Division upwards of 1,400 strong.[10]

[20 August] There was [*sic*] reports on the 20th that Lord Wellington meant to advance, keeping his right on St Jean Pied de Port and his left on St Jean de Luz, but it was more probable that no move would be made until the fall of St [San] Sebastian and surrender of Pamplona.

[21 August] From the movements of the enemy in our front on the 21st, strong suspicions were entertained of their moving to our right and the picquets were ordered to be on the alert & our baggage packed.

---

8 General Jean Drouet, Comte d'Erlon.

9 A ceasefire had been agreed between France and the Allies in Germany, which was thought to presage a peace deal: the possibility of it happening caused Wellington to delay his advance into France. Austria throwing in her lot with the Allies and the crushing defeat of the French at Leipzig destroyed all hopes of a peace.

10 This Guards brigade (1st & 3rd Battalions 1st Foot Guards) had been left at Oporto to recover from a virulent fever which left the troops unable to take part in the majority of the 1813 campaign.

On the morning of the 22 [August] we were under arms at 3 o'clock, but there was no attack on the part of the enemy and all was quiet except the thundering of the cannon at St [San] Sebastian. At noon we took some of the regiments to the ridge of the hill to endeavour to entice the enemy to show his numbers, but our ruse had not the desired effect. The good weather still favoured us and our amusements were shooting in the glens, reading or rambling up and down the adjacent hills.

The joyful reports of peace were still in circulation and that even the preliminaries were entered into and England sent her member to congress at Prague.

[23 August] The French officers with whom we conversed with on the 23rd gave very different information, that Massena was daily expected with a reinforcement of 30,000 men from Italy and offensive operations should again be renewed. This we put down as a gasconade and '*bizarrerie*' [oddity] of our friends '*Les Messieurs*' for want of other news.

On the 24 [August] all our works were finished and we slept thereby infinitely more at ease and secure from surprise, the redoubts, breastworks and fleches, being so very numerous and well connected, that before they could drive us from our ground, innumerable men must they lose and awful would be the carnage. At night the camps of both armies displayed the most brilliant illuminations and every morning as we rose with the sun, the view of the French coast, Bayonne & interior of the country was beautiful and varied. Although every night we laid our heads on the pillow with an idea of an attack before morning, our situation was by no means unpleasant and hopes of either having peace, or orders for advancing soon, animated and kept up our spirits.

On the 26 [August] severe firing was heard from St [San] Sebastian and it was hoped that our heavy batteries had opened, but all at once the dreadful peals discontinued and next day were not reassumed, which arose conjectures of a capitulation. Several conscripts of 14 years of age were joining the French army and 250 louis d'or[11] were paid for substitutes until next draught.

On the 28 [August] no firing was to be heard from St [San] Sebastian which nearly confirmed our suspicions of its fall. Two of our soldiers escaped from Bayonne and having been assisted with clothes and provisions by some American sailors, miraculously made their way into our camp. They reported that everything was in alarm, that the old were made to work, while the young were sent to the army and said that at Bayonne they believed the army had but 25,000 since the Battle of Vitoria.

[29–30 August] Our conjectures respecting St [San] Sebastian were refuted by a heavy and continued fire on the 29th and 30th, which proceeded from our newly erected heavy batteries. In the evening, as the enemy had been seen in the morning to withdraw some of his force from our front to their left, the brigade moved out of their respective camps and forming our light infantry in front, marched out in regular order as far as the advanced picquet and there halted until dark when we returned to our ground.[12] The French picquet lighted a beacon on which their lines stood to arms and probably owing to our demonstration remained so all night.

Next day the 31 [August], the Cacadores in our front pushed on and took one of the enemy's line of huts and a height commanding their camp. This height after a good deal of skirmishing was retaken by the enemy, but at 9 o'clock, the

11 The Louis d'or was worth 20 Francs; therefore 250 Louis d'or was worth 5,000 Francs. The French Franc was valued at 19.5 Francs to an English Pound in 1813; therefore 5,000 Francs was the equivalent of £256 8s 2d – this equates to some £14,000 today.

12 Wellington had ordered this simulated attack

79th & 91st Regiments moved to the front on the right, the Portuguese brigade[13] advancing with the light companies of the left brigade in the centre, again took the height & pushing on still further burnt two lines of huts, advancing until they came to a narrow, deep rivulet, when they halted. Manoeuvring and skirmishing all day and coming to no decisive attack, convinced us that some part of our position had been assaulted and about 1 o'clock there was heard a most tremendous cannonade from not only St [San] Sebastian, but from the positions occupied by the Light and 4th Divisions.[14] In the afternoon after bringing up the 3rd Division in columns, the enemy showed a force of about 4,000 men and it was evident that some had been detached to our left. The Portuguese brigade having advanced too far, but in the most gallant style, were drawn back after suffering considerable loss and all the troops retired to their different camps, the firing on the left likewise ceasing.

This day had been extremely hot and sultry and at 3 o'clock when returning to camp a most severe storm of thunder and lightning overtook us but attended with little rain. The sky at 4 o'clock became again severe and we sat down to our dinner in the tent, which was pitched rather below in a fine spot of ground surrounded by ferns and oak trees. About ½ past 4, when taking our soup, the sky became clouded, the clouds lowered and a shower of hail fell, the most terrific ever beheld. At first, they beat against the tent like a musket ball and immediately became with prodigious fury, the size of an egg, tearing the branches off the trees, mowing down the ferns and obliging us three, to stand, wet to the skin, to support the pole

13 Lieutenant Colonel James Douglas's Portuguese Brigade attached to the 6th Division (8th & 12th Line Regiments and 9th Cacadores) advancing with strong support, convinced D'Erlon that he was under attack and he sought reinforcements from Soult. The Portuguese brigade suffered losses of 11 officers and 238 men killed and wounded. Oman and Fortescue have this brigade under the command of Colonel Madden, but he had been relieved by Lt Colonel Douglas on 22 August.

14 The firing would have come mostly from the Battle of San Marcial, in which the Spanish forces defeated Soult's advance over the River Bidassoa in an attempt to relieve San Sebastian.

of our tent. It had continued unabated for ½ an hour and we dreaded every successive blast would bring the [hail]stones as large as portmanteaus and hurry us to destruction. But the sky brightened and we peeped out, but beheld a leafless desolated waste.

Our little repast was left destroyed & swimming on the table, our horses and goats had fled down the valleys. In the camp, several of the [hail]stones were measured and found to be upwards of nine inches in circumference and were so hard congealed, that several of the men on sentry were knocked down and much bruised, tents torn and three of our brass drums tore in pieces. The few inhabitants who were at the time in camp selling their bread &c, took shelter in the tents, but assured us they never had seen such a tremendous shower.

The sun beamed but for a short moment and the evening came on with lightning & heavy falls of rain, torrents running from the mountains and the storm leaving us in such a miserable situation that we could almost have said with Thomson:

'Here winter holds his unrejoicing court,
And through his airy hall the land misrule,
Of driving tempest is for ever heard;
There the grim tyrant meditates his wrath;
There arms his winds, with all subduing frost,
Mould his fierce hail and treasures up his snows,
With which he now opposes half the globe.'[15]

We were naturally very anxious to hear of the fortunes of yesterday and not until evening did we receive the gratifying intelligence of the storming and capture, by our brave troops of the town and outer works of St [San] Sebastian. Likewise, that Soult's attack of our position had failed and all his attempts on the 4th Division and Spaniards were completely

15 From *The Seasons* by James Thomson. However, 'unrejoicing' should read 'rejoicing'.

baffled and with a very considerable loss. About 9 o'clock at night, a firing was heard on our right towards Los Alduidas [Aldudes] but soon ceased. The castle [of Monte Orgullo at San Sebastian] still held out, but every hope was entertained of its soon surrendering.

On the 2 [September] the Portuguese again advanced and the enemy retired without much resistance, up as far [as] the village wherein their principal force was encamped.

On the 4 September the firing at St [San] Sebastian had ceased and the castle had surrendered, with about 2,000 prisoners. Their number was reduced 2,000 men by the siege and it was said the governor had given up the castle contrary to the wish of the 2nd in command, General St John.[16] Our loss at the storming amounted to 1,200 men in killed and wounded and our cannon during the assault even fired over our men's heads in the breche [breach].[17]

Now that St [San] Sebastian had fallen, the enemy were doubly vigorous in entrenching their position and villages. Pamplona still held out, but on the 6th and 7th September every indication was making by the enemy to lead us to suspect an attack on Roncesvalles or Alduides [Aldudes].

A large supply of every sort of provision and army stores, together with a strong force, was collecting at St Jean Pied de Port, supposed to be for Pamplona, if an opportunity offered.

On the 9 [September] suspicions were entertained that a push might be made on our right by the high hill and accordingly the 94th Regiment of the 3rd Division and our light infantry companies were sent to watch thereon, the enemy's movements. Two deserters from the French reported Count d'Erlon to have

16 He means Colonel Jean de Songon, who was Rey's Chief of Staff at San Sebastian.

17 Allied losses during the entire siege were near 5,000 killed and wounded.

opposed to us, upwards of 21,000 men, but half of them were conscripts.

Forage had already become very scarce, being obliged to send for it upwards of three leagues and then steal it from the inhabitants. The weather had been extremely bad, which together with the scarcity of forage, reduced our horse's condition and made them look quite miserable.

The French officers had the politeness to send us in a *Moniteur*,[18] which contained the news of the Allies having attacked Bonaparte in his position at Dresden & were repulsed, losing 4,000 men. That next day the *Grand Empereur* became the assailant and beat the allies with the loss of 15,000.[19] Little or no credit was attached to these reports of their unreliable *Moniteur*, although it was very probable that ere this a grand conflict had taken place on the continent.

[15–18 September] Sir Rowland Hill on the 15th had an idea that the enemy would make his attack at the Alduides [Aldudes], or here with us and wished to put us on our guard, however up to the 18th instant, no attempt was made on any part of our position.

Our sick in these Alpine and varied regions were very few, although the weather had been very bad and what is always worse, most changeable. It had been for some time very good, but the equinoxes were fast approaching and we dreaded another hail battle, the people asserting we could not possibly remain on the heights in October. It was already stated as certain that the cavalry that were in the rear, had been ordered up and the pontoons on the high road at Irun and everything getting ready for an advance.

18 *Le Moniteur* newspaper was the official mouthpiece of the French government.

19 The Battle of Dresden (26–27 August) saw the Allies lose 14,000 killed and wounded and 24,000 captured.

On the 20 [September] we received a mail from England and we were most happy to find by it, that Austria had added her strength to the allies and that hostilities had again commenced. The same afternoon the officer of the French picquet advanced and placing a paper between two stones, retired when our officer went and took it. It contained extracts in French, English, Portuguese and Spanish of the defeats sustained by our allies, whose army they asserted had been reduced to 80,000 men and the rebel General Moreau killed.[20]

After perusal it was returned in the same manner, with extracts from the *Moniteur* which had mentioned Soult being at Vitoria on the 1 August and that General Graham had been killed, in order to show them what little confidence we put in the news of their *Moniteur*.

It rather appeared now by the labours of the enemy in fortifying his heights that he dreaded an attack, more than he did and Pamplona was the only detriment we had to our advancing.

Towards the end of September we were getting very anxious and tired of our situation, continually being tantalised with the fine appearance of the country below us, whose people were enjoying their harvest with beautiful weather, while we experienced the most changeable. Our little markets in camp had increased and Maya and Elizondo presented everything in abundance, but rather extravagant.

Towards the 1 October the Commander in Chief, whose headquarters had been at Vera [Bera], passed our lines and with some engineer officers, minutely examined the enemy's position, which we conceived a precedent to an advance. His Lordship with his usual celerity went to Roncesvalles with very few attendants and was supposed to have returned to Vera [Bera].

---

20 General Jean Moreau was a French officer and a great rival of Napoleon, and was suspected of plotting to overthrow him. He was banished to America in 1805, but returned to advise the Allies in 1813, and was mortally wounded at the Battle of Dresden.

General Colville[21] soon after, inspected our brigade and gave us hopes of advancing into France next week, which put us all in a flurry, getting our horses, mules, baggage &c in trim for the march. Pamplona however was an obstacle and would yet hold out until the 25th instant at least.

On the 6 [October] a general officer with a grand suite reviewed the whole French troops in our front, appearing to be about 12,000 men, in high order, wearing long blue coats and white overhauls [*sic*]. This evening we had a sudden order again to advance and make a demonstration in favour of our left who were to attempt an advance.

Accordingly on the 7 [October] our Cacadores, brigade of Portuguese and some of the 2nd [Brigade], moved forward and the Portuguese soon turned the feigned, into a real attack, carrying the works and redoubts at the point of the bayonet. At 10 o'clock, our brigade advanced and drove in their picquets, posting our sentries close to their fortified rock. It seemed this was all that was wanted and we retired again at 4 o'clock, when the attack on the left seemed only beginning. The firing was very lively for some time, but we could form no idea of its results.

On the 8 [October] however we ascertained everything had succeeded to Lord Wellington's wishes and that the La Rhune mountain had been carried, the Spaniards also behaving exceedingly well.

On the 9 [October] we were again put in march and found not more than 1,800 men on the opposite hill. A severe firing was on our left and we could perceive the enemy's huts on fire as our troops advanced.

21 Major General the Honourable Sir Charles Colville had temporarily commanded 6th Division from 8 August until Henry Clinton returned in mid-October, when Colville returned to the 3rd Division.

At five o'clock we sent for our tents and encamped in the immediate vicinity of the French position, two miles in front of our old ground. The firing on the left had not ceased at dark and the night came on most tempestuous.

On the 10 [October] no move was made, indeed it was a continued torrent of rain, all day and night, attended with such severe gusts of wind as nearly blew down our tents.

We had succeeded far above our expectations on the left, for the Light Division had taken the enemy's position round the La Rhune and the Spaniards the village of Zarre [Sare], whilst Sir T[homas] Graham had crossed the Bidassoa with the 1st and 5th Divisions.[22] The Spaniards exerted themselves wonderfully and several prisoners were taken and 9 pieces of cannon.[23]

On the 12 [October] we remained in our camp but the light companies were sent up a strong position on our right to reconnoitre where the enemy had a small picquet, who soon retired.

They had a most commanding view of all the French position of the rivers Adour and Nive, on the latter the people were busily engaged in fortifying its banks.

To the very great regret of his corps and the army in general, Sir Thomas Graham from ill health, found himself obliged after seeing the army across the Bidassoa, to give up the command to Sir John Hope and return to England.

We had been very quiet in our camp, sometimes conversing with the French officers on picquet (who however was [*sic*] more distant than they formerly were, owing to an expectation of attack).

Until the night of the 14 [October] when a firing was heard on our left rather close and our picquets stood to arms.

22 The 5th Division crossed at Hendaye and the 1st Division at Behobie.

23 Some seventeen pieces of artillery were captured.

Sleeping generally with part of our clothes on, we soon also were on the alert and gaining the ridge of the hill, perceived the firing to proceed from the ground the Spaniards occupied at Zarre [Sare]. At 2 o'clock in the morning, the skirmishing was very sharp and the fire seemed retiring on our part, when at daybreak, the enemy bringing up some cannon and a strong force, obliged the Spaniards to yield Zarre [Sare] and a redoubt they had before taken.

Towards the 17 [October], the weather became very bad and attended with such severe gales of wind, that blew down & tore our tents in pieces.

On the 20 [October] indeed, the men were obliged to take down their tents and lay exposed to the sleet and wind on the side of the hill. The assertions of the peasants we found by experience, were true and our anxiety to advance or retire was daily increasing as it seemed protracted. The fall of Pamplona was our only hope and it was known by intercepted letters that it could not hold out longer than the 1st of the month [November], as its governor proposed to Marshal Soult to send him troops to meet him and he should endeavour to escape.

Although not mentioned previously, James must have applied to serve with the Portuguese Army, which would immediately give him a step up to Brevet Captain. At the same time, his father made his way to the coast and returned to England. The cause of these changes are unknown, but it is highly likely that the two were linked.

On the 22 October I found myself nominated to a grenadier company of Portuguese and in the 11th [Line] Regiment of the 4th Division.[24] Accordingly, I lost no time in joining my

24 The Portuguese Brigade of the 4th Division consisted of the 7th Cacadores and the 11th and 23rd Line Regiments. The brigade was commanded by Lieutenant Colonel James Miller, 23rd Line Regiment.

new service and accompanying Colonel Stirling on his way to England, we set off to Passages [Pasaia], coming to Echalar [Etxalar], the quarters of the 7th Division, the first night. We crossed over the greatest parts of our most formidable position, a country more remarkable for its strength and wildness, than for cultivation or beauty. The road to Echalar [Etxalar] was only for men and mules, laying sometimes on the very edge of a precipice, rendering our situation at times rather precarious and awakening not a little our nervous system. Just as we were entering Echalar [Etxalar], we had our faces washed and bodies besprinkled with a copious shower of rain and stood under it, until the Mairee and Quarter Master General got us a habitation, which was by no means superb, or elegant, but served to shelter ourselves and cattle from the impetuous elements.

Echalar [Etxalar] is in one of the fertile Peysurean [Pyrenean] valleys and has the Bidassoa running through it, by no means an insignificant river even here.

Next morning by the banks of the river, we continued our road to Vera [Bera] and found yesterday and last night's rain had by no means improved the roads, which were almost impassable before. We however paddling through clay and dirt, arrived on the Bidassoa, where we were throwing across a bridge of pontoons and we forded it although very rapid and deep. The country here seemed to be abundant in mines of iron and tin, but they were little wrought, although we found some iron manufactories, but apparently much neglected. The weather was good and the fine romantic country made our ride very agreeable, until we reached Vera [Bera], which is a tolerable large village, containing several good houses, a large church and a square.

We halted this day at Vera [Bera] and had the honour of dining with the *Hero of the Age*, whose splendid achievements and fortunate services has bestowed on him an unprecedented military character, whilst his urbanity of manners and affability (seeming to forget the knowledge of his transcendent victories) makes all around happy and himself beloved by the army in general.

The road from Vera [Bera] to the point of high road leading from Vitoria to Bayonne was really impassable and we found ourselves obliged to leap into the fields, over ditches and hedges until we came to the grand high road. It was near Irun and the river was navigable to Fuentarribia [Hondarribia], where it fell into the sea. Our artificers were establishing a bridge over the river of pontoons, the former having been carried away. Above on the steep bank, here bivouacked the Spanish corps of General Freyre [Freire][25] and were daily improving in discipline.

The road was now excellent and we soon passed through Irun, a pretty village, with several good houses and shops. Turning to the right, towards Passages [Pasaia], we again got bad narrow roads and at Lasso [Lezo], the hill on which it winded along was very steep, on the tinge of the Bay at Passages [Pasaia]. We came all at once above this extraordinary town and everything was bustle and hurry, loading mules with provisions for the army, others returning, [with] men and stores landing from England and boats sailing to and fro, rowed by females. The scenery to us was novel and most interesting, but the entrance to the town was completely blocked up with mules coming and going with their cargoes, so that we could hardly pass.

Passages [Pasaia] is situated on the foot of a rock and has only one very narrow lane and is all the communication except by water throughout the town. This lane runs for more than a mile and is terminated by a redoubt or strong post,[26] commanding the entrance of the harbour, which is rather a dangerous one, being very narrow and between two high ridges of rock.

25 General Manuel Freire de Andrade.

26 This strongpoint is on the eastern bank at Pasai Donibane: it has been converted into a house.

The number of people running through this place was immense and consisted of a mixture of every nation. Every article of life from Spain, France and England, were here concentrated and sold cheap. There were two dirty inns

Spanish muleteer.

> in the town, but whose charges were enormous and but ill attended. Two tolerable Spanish regiments did duty here and our detachments and convalescents were in camp outside the town.

James now transferred to the 11th Portuguese Line Regiment, as a Captain, British officers being given the next brevet rank on joining the Portuguese Army; but reverting back to one rank lower if they later returned to the British Army. The 11th Line, with the 23rd Line and 7th Cacadores, formed the 9th Portuguese Brigade, attached to the 4th Division. These two line regiments were deemed to have distinguished themselves at the Battle of Vitoria, along with the 9th and 21st Regiments. All four regiments were granted a special inscription, which was added to the central white field of the Royal Arms on their Colours.

> **On the 27 October** [I] returned from Passages [Pasaia] and joined the 4th Division near Vera [Bera], a short distance from the La Rhune mountain taken by the Spaniards and Light Division last advance. Our division were encamped in rather a pretty situation, but the ground being clayey and the men confined to so very small a spot of ground, the bad weather had made the earth ankle deep and to pass from each other's tents, we were forced to cut down large trees and with them make a sort of bad footpath.
>
> The colonel of my regiment,[27] had made himself a little separate territory by enclosing his tent, servants tent, stable and an excellent little wigwam, with large branches of trees & there being a very tolerable chimney in the hut, we enjoyed ourselves in the bad weather, with smoking and drinking and eating, despising the luxuries of 'England' and its epicures.
>
> The salutary effects of smoking in camp is indispensable and may be seen by the following 'Address to a segar [*sic*]' by a very particular friend, who did me the kindness to send it me, advising the use of that inestimable vegetable.

27 Lieutenant Colonel Alexander Anderson commanded the 11th Line Regiment.

Address to a Segar – Pyrenees

Hail!, blest segar thou comfort of my life,
Thou source of joy, my ever darling wife,
Come sweetly moisted from the dewy vine,
And drive these vapours from this mouth of mine.

Thrice happy was I, when in India's clime,
I first did feel thy effects benign,
When up in water to the chin
Yet ne'er a drop did get within.

Full many a night in Albion happy land
I've thee enjoyed; while tumbler in my hand.
I have often drank to friends and war
Thee in my cheek my loved segar.

In foreign lands, thee I have known,
On Egypt's shores and Port Mahon,
In Gibraltar, thy fame I've spread
While snug reclining in my bed.

In Lusitanian and Hispanias lands,
Thee have I smoked by chosen hands,
At morn, at noon, in gloomy night,
E'en in the hostile bustle of the fight.

Then let my tongue thy praises sound,
Till all the earth, thy fame rebound,
I'll echo still in peace and war,
Thy glorious worth, '*My loved Segar*'.[28]

By a road considerably higher than our camp, some nine pounders were drawn down towards Zarre [Sare] with bullocks and posted in front of our position.

28 This is clearly the anonymous officer's own composition.

On the 1 November, Pamplona at last surrendered and its garrison marched out prisoners of war next morning, an event which had been greatly protracted and surpassed all the calculations formed at first. Now our future operations would soon be decided, indeed at headquarters, an advance was immediately anticipated and confidently spoken of.

Our winter quarters as yet had been very indifferent (not to say more) and we trusted our illustrious chief, notwithstanding the awful preparations made to hinder us, would grant the army permission to establish ourselves in the South of France.

Mails from home arrived, which enumerated the great successes of our allies and filled us with envy to cooperate with them. Medals and gold clasps had arrived as a donation from the Prince Royal [Regent] to officers commanding regiments at the siege of Badajoz and Salamanca and had a great effect on the army and would have been even more so, had it extended to meritorious officers of a lower class and deserving soldiers.

The 5 and 6 [November] the weather was considerably better and dried up the ground and roads so much, that our artillery came up and here encamped in a small valley on our left. The Spaniards were posted close to the village of Zarre [Sare], which was protected by two very strong redoubts, houses barricaded and filled with troops.

On the 7 [November] everything appeared in order and readiness for an immediate grand attack, for as we had suspected, the order came in the afternoon to be ready to march at 3 o'clock in the morning, right in front. At 8 o'clock however, a counter order arrived to march, not till further orders owing to some interruption caused by the roads and General Hill's column not being able to arrive at its destination in time, to co-operate with the rest of the army.

Next day [8 November], a deserter came in from the enemy and informed us that they had been expecting an attack for the three last days, occupying the lines and redoubts every morning at 2 o'clock and remaining until 7 o'clock, determined to make us buy our lodgings dearly.

On the 9 [October] no orders came until very late, when the same were repeated as on the 7th and we were fully convinced the 10 November would be a glorious, but hard-won day.

The Battle of Nivelle

Having crossed the Bidassoa a month before, Wellington now launched an attack on the ridges studded with redoubts around La Rhune Mountain with the aim of gaining the defensible river line of the Nivelle. The 4th Division was tasked with capturing the redoubts near Sare, the 9th Brigade taking two redoubts; the 7th Cacadores who led suffering heavy casualties. Once Sare was cleared, the Division continued moving north to the River Nivelle.

[10 November] At 2 o'clock we got under arms and at 3 began to grop[e] our way in the dark until we arrived at the Spanish camp at 4 o'clock. We were drawn up in contiguous columns and we halted until day broke over us and gave hopes of fine weather.

Lord Wellington & Staff then came up, bringing the artillery against the redoubts and sending our little battalion of [7th] Cacadores to skirmish on the left of the village and the 2nd and 53rd Regiments[29] against the redoubt.

The first gun fired by the 4th Division was the signal for the army to begin the attack and at one we heard on all sides the reverberations of the dreadful implements of war.

29 The 2nd and 2/53rd were so depleted in numbers that they had been formed into the 2nd Provisional Regiment and commanded by the officers and NCOs of the 53rd Foot, the officers and NCOs of the 2nd Foot returning home to recruit.

Lord Wellington appeared anxious, but with a smile on his countenance and rubbing his hands at every gun that was fired, seemed to say I'll diddle them. The 7th Division were advancing on our right in fine style and drove the enemy before them, taking the redoubt on the left of Zarre [Sare].

Our redoubt (as we already called it) kept up a heavy fire of artillery, but the two regiments advancing in fine style to the storm, came up to the ditch without firing a shot, threw in their sacks and took it immediately with 200 prisoners at the point of the bayonet. Our noble Cacadores were equally successful in the village, but although we heard the firing, yet we could not see its effects on the left.

The whole division now in columns advanced to the attack of the grand position and passing through the village, suffered a little from the well-directed fire of the enemy's artillery and redoubts. The position before us was the most imposing ever beheld, fortifications on its summit, the works of three months hard labour and filled with troops. The attack on our right and left had begun and we had already seen the Light Division driving them on our left from post to pillar, in gallant order.

The 7th Division advanced in line with us and gained one of the heights of the enemy's ridge and keeping their ground, kept moving on until they joined our division on the summit of the position, gaining it with comparatively little resistance.

The enemy seeing his flanks turned retreated, but in good order, leaving a redoubt with 800 men and several battalions of light infantry. The redoubt soon surrendered and we pushed them until 2 o'clock & took up a position in front of Zarre [Sare], about 2 miles. The left was ordered to make a feigned attack and our right had been well pushed on. The enemy in the night retired across the Nive and left us of a position that in the possession of Britons would have been impregnable.

The taking of this formidable position gave us a clear passage into France as far as the Adour and the further advance of Lord Wellington would at present greatly depend on the state of the weather and we had secured in St Jean de Luz, Ustaritz and the intervening villages sufficient winter quarters for the army.

The 11th Line Regiment reported three officers slightly wounded (Lt Colonel Alexander Anderson, Brevet Captain Ignacio Pereira de Lacerda and Lieutenant & Adjutant Simao Clemente), with one man killed and twenty-five men wounded. In comparison, the 7th Cacadores suffered seventy-seven casualties.[30]

Routes and Distances marched from 1 December 1812 to 11 November 1813

Names of Places	Leagues	Miles	Remarks
Carried over to Cea [Seia]	328½	1252	Winter Quarters
Marched [Remained?] at Cea [Seia] until 29 April	42	168	By Brigade
Midones [Midoes]	4	16	Fine country. Roads bad.
Moimenta da Serra	6	24	Good roads.
Celorico [da Beira]	5	20	Encamped
Trancoso	4	16	Encamped
Marialva	3	12	Good roads.
Total	**392½**	**1508**	
Villa Nova de Foscoa [Vila Nova de Foz Coa]	3½	13½	
Serra de Moncorvo [Torre de Moncorvo]	3	12	Plentiful Country
Fornos	4	16	
Villa Della [Vila de Ala]	3	12	Good Forage
Malhada[s]	3	12	Good Forage
Paradilla [Paradela]	2	8	Good Roads
Caravajales [Carbajales de Alba]	3	12	Barren Country
Palaseos [Palacios del Pan]	3	12	Crossed Esla

30 Gaudencio & Burnham, *In the Words of Wellington's Fighting Cocks*, pp. 192–3.

Names of Places	Leagues	Miles	Remarks
Zamora	3	12	Good Roads
Tagara Bunena [Tagarabuena]	5	15	Good Country
Morailes [Morales de Toro]	4	12	Good Country
St Salvador [San Salvador de Hornija]	2	6	Fine Country
Penaflor [de Hornija]	2	6	Fine Country
Villa Alba [Villalba de los Alcores]	4	12	Ground Bad
Villa Gimene [Villajimena]	4	12	Flat Country
Samara [Tamara de Campos]	3	9	Most Romantic
Stera de la Vega [Itero de la Vega]	3	9	Pretty Country
Villa Silos [Villasilos]	2	6	Pretty Country
To Name Unknown	3	9	Wild Country
Villa Mure Depuresta [Villanueva de Puerta]	5	15	and very bad
St Martin de Hellenes [San Martin de Elines]	6	18	rugged roads
Mandanega [Manzanedo]	4	12	Crossed Ebro
Villalcayo [Villarcayo]	2	6	
Medina de Pomar	1½	4½	Flat Country
Quincoces [de Yuso]	4	12	
Total	**475½**	**1781**	
Anda	5	15	
Vitoria	4	12	
[Arrasate o] Mondragon	5	15	High Road to
Vitoria	5	15	Bayonne
Penacerrada [or Urizaharra]	6	18	Beautiful
Logrono	6	18	Country
Lodosa	7	21	
Levin [Lerin]	2	6	Hilly Country
Puente de la Reyna	4	12	
Near Pamplona	3	9	
Ostitz	3½	11½	Very bad
Lanz [Lantz]	3	9	Rough roads
St Estevan [Sanesteban/ Doneztebe]	5½	16½	Hilly Country

Names of Places	Leagues	Miles	Remarks
Sumbilla [Sunbilla]	1½	4½	
St Estevan [Sanesteban/ Doneztebe]	1½	4½	
Lassaca [Latasa],	5	15	Wild Country
Opposite Sorauren	3	9	In position
Opposite Sorauren	½	1½	against enemy
Village near Ostitz	2½	7½	
Burguete [-Auritz]	6	18	Bad Roads
Roncesvalles Pass	4	12	& Steep
Los Alduides [Aldudes]	4	12	Fine Valleys
Heights above Los Alduides [Aldudes]	2	6	
Heights above Maya	4	12	On the
To Position	3½	7½	Pyrrenean
In Position	6	18	Mountains
Total	**578**	**2086½**	
Maya	1½	4½	Cold Weather
Echalar [Etxalar]	3½	7½	
Vera [Bera]	2	6	Narrow Roads
Passages [Pasaia]	5	15	Hardly Passable
Camp near Vera [Bera]	5½	16½	
Attack of Fortified position	3½	11½	
Passed Nive	2	6	Bad Clayey
Into Quarters	1	3	Roads
To 11 November 1813	**602**	**2156½**	

On 9 December, Marshal Soult launched a major attack on Hill's troops, which were isolated on the eastern bank of the River Nive and the fighting continued on both banks over the ensuing four days. The 4th Division remained in reserve for almost the entire battle, being at Arbonne on 10 December. James does not mention anything at all, but the 7th Cacadores and a single company of the 11th Line Regiment were engaged, there is no known loss for the 11th Regiment, the 7th Cacadores only reporting five wounded. It can be safely assumed that James was not involved in any fighting.

1814 – South of France

We unfortunately do not have any journal for this year from James Stirling, but knowing that he remained with the 11th Portuguese Line Regiment until September 1814, we can reconstruct in some part his experiences during this period.

The Duke of Wellington was forced to retain the troops in winter quarters until mid-February as the incessant rains turned the roads into quagmires, seriously hampering both troop movements and the commissariat supply system; added to which putting the troops on the march in such conditions was sure to give rise to huge numbers of sick.

For the coming campaign, the 9th Portuguese Brigade, still consisting of the 11th and 23rd Line Regiments and 7th Cacadores, was commanded by a Portuguese officer, Colonel Jose de Vasconcelos e Sa, Colonel of the 23rd Line Regiment. This brigade remained attached to the 4th Division, which along with the 7th Division, formed the left of Wellington's army under the command of Lieutenant General William Beresford.

Beresford's force marched on 15 February, facing very little French opposition, as General Hill's force threatened their left. Heavy rains re-commencing on 18 February, further operations were stopped for four days. On the 23rd, the 7th Division drove Foy's troops back from Hastingues, the 4th Division in support.

On 27 February, Soult stood at Orthez and the 4th Division was involved in the assault of Soult's position to a large extent. The Brigade remained in Reserve until the village of St Boes was captured, when it took part in two unsuccessful attempts to gain the ridge line, being driven back with heavy losses. James served at Orthez and survived unscathed, Lt Colonel Daniel Donahoe; Major Joao Guedes; Captain Joze da Costa; Lieutenants Ignacio Pereira de Lacerda and Antonio de Gouvea Vasconcelos; Ensigns Thomas de Magalhaens, Joaquim Maria Lucena de Beltrao, Antonio de Carvalho Savedra and Valentim de Almeida were wounded, Donahoe dying of his wounds a few days later. The regiment also suffered 17 men killed and 121 wounded, with a further 20 missing. General Hill then sent Beresford's force on the road towards Bordeaux.

At Toulouse on 4 April Beresford with the 3rd, 4th & Light Divisions managed to cross the River Garonne 20km downstream; but heavy rains then cut the bridge, isolating this force on the French bank for three days, which luckily passed without incident, when the bridge was restored. During the Battle of Toulouse, the 4th and 6th Divisions were ordered on a long flanking march, to attack the main French position on Mont Rave, the 7th Portuguese Brigade of 6th Division suffering particularly high casualties. James fought at Toulouse and was again lucky enough not to be wounded. The 11th Portuguese Line lost one officer and five men killed and sixteen men wounded.

With the end of the war, Wellington's army congregated near Bordeaux, where in June 1814 the Portuguese troops formed and marched for Portugal, the British troops forming a Guard of Honour on their departure. James would have proceeded with the regiment, giving up his commission when they had safely returned to Portugal, remaining with them until 13 October 1814 and then presumably took passage from Lisbon for home.

He then became a Captain in the 42nd by purchase[1] on 11 May 1815, but did not serve in the Waterloo campaign. He had served at Corunna, Walcheren, Salamanca, Burgos, the Pyrenees, Orthez and Toulouse.

He retired from the army in 1817, presumably from ill health, and unfortunately died on 20 January 1818 aged only 25 years old and was buried in St Michael's Churchyard, Inveresk, Midlothian, Scotland. His father died in 1834 and he was buried alongside his son.

A single letter exists regarding James' death in 1818, which is now held in the Black Watch Museum Archives in Perth.

1 Vice, Captain Walker retired.

Cheltenham 9 February 1818[2]

My dear General,
Your letter with Mr Harris's reached me this morning. I would have written to you on the death of your son, did I not know from experience that the kindest condolence of friends on such melancholy occasions, as the last irreparable breach in your family, is more apt to summon up, than to compose those acute or affectionate feelings of distress arising from such affliction; but be assured I sympathise most sincerely with you & your family. Many thanks for your enquiries about Lady Huntly, she is now much better, but her affliction was equal to her loss; and that has been very great indeed.[3]

I really think it most natural at your time of life, that you should be anxious to have your daughter & Mr Home near you;[4] and it would be very gratifying to me to be able to persuade Lord Palmerston to do what would be agreeable to Mr Home. I shall write His Lordship once more on the subject and by this post. I beg to offer my regards to Mrs Stirling and all at your fireside & believe me my dear general, with perfect friendship, yours most sincerely, Huntly.[5]

---

2 Archive reference BW141/1/4.

3 Elizabeth Brodie married the Marquess Huntly in 1813, becoming Lady Huntly. She never had any children and it is likely that the loss mentioned was a miscarriage as both her parents were long dead.

4 Jean Stirling, our James' only sibling, was born on 20 May 1785. She married Paymaster John Home of the 42nd Foot in 1805.

5 General George Gordon, Marquess of Huntly, was the heir to Alexander 4th Duke of Gordon. He created the 92nd Foot (Gordon Highlanders) and commanded them in Holland in 1799. In 1806, he became Colonel of the 42nd Foot. In 1820 he transferred to command of the 1st Foot. He was Grand Master of the Grand Lodge of Scotland.

Bibliography

Anonymous, *Army Lists*, Various.

Anonymous, *Personal Narrative of a Private Soldier Who Served in the 42nd Highlanders for Twelve Years*, London 1821.

Anonymous, *Officers of the Black Watch 1725-1986*, Salisbury 1989.

Anton, J., *Retrospect of a Military Life*, London 1841.

Cornford, L. Cope, and Walker, F.W., *The Great Deeds of the Black Watch*, London 1915.

De Laborde, A., *A View of Spain (5 Volumes)*, London 1809.

Forbes, A., *The Black Watch, The Record of an Historic Regiment*, London 1896.

Fortescue, J.W., *A History of the British Army (20 Volumes)*, London 1900–30.

Gaudencio, M., and Burnham, R., *In the Words of Wellington's Fighting Cocks*, Barnsley 2021.

Groves, Lt Col P., *Illustrated Histories of the Scottish Regiments Book 1 The Black Watch 1729-1893*, London 1893.

Hall, J., *A History of the Peninsular War Vol VIII*, London 1998.

Hutton-Wilson, G., *Merely a Memorandum, From Spain to Portugal in Wellington's Army*, Kinloss 2005.

Jones, Sir J.T., *Journal of the Sieges carried on by the Army under the Duke of Wellington in Spain 1811 - 1814 (3 Volumes)*, London 1846.

Maxwell, M., *Peninsular Sketches (2 Volumes)*, London 1844.

Oman, Sir Charles, *A History of the Peninsular War (7 Volumes)*, London 1902–30.

Page, J., *Intelligence Officer in the Peninsula, Letters and Diaries of Major Edward Charles Cocks 1786-1812*, Tunbridge 1986.

Schofield, V., *The Highland Furies, The Black Watch 1739-1899*, London 2012.

Index